hot
jobs

hot
jobs

**THE NO-HOLDS-BARRED,
TELL-IT-LIKE-IT-IS
GUIDE TO GETTING THE JOBS
EVERYONE WANTS**

Charlie Drozdyk

HarperCollins*Publishers*

HarperCollins books may be purchased for educational, business, or sales promotional use. For information, please write: Special Markets Department, HarperCollins Publishers, Inc., 10 East 53rd Street, New York, NY 10022.

FIRST EDITION

Designed by Alma Hochhauser Orenstein

Library of Congress Cataloging-in-Publication Data

Drozdyk, Charlie, 1964–
    Hot Jobs : the no-holds-barred, tell-it-like-it-is guide to getting the jobs everyone wants / by Charlie Drozdyk.—1st ed.
      p.   cm.
    ISBN 0-06-273245-5
    1. Job hunting. 2. Vocational guidance. I. Title.
HF5382.7.D76   1994
331.7'02—dc20   93-36428

---

94 95 96 97 98 ❖/RRD 10 9 8 7 6 5 4 3 2 1

Contents

Acknowledgments

A very sincere thank you to everyone I interviewed, including the people who, for whatever reason, I wasn't able to include in the book. Without them there would be no book. Thanks to John E. Prunier at Veronis, Suhler & Associates and to John M. Diat at Standard & Poor's Corporation for the wealth of statistical and economic information they made available to me. Thanks to Keith Baptista from *Interview* magazine for help on the fashion chapter. Thanks to Sam Paul for encouraging me from the beginning to do this book, and for his belief in my ability to do more than eat free meals. Thanks to Alix Koromzay and Michael Kastenbaum, my L.A. pals, for their extraordinary hospitality whenever I visit. My agent, Ellen Geiger. My brother John ("Droz") for all sorts of stuff (money) and for being the coolest. My wonderful editors, Lauren Marino and Jenna Hull, and everyone at HarperCollins. And, at the risk of making this book out to be a bigger deal than it actually is, to my mother, a great person and inspiration who started this whole thing of not settling for a boring life or desk job by infusing this piece of advice in my brain since I was a kid: "You never know, you could be run over by a truck tomorrow." Thanks, Mom.

Author's Note

"What am I going to do with my life?"

Not a fun question. And not an easy one to answer. After graduation, I avoided it and went to an island for a year. Others with less direction than myself took dumb jobs from firms that had recruited on campus. One particularly cool friend of mine took a job with a railroad company. Why? Why not? He didn't know what else to do. And, he needed a job.

Maybe I was too idealistic. Maybe I didn't want to grow up. Whatever the case, I just couldn't take a job that I knew was going to suck, be boring, and turn me into an uptight, depressing working stiff who hates his job and lives for the weekend and two weeks off a year. Nope.

But the thing is, how are you supposed to know what to do with your life—something hip and interesting as opposed to meaningless and boring—when you don't know what you *can* do with your life? When you don't know what your options are? When you don't know what's out there? You've been in school pretty much all your life, isolated from the real world. You need exposure. Ideas. Advice. Role models.

I would devour interviews with really successful people in *Rolling Stone* and *Details*, and see them on "Letterman," "Leno" and "Entertainment Tonight," all the while looking for clues and for the paths to their success. How they did it. You know, how did David Geffen, mailroom kid at William Morris, get to be David Geffen, god.

And it would piss me off, because all the time you'd get the same reportage by these moguls that would always go something like this:

"Well, I started out as a messenger boy, you know, delivering scripts to stars around town and—Oh, excuse me a second (Mr. Hot Shot tells the waiter to ask the chef if he would make him a simple peanut butter and banana sandwich). OK, where was I? Oh yes, so then when I became president of Columbia Pictures, Def Jam Records, and Grey Advertising all in the same year, I thought, 'Hey, this is the same thing I used to do when I was a messenger years back—just giving the people what they want.'"

It used to drive me nuts. Their ascent, their career path—the thing I thought would be most interesting to hear about—was always completely glossed over. But the thing is, even if a big successful Mr. Hot Shot were to go into detail on how he moved out of the mailroom—started as an assistant, did this, did that, and then became huge—I doubt it would motivate me to say, "Hey, I can do that." I mean, how can you possibly relate to a David Geffen or a Mike Ovitz? And the thing is, they're not going to tell you the real story anyway. By now it's folklore.

It dawned on me that I needed to find role models who were young and not too high up the career food chain. Twenty-somethings who still remember how they got their first "real" job as a low-level grunt, and who can recount how they went from being an assistant to having one. Someone who has achieved enough success to be able to give advice on not only how to get a job, but on how to get ahead. Someone who is going to paint an honest picture of their work life— the highs, the lows, the politics, the truth.

WHAT THIS BOOK WILL DO FOR YOU

I think these candid and informative interviews with people only a few years older than yourself—people you can relate to—will wipe away that mystique of unapproachability that surrounds these high-profile, glamour careers. Instead of saying, "Yeah, sure, great job but who do you have to know?" after reading the interviews you'll probably say "Hey, that's what they do, that's how they did it? I can do that!" And then maybe you won't do something stupid like go to law school, or take the first job offered to you from some chump company recruiting on your campus.

I also tracked down, begged, and pleaded with personnel directors or top hiring people—one for each industry—from major companies who, under slight duress, tell you about:

- How they go about hiring
- What they look for in a candidate
- How people blow it in an interview
- What qualities get people hired
- Creative ways people have gone about getting interviews
- Resumes, cover letters, personal hygiene, etc.

The chapters, "Strategies for Landing the Hot Job" and "Moving up the Ladder: From Being an Assistant to Having One," are exactly what they say. They give you real, honest, in-your-face, totally irreverent advice for a competitive, ruthless, cruel, and heartless working world. Please do not hold me accountable if these tips and strategies get you into trouble of any kind. I do not recommend or endorse the shady, more controversial ones. (But do I think they'll get you ahead? Absolutely.)

Just so you know, I didn't just make up all the statistical stuff and economic forecasts that you find in the introductions to each chapter. Unless otherwise noted, it is based on research by Veronis, Suhler & Associates and Standard & Poor's Corporation, two undisputed leaders of economic research.

PART ONE

Strategies for Landing the Hot Job

1

The Job Search

Looking for a job sucks. No doubt about it. I'm not going to give you worthless encouragement, as other career books may, such as, "Make it an...*adventure*." Or give you ridiculous advice like, "Don't give up because it can be discouraging. Form a support group. Consider it as if it were a job. Get dressed up every morning. Put on a tie! Blah blah blah." Wear women's underwear if that's what's going to get you motivated. (That's for the guys. Women, you should already be wearing them. 'Nough said.) I don't care. Do whatever you have to do.

The truth is, it's more dog-eat-dog out there than ever. Due to the recession in the early nineties, companies have trimmed their staffs. Duties that three different people used to do in the eighties are often done now by one person. So not only has it gotten more competitive and harder to find a job, I think that in the workplace as well, there's a heightened understanding that one must *really* perform or they'll get sacked.

What's good for you though is that most young people go about their job hunt either half-assed, totally inefficiently, or both. Therefore, if you're hungry, if you really want it, if you're not hanging out at home watching MTV and Oprah, but instead are calling and calling and calling, looking and asking and searching, not making stupid mistakes, and taking advantage of every opportunity because you read this book, then eventually you'll get a job, don't worry about it.

THE PERFECT JOB. IT DOESN'T EXIST, SO GET OVER IT.

Again, unlike other career books, this one won't help you identify what skills you have and then match that with an appropriate career in which you would utilize them. You know, using charts and filling in the blanks with your skills and all that bull. That's nonsense. I think someone in radio could be just as successful and happy in TV, or advertising. **There's no *one* right job or industry for you, so don't kill yourself worrying about it.**

I remember that I was so hesitant and half-assed about my job search when I got out of college because I was like, "Shit, I don't know if this is *really* what I want to do, and if I do it then I'm stuck in it for good." Not the case. It's just a starting point and will invariably lead you in other directions. You've got to be in the working world in order to *see* the working world and the different jobs and opportunities that exist therein.

Who Me?

So the best advice I can give on this is just pick the one career or industry that seems the coolest to you and go for that one. For me, after graduating, I probably would have said film. The thing is, back then I didn't know anyone who worked in film. I was so intimidated by the idea of *me* working in *film* that there was no way I was even going to attempt getting a job in it. Impossible. That was for other people. So my first advice is, get over it. Don't let it intimidate you. The people working in these jobs are no geniuses, with special gifts. I know, I've met them and worked with them. They are ambitious though. And they are smart. Usually.

"It's Hiring Season!"

Let's clear something up right now. You always hear people say, "Oh, it's a really bad time to be looking for a job." Or, "Nobody's hiring right now." Don't listen to them. As Greg Drebin, program director at MTV says, "When people say, 'Well now is a really hard time for the industry,' and all that—well, it's *always* a hard time. There's no such thing as: 'Oh, it's hiring season; we've got all these jobs that just became available. This year for some reason we have tons of jobs.' It's never like that. It's always hard. And you know what? There's always jobs and there's never jobs."

So don't be like others and use that as an excuse not to look for a job. People are always retiring, getting sick, quitting, dying, getting fired, getting promoted, moving....

Pick the Company, Then Your Title.

If I were starting over again, what I'd do first is pick the industry I most wanted to work in, e.g., radio, film, advertising. And then, instead of trying to scheme up a job title that sounded good, I'd pick the companies in that industry I would most like to work for.

You see, you don't want to limit yourself with a title by saying, "I'm going to be a market analyst or development executive." Sure, maybe you'll wind up doing that, but the truth is, you might get a job doing that with some stupid company and realize you hate it. But the reason that you'll probably hate it is not because of the job title, but because the product that your second-rate employer produces— whether it be TV shows, blouses, radio shows, whatever—is just that, second-rate. There's nothing like the excitement of working with a first-rate company, with first-rate clients, that does first-rate work— even if you're sweeping the floors. The energy of the place will motivate you.

What's in a Name? A Lot.

Therefore, I think it's imperative that when you're starting out you should try to get a job with the most prestigious and successful company possible. I wish someone had told me that when I was starting out.

With my first job I made the mistake of going with a title rather than a company. I accepted an offer with a very small, unknown PR firm because they hired me straight off as a "copywriter." I was thrilled—at first. After three months I left. Problem was, there was no room for growth because the office was so small. And it was unchallenging because our clients were a bunch of schlock doctors who cured hemorrhoids. Meanwhile, I had turned down an offer from a great and big company because they told me I would be an assistant for at least a year before I could do any writing.

What's most important though about starting with a great company is how it propels your career. You see, the better the company you start out with, the better your second job is going to be. **People love hiring young people from brand-name companies.**

So pick around twenty companies that you would want to work for. In your opinion, the best companies. What radio stations do you like? Who makes films that you like, clothes that you like, records, ads, books? Then, figure out what entry-level jobs are available with those companies.

What Is Entry Level?

This might be completely obvious to some, but might not be to others. You get out of college and you think you're ready for the working world. College has prepared you for a job, so you're not quite entry level, right? Wrong. **A college degree is simply a way of allowing you to get an entry-level job that requires no college education.** An employer will say "college degree required" as a way of weeding out people. But it's not a requirement as though college has given you anything that could be of value to them. Because it hasn't. So this is another reason to ignore titles and just go for the company when you're starting your job search—reason being, you're basically going to be a grunt or glorified secretary anyway.

Job Boards

A great little trick. Most companies post them. Tip: they're usually in the hall near the bathroom. But how do you get access? From a friend. Or drop off a fake letter to Personnel from Joe Schmoe, and while you're there, ask them if you can use the bathroom. Snoop around. Hide a camera in your pocket, or something. If the receptionist says it's down the hall to the left, then take a right. Get lost. Take a look around. See if it's a place you could imagine working at as well.

Floating and Temp Pools

The big companies, the Calvin Kleins, the Paramount Pictures, the Grey Advertisings, the Sony Musics. A lot of these big companies have what are known as temp pools. The personnel office either calls up people they know who are flexible and can work on a day's notice, or they use a temp agency to fill the void. A lot of these big companies have what are known as floaters (call and ask Personnel if they have such a thing), people who cover for assistants when they are out sick. When all the floaters are taken, the temps come in. Getting into this floater or temp pool is a great way to get your foot in the door.

Temporary Agencies

I've heard it dozens of times: "I started out temping and never left." It's a very common thing. But why and how does it happen? Two ways. First, when someone's out sick for a day, either the boss will go for a day without an assistant or the office manager will pull in someone from the mailroom or a floater. But if the person will be out sick for a week or is on vacation, or a couple of people are out sick, or there's a special project that needs doing like massive filing or data input in a computer, then they'll bring in a temp. If you're really good on one of these temp assignments, then they will ask for you specifically next time. And if you're a good worker and you're smart, you'll give the office manager your number, telling him or her you'd love to be considered when a full-time position opens up. If they like you, they'll remember you. You're a proven commodity, plus it saves them the effort of interviewing.

The second reason why a company will take on a temp is because they're actually looking to fill a full-time position. So what they do is tell the temp agency that they've got a full-time position to fill, and to send over the people who are interested in landing a full-time job. The company then tries out different people until they find someone they really like. It's like test-driving different cars.

Personnel—A Last Resort

The thing is, when someone's got to fill a position, they're going to try to fill it with someone who was recommended to them by a friend or an associate. Or else they'll do their own little search. Personnel is often the last place a boss will go to fill a position.

Example. I was hired at the Brooklyn Academy of Music (BAM) by answering an ad in *The New York Times*. The general manager's office avoided their personnel department and put their own ad in the paper, looking for an administrative assistant. The two guys who hired me were looking for a specific type of person and personality to join them in their office, and they weren't getting that type of candidate from Personnel.

Not that Personnel cares that they're often bypassed, mind you. If someone from a department wants to do their own assistant search, then it just frees them up to do other things.

Even though you might make it in the door by a circuitous way other than Personnel, you're probably going to have to interview with them anyway to get their blessing and approval. Because often the Personnel person doubles as office manager or director of administration or something like that.

CONNECTIONS

What you need now are people to help you. You need to find people who work at these companies you've selected or people who know people who work at these companies, and get them to talk to you. Get them to give you the inside scoop on who might be hiring, whose assistant might be leaving soon or getting promoted. You want to make as many contacts at each company as possible.

For some reason, connections, or contacts, for a lot of young people is a dirty word. Friends will snivel, "He only got that job because he knows somebody." Damn right! Get used to it; it's how the game works. When I got out of college I didn't pursue any contacts because I didn't think I had any. My parents weren't

very social people, so I didn't know many friend[...]
worked for IBM anyway, not a place I wanted to g[...]

But what about my neighbors? Did any of the[...]
a company that I would be interested in workin[...]
thought of it. If I'd known then what it takes to g[...] [...]about a
doubt I would have knocked on their door at about seven-thirty at
night and introduced myself. "Hi, I'm so-and-so's son. I live down
the street and I know you work in advertising. I don't know anyone
in the field so I'd really appreciate an opportunity to talk to you. Can
I give you a call at the office this week to set something up?"

Perfectly acceptable. And who can say no to a neighbor? If he
said no, word would get around quickly that he was a jerk and his
house would probably get egged.

People Like to Play God.

But the cool thing, and something that surprised me, is that people actually like to help the little people. Sure, there are idiots you
hear about who wouldn't even help out their cousin. But generally,
people seem to get a vicarious thrill out of helping someone get a
job. At the present time, I'm trying to get two people I know jobs.
Why? Partially because I'm a good guy. Partially because I like these
people and know what it's like to be in their shoes. Partially because
it makes me feel like god. Partially because they're going to owe me
one. And partially, because it just adds to the network of people I
know out there in the entertainment industry. So if I ever need
something from that company where I helped place a person, I've
now got someone who will, or *should* at least, do anything for me.

People Trust Referrals.

The reason connections are so important is that when someone
needs to fill a position, they usually start by calling all their friends and
associates asking, "You know anyone?" It saves them the hassle and
time of dealing with their personnel department and meeting a bunch
of random strangers. So ask everyone you meet and everyone you
know whether or not *they* know anybody who might need somebody.

s how Farrah Greenberg (fashion editor, *Elle* magazine) found er assistant. "With my assistant, my friend said, 'My cousin has a friend who wants to get into the industry, will you meet her?' So I just hired her."

It's also how Jenna Hull (editor, HarperCollins) got her first job in publishing. "This guy called me and said, 'A friend of mine at Random House needs an assistant, do you want a job?'"

Jenna is living proof of how beneficial it is, "if you know anybody who's peripherally anywhere who knows anybody...because it certainly helps if you can get something in the mail and somebody says, 'I'm a friend of so-and-so's.'"

Ask Everyone.

When I went out to L.A. I had one connection: a guy I had met once or twice back in New York. After my informal interview with this guy's friend, I left her office, and before walking out the building I thanked the young guy at the reception area and struck up a conversation with him. We chatted for a while and I said, "Listen, I just moved out here and I don't know anyone. I'm looking for a job in TV, do you know anything?" In fact he did. He gave me *two* leads actually. So, ask everybody.

COLD CALLS

Alright, say you've got no leads, no contacts. You're a veritable alien from another planet. Which is to say, you're straight out of college. What do you do? Where do you start? Who do you call? This is where it gets challenging.

If you don't know anyone who can set you up on an interview with someone at a company you want to work at, then you've got to make your own connection.

If you're interested in doing publicity at Miramax Films, the first thing you've got to do is find out who the director of publicity is, or whatever title the boss might have. If you don't know who that person is, call the company and ask the receptionist, "Who's the head of publicity there?" Simple as that. Then give them a call—*before* you send them your resume.

You could just send your resume and letter at this point as others would do. Don't. Here's why. You want to have as many personal encounters (phone calls are personal) with this office as possible; with the receptionist, with the assistant, and with the boss if possible. This is what you do.

Make the Call.

Call and ask for the person you've already targeted. We'll call this person "Ms. Boss." The receptionist will put you through to her office, and chances are her assistant will answer the phone. We'll call the assistant "Bob." Ask for Ms. Boss. When Bob asks your name, tell him. If it doesn't sound familiar he'll probably ask you about the nature of the call or if Ms. Boss is expecting your call. Tell him the truth. Tell him the reason you're calling.

This is your reason: You're looking for a job and you'd love to work for that company. Tell him that. Therefore, you're interested in meeting with his boss to discuss potential jobs that might be opening. Ask him if it would be possible to meet with Ms. Boss even if there aren't. If you can't get an appointment, then say, "Listen, would it be alright to send in my resume?" He'll say, "Of course, even though we're not really hiring."

Now you have a specific person to send a letter to, instead of sending it to Personnel. Plus, in your letter you can make it sound as if they *requested* your resume by starting the letter as such:

Dear Ms. Boss:
    After speaking with your assistant Bob on the telephone today...

Even though you and Bob spoke of nothing really, the fact that you got their approval to send your resume makes it much more likely that he and his boss will actually read it and not throw it away. The "After speaking with..." line is a great advantage over the hundreds of resumes that come in unsolicited. Your letter is now more familiar, and it's as if they're expecting it.

Make a Follow-up Phone Call.

Your resume has been there for two weeks. It's now perfectly acceptable to call Ms. Boss to see if she got it and to try to get an informational interview. Say you get the boss on the phone. You've got about ten seconds to state the reason for your call. This is your reason:

"Hi, Ms. Boss. Thank you very much for taking my call (or, calling me back). I sent in my resume, and I was wondering if I could come in and meet with you sometime in the near future." If she says, "Well, we really aren't hiring right now," say, "That's OK, I'd just love the opportunity to meet with you to discuss jobs that might become available in the future, and to learn more about your company." Chances are she'll say yes. Remember, you don't get things if you don't ask.

But chances are you won't get Ms. Boss on the phone. Instead you'll probably get Bob.

Get Bob on Your Side.

The first thing you want to do is get Bob, the assistant, to sympathize with you and your cause. Schmooze and charm him to death. Make him like you so he'll want to help you out. If you're any good at schmoozing at all, you should expect Bob to help you in at least one, if not all, of these ways:

- Set up an interview between you and his boss.
- Give you information about a job that might be opening somewhere else in the company.
- Give you a lead about a job opening at another company.

Bob Might Be a Jerk—Bad Bob.

Bob might be professional and courteous, but he also might try to keep you from speaking with Ms. Boss. Maybe he's paranoid or insecure about his job, desiring no competition from upstarts like you. Or he might be one of those watchdog assistants, protecting Ms. Boss from evil, unnecessary calls. Therefore, he might not even announce your call to Ms. Boss. He might not even be giving her your messages, even though he tells you that he has. Bob will do this. Therefore, ask Bob really politely to tell Ms. Boss that you called and that you'd like the opportunity to meet with her for five minutes for an informational interview. Leave your number and pray.

Bob Might Be Your Friend—Good Bob

But say Bob's a really nice guy. You two hit it off, and he's explained to you that there's no way his boss will meet with you, even for an informal interview. That's cool. Don't push it. Never push it. Make Bob your contact person. Give him the opportunity to help you out—to be the person with the information. Let him feel important.

So, for the next couple of months, or for however long it takes you to find a job, stay in touch with the Bobs out there so they remember you. So when a job does become available, you're the first person on their mind.

Make Friends With Strangers.

I can't stress this enough. **The job search is about building relationships with strangers over the phone.** You're going to be calling and talking to people about jobs at their company. Chances are they're going to tell you that nothing is available. In this process of being blown off, however, your goal is to strike up a conversation with someone there. Make a phone pal. Be honest with the person. Say, "Listen, I really would love to work for you guys, but I don't know how to go about it. Do you think I can check in with you every two or three weeks or something?" Nine times out of ten they'll say sure. Then when something opens up, this person might even call you.

When you do get hired, it will probably go something like this. Bob, the assistant you've been talking with, hears that there's an entry-level position open answering the phones or something. Bob's boss doesn't want to deal with it. She's probably thinking, "Shit, our phone answerer is leaving. I don't want to waste my time looking for someone to do this basic function. Bob, you do it. Besides, it's such a shitty job, who would want it?" You, that's who. That's where Bob—who's always looking to be helpful (or should be)—pipes in, "You know, there's this guy Charlie who's been calling here every two weeks for the past two months looking for a job. Says he'll do anything. He's real persistent. Maybe I should give him a call. What do you think?" His boss replies, "Fine, whatever. Get him in here."

But none of this phone stuff will work for if your phone manner isn't right. By right I mean you must be extremely pleasant, non-arrogant, and a sense of humor doesn't hurt either. **So don't call when you're in a pissy mood, or when you have a cold, or when you're feeling sorry for yourself.** You must be smiling on the other end of the phone. Sounds stupid, but it's true. You must be cheerful. You cannot be a burdensome call like most of the others they receive on any given day.

A Receptionist Tells All!

Listen to these words from the receptionist at a major film production and distribution company:

"Be really pleasant when you're speaking to the receptionist, because they take shit all day long, and speaking to a pleasant person on the phone always breaks my mood. I've had twenty-minute conversations with people on the phone just because they were really nice. I had a guy call a few weeks ago looking for a job and he was really pleasant. So I told him that there were no jobs available and ended up giving him total inside background information about (her company) and how they were doing mass firings and blah blah blah. And I said you might want to try an internship because the turnover rate is so high you'd probably get hired really quickly.

"I said, 'What department are you interested in,' and he said, 'I have no idea, I just want to work in film.' And I said that I would suggest Acquisitions because they're the nicest people in the whole company and it would be a really good place to get your feet wet. At that moment the head of Acquisitions walked by and I asked him if he wanted to pick up (the phone) and talk to a potential intern, and he said, 'Yeah sure.' And the guy was in a half an hour later interviewing and started the next day. And then got hired full-time soon after.

Why did you give him all this information and help?

"Because he was nice, and, I liked the sound of his voice."

What if people aren't nice, if you don't like the sound of their voice?

"I've given out false information. I've hung up on people. I've spelled names wrong. (Laughs.) They'll never even open up your letter if you've spelled their name wrong. So call a couple times, a couple of different days, because receptionists take all the shit all day long. So it's worth it to find one who's in a good mood."

What should they say to you when they get you on the phone?

"First off, when they call they should immediately lower their status so that they know that I'm doing them a favor by giving them any information at all. That's always what opens me up and breaks my mood, for them to say, "I know you're incredibly busy, but I just graduated from college and I was just wondering if you could..." Just in a language that lowers your status. Not because I'm an egomaniac, but because I realize that you must know what I'm doing, or that you're faking it really well."

Brutal, huh?

When I asked Robin Danielson (president, Mad Dogs and Englishmen Advertising) what she did with resumes she received she said, "I usually toss them away."

Are cold calls OK? I asked her. "Yeah, they're fine with me. Because I'm more likely to say, 'Yeah I'll meet with you' over the phone than I am to actually read a letter and make any response. Reading a letter is time-consuming."

"You never know," says Emily Gerson (agent, William Morris Agency) about cold calls. When she moved back to New York she knew nobody, so she "called everybody that I possibly could. I got one very famous producer, David Brown, on the phone directly. This assistant put me through for some reason, and he had me come in to meet him. He said, 'Come on in, let's talk.' He didn't know me from a hole in the wall. He wound up sending my resume around New York to the most important people."

Drop a Name.

When making a cold call, if you know anyone who has ever worked at the company, or who knows, even vaguely, the person you're calling, drop that name! And make sure it's the first thing out of your mouth. As Greg Drebin from MTV says, "I get calls all the time, 'Hi, I'm a friend of so-and-so's that met you at a party.' This isn't even someone I met at a party, but a friend of theirs."

When to Call

Don't call on Mondays, it's usually a hectic day. Don't call in the morning, it's when most work is done. Don't call from twelve-thirty to two-thirty, they're probably at lunch. So, from three PM on, Tuesday through Thursday (Fridays people want to book out of there), is your time to call. A great trick is to call after six PM. You often catch the people you want to talk to picking up their own phone because their assistant has left them.

Oh, and if you get voice mail, do not leave a message. Call and call and call until you get a real person. Better to wait to make that connection.

So, there you go. Cold calls. Just be very friendly and don't be a jerk and you've got nothing to lose—and possibly more to gain than you even know.

RESEARCH

You'd think this would be obvious to everybody—know what the hell a company does before going in to meet them. Find out who owns the company. What kind of films, clothes, ads, pillows, radio shows, records do they produce? Who are their clients? What do they sell?

Say you're interviewing for a job with a small production film company. When you go for the interview you should know the names of all the films that company has produced. Hopefully, you've rented and watched them all. Therefore, you should know what kinds of films the company makes.

If you have an interview with "CBS This Morning," it goes without saying that you should watch as many episodes of the show as possible (have someone tape it for you every morning). You should get *Variety* magazine and check out its ratings and share. You should watch the other morning shows so you can talk with insight about what makes "CBS This Morning" different, better, or the same as the other shows. You should go to the library and do a word search to see if there have been any articles about "CBS This Morning."

All this information is accessible to you before the interview. Get the company's annual report if they're a public company. If they are, they also have to file 10-Ks with the Securities and Exchange Commission. This is something they'll send to anyone who calls and asks for it. These are great. A lot of the stuff inside is all numbers and impossible to understand, but about half of it is very straightforward information about the company and the industry as a whole. If they're not a public company, they might still have literature about their company that they can send you. Just call and ask.

A Personal Story of Failure and Sloppiness

I'll tell you a quick story of how I blew an interview and a great job so that you don't do the same stupid thing. Remember, you don't get that many chances. At the time I did not know this, so I was sloppy.

First off, I had never heard of this company, they were small. I was like, "No big deal, a small unimportant company; no big loss if I don't get the job." Well, it turns out they're one of the most successful companies out there in their field.

I knew that the company made movies for TV, but I hadn't bothered to find out what kind. Turns out they do movies based on tabloid news stories like Amy Fisher. I didn't know this, so when the hiring person asked me what magazines and papers I read, instead of saying *People, USA Today, The New York Post,* I said, *The New York Times* and *Esquire.* Then she asked me what TV shows I liked. I could only name two shows on TV, period: "Doogie Howser" and "L.A. Law." "What books have you read recently?" she asked me. "I just finished *The Sun Also Rises* by Hemingway," I replied.

If I'd been at *The New Yorker* or PBS they might have made me vice president. But here, they were not impressed. I buried myself. Here's a company that makes sensationalist movies-of-the-week about girls falling down wells, and I'm talking Hemingway. She gave me some advice. "Go home and turn on the TV."

Apply this to whatever industry you're going after. A record company: what kind of music do they put out? An advertising agency: what kind of ads do they make? Fun, irreverent stuff, or conservative? Who are their accounts? Nike? Gerber baby food? Just do a little homework so you don't look like an idiot. So there you go. You've learned from my mistake.

SENDING YOUR RESUME (AND/OR COVER LETTER)

Sending a resume should be a last resort, that is, if you've been unsuccessful at getting someone at the company, hopefully the hiring person, to meet with you via a phone call. If they tell you to send a resume, you can do that along with the thousands of others they've told to do the same thing. Or—a big *or*—you could send a letter that contains the same information that you'd put in a resume.

Here's an example off the top of my head. This would be me a couple of years ago. Names have been slightly changed to protect the unsuspecting.

Dear Ms. Executive:

As I mentioned to your assistant Gary, Bryan S. suggested that I give you a call when I get out to L.A. I know Bryan from New York where I was the assistant to Mr. Man, the producer of Bryan's Off-Broadway musical, *Spuds*.

Besides assisting Mr. Man on several Broadway and Off-Broadway shows, I also served for two years as theatre manager for the Criterion Center, which housed a Broadway theatre as well as a three-hundred-seat cabaret. For all the shows that came in to both theatres, I represented the house's interests. This included overseeing a staff of ten, being accountable for all monies that came into the box office, and generally doing everything and anything that needed doing—including going on the roof when it rained and finding the clogged drain responsible for causing embarrassing leaks on patrons.

Previous to that, I worked for a year at the Brooklyn Academy of Music as the assistant to the general manager. There I prepared contracts and budgets and was integrally involved with all aspects of mounting the many shows that came in to one of the five theatres.

I'm making a bit of a career change, and would greatly appreciate the opportunity to meet with you to discuss the TV industry in general, as well as future entry-level positions at ___ Productions.

Thanks for your time in reading this letter. I'll give you a call next week to see if we can set up a time to meet.

Warmest regards,
C.D.

This type of letter-resume is so much more personal, besides being different, that it is a lot harder to throw in a pile and ignore.

For those of you who are not willing to try your hand at a bio letter, and still insist on sending a traditional resume, for god's sake make it a little bit different and interesting. Make it stand out.

Set Yourself Apart From the Crowd.

You know that stuff you'd just as soon put behind you, or maybe even are embarrassed about? You know what? You might want to throw it on your resume—even if you think it has absolutely nothing to do with the job you're applying for. Often these jobs or experiences I'm referring to can tell an employer more about you than time spent in an internship at Disney or Calvin Klein.

For example, a friend of mine was an assistant coach for a Little League baseball team and he included it on his resume. It worked great for him. Not only does it demonstrate that he must have a considerable amount of patience, it also shows that he has interest in management and in working in a team environment.

He included something like this:

LITTLE LEAGUE, Assistant Coach—Responsible for controlling incredibly difficult, petulant and bratty ten-year-olds. Had a great time.

Believe me. This will get noticed. And appreciated. A little well placed, conservative levity can make the difference.

Don't Take My Word for It...

"When I was in college I was a nanny," says Claire Raskind (publicist, Skouras Pictures). "When the woman who hired me saw my resume—more than other people who had, like, an internship at a major studio or something during college, which I didn't have—she thought it was really interesting that I was a nanny. Because somebody who was a nanny could really put up with a lot of bullshit work."

Padding the Truth

What's a resume anyway? Just a piece of paper, I say; not a legal document. Now take it easy, I'm not saying make things up. Just fudge a little if you think it can help. For example, how is someone to know whether or not this so-called "assistant coach" for that Little League team wasn't in fact just friends with the coach or assistant coach and came out to help every once in a while? As long as the guy could bullshit a little bit about the subject in an interview, and had a few good stories to tell—you know, about wild, ten-year-old pitches and concussions or something—then our applicant's alright.

Responding to Want Ads

I wouldn't bother answering want ads unless they list their phone number, and unless you happen to be a very charming salesperson on the phone. I got one job listed in *The New York Times* this way. I called and was one of the most charming, upbeat little campers you've ever heard.

If you have to send your resume to a want ad, however, along with a thousand others, it's got to be a doozy. I suggest either doing a bio resume, or else doing something very bold and out there. For instance, what follows is part of a cover letter that I sent along with a resume in response to a want ad listed in *The New York Times*. It was that PR job I mentioned earlier. I sent this same cover letter blindly to Personnel to about fifteen major public relations companies and got three or four interviews and two job offers.

> To whom it may concern:
>
> At dinner last night a friend of mine told me that a cover letter should tell a little bit about you that a resume doesn't. So here goes.
>
> Getting to know Charlie in "quotations" and (parentheses):
> "Crazy, mixed-up Kid. He's totally lost." Dad (wanted me to join IBM like him).
> "He's too short. His shots get blocked every time. Helluva kid though. Writes pretty good." Junior High School Basketball Coach/English Teacher (explaining to my mom why I went the whole season on the bench, and inadvertently, why he lists "Basketball Coach" in title before "English Teacher").
> "He's cute, but I can't imagine *dating* him." First girlfriend in college (overheard her saying to a friend at a large dinner party. Obviously had more imagination than she gave herself credit for).

The letter got their attention. It made them laugh, I'm sure. It also shows that I'm creative, can write well, and am also a little different. Some people liked it, some didn't. When it's going unexpected and you have nothing to lose, you might as well send something bold.

But, if you're sending a letter to someone you've already talked to, or an acquaintance of someone you know, don't send a resume at all. Go straight for the interview.

If you have to send a resume, make sure your cover letter isn't stupid. You might want to consider what bothers Robin Danielson about cover letters:

"I hate when people try to impress me. I hate cover letters that are full of catch phrases. I mean, I think people who are starting out trying to get jobs make the mistake of believing that there's this language that they have to use. Letters that don't use normal language really piss me off. You know, 'As a marketing executive, you are aware of the need for brilliant solutions.' You know, 'I can bring the power of...' Its like 'fuck off you stupid wanker.'"

THE INTERVIEW

Alright, let's talk about the interview. Say you're lucky enough to get one. This is probably your hope. "Uh, I'm going to go in there and hopefully they'll give me the job." Wrong! Nobody gives you nothin'. Got it. You've got to sell. You've got to sell yourself. Here are the things you're selling:

- You want the job.
- You've got tons of energy.
- You've got personality, i.e., you're pleasant, if not fun, to work with.
- You're optimistic.
- You're ambitious, but you're willing to do anything. You're ready to pay your dues in order to prove yourself.

Let's start at the beginning. Who is the person you'll be meeting with—the employer?

Employers. They're Just People.

Before we get into this interview stuff, I might as well clue you in to something that will put you at ease. Interviewers—bosses, people who hire—can be, and in most cases, *are* people too. A realistic age for the person interviewing you might be, say, thirty-five years old. OK, it's 1994, so if this person graduated from college in 1981, then they can't be that bad. That means that they grew up in the free-wheeling, pot-smoking, sex-laden (pre-AIDS) seventies. They're probably more liberal than you are. Not that the person is likely to light up a joint in the interview (but chances are they will later that night).

You're Among the Hip.

The thing to realize is that most of these glamour industries are run by young, generally hip people who are working these cool jobs because they're not boring, status quo fools who settled for whatever company landed on their college campus and would have them. So don't treat them like your parents. Even though they may be fifteen years older than you, but only ten years younger than your parents, it doesn't necessarily follow that they're more similar to them. They're not. So the point is, you don't have to be all stuffy with them when you meet them. Don't act like they're your parents' best friends. Relax. Don't be afraid to laugh or have fun in interviews. The candidate who does this—relates the best, not acting all stuffy and nervous and formal—will get the job.

Hang Out.

Since most of these jobs are very people-oriented, employers are looking for people who feel comfortable hanging out with veritable strangers. So relax. Be friendly and show a little personality. It's either this or be taken for a wallflower, whether you are or not.

Don't Take My Word for It...

Robin Danielson: "Don't think that because people are older than you, they're somehow another species. Your bosses are not really *that* different from you. Kids forget that grownups are people. You get all intimidated and think that it's all so fucking complicated, and it's really not."

Be Humble. Be Nice.

You're there. You're in the lobby, in the reception area. Walk in the door five to ten minutes ahead of time. Sure, get there a half an hour beforehand, but just sit in your car. I don't suggest getting a cup of coffee, unless you're a die-hard coffee drinker. The stuff will make you nervous and your hands clammy.

When you tell the receptionist you're there to see Joe Blow, for god's sake be nice, and charming. If you rub them wrong, and if they're friendly with the person you're interviewing with, then you're history. If you're nice, and I don't mean, "Oh, what a nice bracelet that is you're wearing," but just nice, then they'll probably say, "Yeah, he was alright," instead of saying, "He was an asshole."

"Coffee?"

A lot of times the boss will send their assistant out to meet you and offer you something to drink, per their boss's order. All assistants

I've ever known resent this ritual and resent the jerk that takes them up on it. If you say, "Sure, I'll have a Diet Coke," you're not scoring any points there. Just go to the bathroom and get some water.

OK, You're in the Room.

You've got one goal. Two really. First, you've got to get this person to like you. People hire people they like. Yes you have to be smart and have the general goods that they're looking for, but when it comes down to deciding between you and five other people with basically the same experience (very little), they're going to hire the person or call back the person they remember the most. That is, the person they had the strongest connection with. Which leads me to...

Connectconnectconnectconnect.

The thing is, nobody is going to hire someone they don't like or feel comfortable with. Why would they? What are they thinking? They're thinking, "I've got to spend about ten hours a day, five days a week with this person. Fifty hours a week." That's a lot of time to spend with someone. So, after you've convinced them that you're hungry, that you're ambitious, that you're willing and looking forward to working hard, your last and most important mission is to get them to like you.

It's such a common testimony of how someone explains how they got their job. "I just connected with this person." "We clicked."

I don't know what people think interviews are. They have your resume. They already know about your experience. They obviously consider you experienced enough for the job if they're interested in meeting with you. So what's the interview for? For the person to meet you. For them to see if they like you. If they feel comfortable with you. These are the things you're selling. You're selling personality. You're selling character.

Don't Take My Word for It...

Check it out. John Verrilli (managing editor, Fox News) had studied in Florence for one semester and put that down on his resume.

He recounts, "It turns out the news director loved Italy, had gone there several times, he loved Italian food, is just a real Italian lover. I have this interview and all we talk about is Florence. He asked me one or two questions and then we sit there and talk about Italy." He got the job.

Now, obviously he didn't hire John because he spent time in Italy. The point is they connected and the guy just felt comfortable with him. Italy was just the connecting device.

Jenna Hull: "I do a lot of informational interviews with young people. This woman who came in to meet me, I liked her and we sat around and talked forever. And now every time I know someone who's looking for an assistant, I call her."

Claire Raskind: "Once you're in the interview just act confident. Act confident and not stuffy. Make it fun. I met with the woman I'd be working for and there were pictures on her desk of her grandchildren or whatever. And I was like, "Oh, who are those kids?" And we started talking about kids, and it was something that was bonding. Latch on to anything you can, you know? Something that can bond you with these people."

Don't Mince Words: "I Want This Job."

I already mentioned that the interview is there for you to sell yourself. Making a connection is imperative if they're going to remember you and feel comfortable with you. But you also should make it clear to them that you want the job. Tell them so. Maybe they think your mother made you go on the interview. Or that it's just one in fifty that you're going on, just sussing things out.

You've got to remember where they're coming from. They've got a bunch of people interviewing for the job. They know that the job is demanding. **Some bosses might think the job available is so demanding and shitty that they can't imagine why someone would want it.** They know the long hours, the stress, the bullshit. They know their candidate has to really want it. That they have to be really hungry.

I actually went on an interview where the man told me in no uncertain words that the job available was a total headache. He couldn't imagine why anyone would want to deal with it. He said, "You don't want this job, it really sucks. This is why it sucks..." He said "Why don't you get back to me, think about it." I told him, "I don't need to think about it, I know I want the job. I know it's going to be difficult and it might suck but it's a great opportunity for me. At least I won't be bored." He told me months later that he was testing me. He wanted to make sure that I really wanted it bad enough, and that if I had had any hesitation then forget it, he would have looked for someone hungrier.

Don't Take My Word for It...

John Verrilli: "In interviews I'm interested in enthusiasm. You want to see people that are really enthused and want the job."

When Claire Raskind was making a career change she had to do some selling. "I interviewed with him four times. Every time I went in—and I think this has a lot to do with it—I told him how much I wanted the job. I wasn't just passive. I mean, every time I went in I said, 'I really want this job. This is really the direction I want to go.'"

Do What You Gotta Do, Say What You Gotta Say.

What I'm going to tell you next is actually pretty common. Over the years I've heard this applied to success over and over again in getting jobs. That is, **sometimes you have to lie.** What I mean is, there are certain things that shouldn't bar you from getting a job, things that have to do with experience. I'll give you an example.

I was interviewing for a job with a Broadway producer/general manager. I knew he was looking for someone a little older, a little more experienced than myself. So when he asked me, "Are you familiar with Actors Equity contracts for the larger size venues?" I said that I was. The truth is I wasn't at all but I knew it was something that I could teach myself over a weekend. I knew of a place where I could get the different contracts and read them over and over until I knew them better than he did.

He also asked me if I knew the Lotus computer program. "Sure," I said. Not. Never used it in fact. But I'd be damned if some stupid program that I could learn in a few hours should keep me from getting the job. Well, I got the job and then I did my homework. No big deal. After a couple of days, these were no longer lies.

David Geffen Lied.

Look at David Geffen. Arguably one of the most successful entertainment businessmen in the world. Mr. Geffen got his start in the mailroom at the William Morris Agency, a job that required a college degree, even though it was completely menial. So Mr. Geffen forged a letter from UCLA, indicating that he was, in fact, a graduate, even though he wasn't.

When Ray Rogers heard about the job at *Interview* magazine, he was told he needed to know desktop publishing. He said, "'Of course I know it.' I sort of knew it. If I could teach myself to type from eighteen to thirty-eight words per minute in a week, I figured why not? I learned it over the weekend. I got the manual and stayed at the computer while no one was here for like ten hours a day over the weekend. And then I went home and read the book. I just made myself learn how to do it. I came in after the weekend and said, 'Oh, I learned Quark Express.' And everyone was like, 'You what?' I mean, I needed the job."

Any Weaknesses?

This is a trick question. If someone in an interview asks if you have any weaknesses, no, you have none. Other than maybe the fear that you demand too much from yourself, or you wish you had more time to read. This person is not your therapist, or god. You do not have to be honest with them. So, you do not, ever, get short-tempered or angry with people. You never lose your cool. Got it?

Any Questions?

"When I do interviews I always say, 'Do you have any questions for me?'" says Robin Danielson. "I'm very suspicious when somebody doesn't. Because if they're not interviewing me while I'm interviewing them, I'm not interested in them. If they're not critical about wanting the right thing for themselves as I am about wanting the right thing for my company, then there's something wrong with them. So, it would behoove somebody before an interview to think about some of the things that they'd like to know."

Stupid Things to Avoid

1) "Immediate turnoff, 'How late do you work?' I've had that one. Goodbye," says Robin Danielson.
2) "Never talk bad about anyone," says Michael Catcher (casting director). For instance, "'Oh, I went into this interview and they were such a fucking asshole.' If you don't like someone, tough. (As an interviewer) you'll think this person's going to say the same thing about me one day."
3) In a competing career book out there, you know, the one with the parachute on it, the advice is given that if you've asked for a fifteen-minute interview, at the end of that fifteen minutes say something like, "It's been fifteen minutes, so I'm going to go now," even if the guy says "No, it's OK, stay." I don't get it. What's the point, why would you do that? What, because now the interviewer knows that you're a man of your word or something? You're also an idiot. The guy might be bored and want to hang out and talk, which is great for you because the longer you're in there, the better he'll remember you. And if it's not you, it'll be the smart guy who hung out and drank cappuccinos and then cocktails. Set up camp, for god's sake. He'll kick you out when he's ready.

"I Want to Hire You, But..."

For whatever reason, the person you're interviewing with might have reservations about hiring you. Maybe you lack the experience. Maybe he was looking for someone older, or a woman, or a man. Whatever. If you can tell that the person is reluctant, you can do what I've done before, and that is, offer them a trial period. Tell the person, "Listen. I know you have some reservations about my experience or whatever. Therefore, how about if we do a three-week trial period. At the end of three weeks, if you're not happy with the way things are going, then just let me go." This way it's easier for them to take a chance on you, without their having to do all the paperwork and being committed to paying unemployment should they fire you right away. It's a great way to prove yourself. Another good thing about this approach is that it proves to the person that you are confident about your abilities to pick things up, and that you're a person that will do whatever it takes.

"I'll Work for Free."

Listen to how Becky Coleman (free-lance commercial and music video producer) did it:

"When I started working free-lance I would go to companies and say, 'I'll work for you for free on the next job.'" I would do that, and then I would get hired over and over and over again. They're little investments that you have to make. **You have to be able just to be a slave and accept that you have to grovel a little bit.** I mean, who's going to say 'No, I don't want you to work for free.' They'll say 'OK, we'll give you stuff to do.'

"Just to get in the door of a big company. You know, you have to say, 'I've really wanted to work here forever.' You just kiss ass. I *begged* to work for them for free. You've got to stroke these big companies and say, 'I'll do anything to work here. I'll do whatever it takes, I'll work for free.' You have to literally *say* these things. If you do that, you are *going* to get hired. It's a guarantee."

AFTER THE INTERVIEW—YOUR SECOND CHANCE

Unless you are offered the job on the spot, at the end of the interview, nothing should be assumed. Don't assume the job is in the bag if you think you did great. Likewise, don't write it off even if you think you completely fucked it up. You've still got one more shot.

Don't Skip the "Thank-You" Letter.

I've spoken with friends (high up the in the food chain, bosses, people who hire) who claim they've blown off otherwise excellent candidates for a position solely because they didn't receive a thank-you note from that person. Why? Rude, they say. Or stupid. Or it shows they don't want the job enough. Got the point?

The first thing you should do in a thank-you letter is thank them. "I just wanted to thank you for meeting with me yesterday." Now, you can write what every other schmuck writes, which is basically this, "I enjoyed speaking with you about the position and learning more about your company. As I said in the interview, I know I could be a valuable asset to your business." This letter doesn't completely rot and so I don't think it would be detrimental. But it ain't gonna help you either. Which might be what you need.

Say the boss can't make up his or her mind. He's interviewed fifteen people and he's having a hard time deciding between you and one or two others, which is a very common scenario. So what do you do?

Personalize It.

I couldn't say it better than Robin Danielson...."We hired a guy who sucked in the interviews, frankly. But that day he had thank-you letters to everybody he saw. And they were personalized. It wasn't just 'Thank you very much for seeing me.' It was, 'Thank you very much for seeing me. The next time you're at so-and-so bar, we'll have to get together,' to one guy who talked about that. To me it was, 'Thanks for seeing me. It was really interesting to talk about planning. I didn't really understand it before, but now I do, and I think I'd really enjoy working with you.'

"After the interview write down a note to yourself about a way to do that. It showed initiative and it also showed that he had writing skills, which I hadn't expected because he wasn't that articulate. There's no way we would have hired him if he hadn't done that."

Put a Pig on It.

"Do something to make yourself different," says Claire Raskind. I think people waste way too much time typesetting their resumes— what color ink or what color paper. That's not it. Nobody's interested in how your resume's typeset and goes, 'Ooh, this person's creative, let's get him in here, look at this lettering.' They know PIP did it. You just have to do something else."

"In an interview," Claire continues, "(this guy) told me a funny story about a pig. And I just thought it was really funny. So when I sent him a thank-you note, I sent him a card with a pig on the front. He remembered me."

No Word? Find Out What's Going On.

People are busy. People are indecisive. Maybe they're waiting for the final budget approval to hire another person. People can be lazy. So if you haven't heard from the people with whom you interviewed after about two weeks, go ahead and call them, and call them, and call them, until you find out what they did, whom they chose. If they hired someone else they'll tell you. No big deal.

John Verrilli: "You have to call back after an interview. Because people in this business are always busy, they've always got calls coming in. If someone doesn't return your call, it's because they're too busy, so you should take the initiative to call again. If it looks like they really need somebody but they're just too busy, then you should be persistent and find out what's really going on there."

"Specifically, Bug People."

After Claire Raskind's first interview with Orion Pictures she recalls, "I didn't hear anything. So I just kept calling and calling and calling. I called every day. I felt really comfortable there and I wanted to work there. So I was calling every day and he said, 'OK, I'll let you meet with the woman (who's hiring).'" She got the job.

"I think the squeaky wheel gets the grease in terms of getting your foot in the door," says Greg Drebin from MTV. "Specifically, bug people in terms of calling and sending resumes and checking up with them. Remind people. People ask me about positions here and send me their resumes. And they may be very qualified but I don't have anything available. Unless they are constantly reminding me that they're out there, they're going to fall in a pile of resumes like everybody else."

Typing—An Unfortunate Evil.

I know it sucks, but typing is the one skill that almost all employers look for first. It's the first phase of weeding out the tons of qualified applicants for a job. Remember, you're not going to be hired entry level because you're so wonderfully smart and talented; uh-uh. They need to get some basic grunt work out of you. So, it doesn't matter if you can type alright, if you don't match their words-per-minute requirement (it usually starts at 45 wpm), it will be tough.

After a year in Hollywood, having worked on two shows that aired on CBS produced by an independent production company (I was not a CBS employee), I was in a good position, I thought, for a job there at the network. Besides my association with the network, my very good friend was practically best friends with the head of Personnel there. I had an interview with her. It went great. Then came the typing test. I'm a decent typist, but under pressure? Forget it. I did like 30. No can do. I couldn't even get a job in the mailroom. No sense complaining, that's just the way it is.

Obviously, not every company is so strict, and there *are* many ways around it (beg), but the sad truth is, if you can type over 50, a lot more doors will be open for you. Not to mention the benefit of signing up with a temp agency.

Some of you are probably saying, "Well I don't want a secretarial job anyway." You're wrong. Secretary, assistant, whatever—it's entry level and it's the only way in. So it would behoove you to practice. 'Nough said.

INFORMATIONAL INTERVIEWS

The good thing about informational interviews is what you don't know—the unexpected. First off, what is an informal, or informational interview, as they're called? It's basically someone at a company being a good guy and agreeing to meet with you for these reasons.

1) Because you're interested in learning more about the field he works in.
2) Because you're interested in learning more about the company he works for.
3) Because you want a job from him (even though you haven't said such, he knows it).

Informational interviews are very common things. If you make a contact through cold calling, or however, and they tell you there's no job available, always ask for an informational interview without calling it that (that's just a term common to most people in the working world). Say, "I know there are no jobs available at your company, but would it be possible to come in to talk with you for ten minutes to discuss the industry in general, and maybe gain from you some ideas about how to go about finding a job in it?" If they're at all cool they're going to say yes.

The thing is, when you ask someone for an informational interview, they know, even if you tell them otherwise, that you'd be interested in working for them. In fact, the main reason you are meeting with them is because you would like to land a job at their company. They know this, they're not dumb.

It goes the other way as well. An employer may have their own agenda in meeting with you. There's turnover all the time everywhere. Employers will therefore agree to informational interviews in order to line up prospects for when a job opens up, so they don't have to start at ground zero. Also, they may be thinking about firing their assistant but are too lazy. It might also be uncool to do an official search in front of the assistant who's getting canned. But if a boss meets with you because you've requested it, then the guy getting canned has nothing to be suspicious about.

So, when you go in to meet with someone, realize that they may be actually considering you for a job and haven't told you this. Therefore, be very specific about the fact that your goal is to get a job with a company such as theirs. Don't go, "Oh, I don't know, I was thinking about marketing but I'm not really sure. There's some other directions I'm thinking about going in. What do you think?" He'll think you're a flake. You're outta there. Let him know that you're seriously hungry to start out doing whatever you have to to work in that field.

And before you leave, ask them if you can leave a copy of your resume for him to keep on file. Some people say you should conclude the informational interview by asking for three names and numbers of people he knows and would be willing to call for you. I personally think that's a little pushy and presumptuous. That's a lot to ask of someone, even a best friend. If the person mentions someone at a specific company during your interview, then you might say, "You mentioned Joe Schmoe at Alamo a little earlier, is this someone I should try to meet with, and can I mention your name?"

Just like in regular interviews, know what the guy's company does so you can sound well-informed. Impress the guy with your knowledge. Make the guy want you to be the next person they hire.

Don't Take My Word For It...

"I was introduced to a senior fashion editor at *Glamour* magazine who said she didn't have a job but would meet me," says Farrah Greenberg. "So I went up there. We were chatting, and I didn't even pull out my resume or anything, and before I knew it she said, 'I think you would be perfect for the job.' And I said, 'What job?' She said she needed an assistant."

INTERNSHIPS—JUST GET IN

What can I say about internships? Not enough. Read the interviews that follow and you'll see how important they are. Get one and work your ass off and you'll be cool.

The Industries

The Industries

2

Film

Wow. Where do I begin? I'll give you a quote that I pretty much agree with, and one that I think most people who work in Hollywood would agree with as well.

> That place (Hollywood) is corrupt and evil. I'm not saying that everybody born in L.A. is automatically an asshole. But there is a certain 'let's do lunch, babe' mentality that I really hate. Here, everybody's in the movie business, everybody's out to make a buck, everybody's full of themselves. This place is a complete cesspool.
>
> (actress Traci Lords as quoted in *Movieline* magazine, Jan./Feb. 1993)

Sure, this is a generalization and there are exceptions. But, if for some sick reason you feel compelled to go into the movie business, which means going to L.A., I don't think it will hurt you to be prepared for the worst.

ECONOMICS

Chalk it up to cheap thrills and couch-potato fever—people are increasingly taking movies home in a box instead of catching them on the screen. While admissions at the box office dropped at a 0.7 percent compound annual rate during the 1987-1991 period, the number of butts on couches soared, causing home video spending to double.

In fact, by 1996 it is projected that spending on home videos will reach $16.2 billion, compared to $6.7 billion expected to be spent at the box office. And although theatre attendence and VCR rentals are projected to grow at the same paltry rate of 1.3 percent annually from 1991-1996 (as opposed to a 13.1 percent increase for videos and a 0.7 percent decrease in growth for box office over the 1987-1991 period), videos will rake in a disproportionate amount of cash due to VCR home penetration increases from 73.7 percent in 1991 to 90 percent by 1996.

So when you think about film production, you've got to expand the idea that it's just about producing things for the wide screen; it's not. Considering that six out of ten movies fail to make their money back at the box office, film production companies, besides trying to bust through with a blockbuster box office hit, also produce movies that go straight to cable or video—ancillary markets that help to support the movie-making machine.

HOW THE BUSINESS WORKS

It's many people's belief that agents run Hollywood and are also responsible for running it into the ground. So let's start with them.

Agents

Here's a couple of agent jokes I lifted from Linda Buzzell's fabulous book called *How to Make It in Hollywood*. (If you're interested in working in Hollywood, it's *the* book to get.)

HOLLYWOOD AGENT JOKE #1

An agent falls overboard in shark-infested waters, yet he isn't attacked. Why?

Professional courtesy.

HOLLYWOOD AGENT JOKE #2

The Devil: "I'll make you the top agent in the business, bigger than Mike Ovitz (super agent voted most powerful person in Hollywood by *Premiere* magazine a few years in a row) But I want the soul of your first-born child and the soul of your first-born grand-child."

Agent (suspiciously): "So what's the catch?"

Not *all* agents are completely heartless, however, agents have the worst reputation imaginable. Become an agent and see if you don't become crazy. The number of calls they make and take in one day is staggering. The pressure to close deals to pull in their 10 percent commission is immense. And the fear of making one false move and losing a star client to another agent is constant. It's just a killer exis-tence. And they love it. As the already legendary agent Bill Block (founder of InterTalent, now with ICM) says, "It's war. Every other agent is the enemy" (*Vanity Fair*, Jan. 1993).

The reason the other agent is the enemy is because agents are only as powerful as the clients they represent, clients that are con-stantly being wooed by other agents. But agents have become so powerful and so feared that it can be argued that it's the other way around: that clients are only as big as the agents that represent them.

Since agents control every facet of a star's career—what scripts they allow them to see, what producers they'll allow them to talk to, what movie offers they choose to tell their client about—they wield incredible power. You can't get near an actor, director, or writer without going through their agent. And try to get an agent to let you give their actor client $3 million for a few months' work without him making you hire a director, cinematographer, and supporting actors whom he also represents and you've done the impossible. It's called packaging. "You want Julia Roberts? That's cool. But if you want her, you've also got to hire so-and-so and so-and-so who we also repre-sent." "Our motto was 'Kill, maim, and package.' There was great camaraderie," says Bill Block, reminiscing about his days as a young agent at ICM. (*Vanity Fair*, Jan. 1993.)

Agencies are prohibited by law to produce films, but since they control all of the creative talent in Hollywood—as well as represent-ing producers—they dictate, as a producer would, what movies will get made. Say, for example, that Michael J. Fox reads a script that he loves written by a writer represented at the same agency as him. See if the agency doesn't find a producer—also represented by the agency—to produce it, and a studio to finance it within a couple of days. They're not just sitting by the phone waiting for offers for their clients, they're creating the opportunities for their clients themselves.

The Studios

20th Century Fox (News Corp.)
Disney
Paramount
Columbia/Tri-Star (Sony)
Warner Brothers (Time Warner)
MCA/Universal (Matsushita)

Besides being the nerve center of filmmaking, the studios' main contribution to the film community would have to be their distribution and marketing force—their ability to release and promote films on a grand scale. Yes, the studios do have in-house producers who initiate projects and get them to the screen, but the majority of movies that you see with the studio's name attached to it are ones that were produced by third parties. The studios will, in effect, finance the production of the film by acquiring the right to show (distribute) the film. And then, of course, profits will be divvied up among the production company, stars, director, and the studio.

The Independents

There are hundreds of independent production companies in L.A. that vary in size from two to fifty employees. Actors have their own production companies as well as do directors and former studio chiefs, among others. The successful independents—with the exception of the really big independents that can afford to be autonomous—have what is known as studio deals. They have their offices on the studio lot and sort of function as in-house producers. They're paid a modest salary, receive free office space and an assistant, plus they still get paid even if they don't get a film made, *plus*, they share in the profits of movies they do get made. It's a no-lose scenario and is therefore coveted.

HOW MOVIES GET MADE

It often starts with a breakfast meeting. Development people—story editors, directors of development, and producers—meet with agents all over town at 8:00 AM. Each has their own agenda. The agent (literary or talent) wants to know what this person's production company is up to—what movie of theirs is likely to get a green light from the studio (so they can pitch their actor-client who would be perfect), what script needs a rewrite (so they can pitch their writer-client who would be perfect), and who's sleeping with whom. The production person wants to be the first to get his hands on the new hot spec script that the agent is about to send out for auction. They each go back to their office and attempt the impossible—getting a movie made and getting their client in that movie.

Production

So, you can be a cog in the wheel of getting movies made, described above, or you can actually make them, which means getting into production. Start off as a production assistant on the set of a movie getting coffee and running stupid errands, and scope out the different opportunities and jobs available. There's too many to name. (Watch the credits at the end of a film.)

LAURENCE SCHWARTZ

Director of Development, New Line Cinema, New York City

Twenty-three years old

Background check—Film production and distribution company with offices in New York and L.A. Films include, besides the ones listed below, *House Party I* and *II*; *Glengarry, Glen Ross*; and *Menace II Society*.

Waiting in the lobby of New Line Cinema. Laurence Schwartz's assistant comes out to greet me and informs me that Laurence, who is already ten minutes late, is presently "on his way." The eager young guy with tie and loafers offers me a coffee, mineral water, or Diet Coke. On the walls of the reception area are posters from the films *A Nightmare On Elm Street 4—The Dream Master,* and *Teenage Mutant Ninja Turtles,* two New Line films. I also notice from the wall decorations that they have also released many more reputable films (by artistic, not monetary standards) such as *Rambling Rose, Torch Song Trilogy* and *Hairspray.*

Ten minutes later Laurence arrives. Things have been a little hectic today, he explains, having just returned from a screening and opening in L.A. A sharp dresser, wearing suspenders, tie, sweater tied around his waist, and an earring, Laurence barely looks older than his assistant. And he's not. At twenty-three years old he is recognized for wielding enough power in this "young is hot" industry—where vice presidents are still paying off their college loans—to be featured in *Premiere* magazine's column, "Flavor of the Month."

So how do movies get made?

Movies get made in different ways. Some of them start with an idea that someone has internally (at New Line). You find a writer to write it, attach a director to it, and then the talent—putting together a creative team to get the movie made. Sometimes a script comes in that doesn't need a lot of development. This is a rare occasion, because things don't usually come in ready to go. You spend a significant amount of time trying to find these, which requires a lot of reading.

Your job title is director of development. What is meant by development?

Development means different things to different people. Most New York development people are chasing books. The studios (Universal, Paramount, Disney, Sony, Fox, Warner Bros.) don't have development offices in New York, they have development adjuncts. They're people that have development titles that spend all their time covering the publishing industry trying to get to the next best seller before it's a best seller, and buy it up before anybody else does. It's sort of a feeding frenzy. We don't develop from books very often at all, so we're different from any of the studios in New York.

How many films does New Line release a year?

We release around twenty-five films a year. Out of these we produce in-house around eight or so. We also have a division of our company called Fine Line that releases more sophisticated types of films.

When did you start here at New Line?

I started working here as an intern while I was still at Sarah Lawrence College around three years ago.

How did you get the internship here, and why New Line?

I didn't know what the hell I was doing when I decided to do an internship program at New Line. I didn't know I wanted to work in the film business at all. My intention was to just try this. I found out who to call and who to send my resume to. This seemed to be the best place. Getting into the internship is difficult in itself, especially in New York where there's not a lot of places to get experience in development. You have to interview and do sample script coverage. **It's very competitive to get an internship that doesn't even pay any money.**

What did you do as an intern?

Basically, I did whatever needed doing. I read a lot of scripts, wrote a lot of script story notes for projects that were in development and for scripts that were coming in. I also started to get involved in bringing scripts in. I did a lot of typing on the computer and filing and Xeroxing—I certainly did my share of that. It was such a small group at the time, and a lot less corporate, that there was a lot of room to sort of pipe in your opinion and get creative, and my boss at the time encouraged that. This was before *Teenage Mutant Ninja Turtles* came out. This film and the *Nightmare on Elm Street* series brought in a lot of money, and the company has since expanded greatly since then.

So what happened was, when the internship was over, I didn't want to leave and they didn't want me to leave, so we sort of figured out together a way for me to stay. I was still in school at the time, but starting to get less and less interested in what I was doing in school and more and more interested in what I was doing here. I was reading ten to fifteen scripts a week and working here around three days a week. I was going to plays at night and screenings, plus going to school full-time. It was just nuts. I was sort of a mess at that time. So we came up with this idea for an apprenticeship, which had never been done. This was an idea I had so that they could keep me but wouldn't have to pay me a full salary while I did more of trying to prove myself. I did this for around four months.

So you sort of created your own position.

Yeah, we figured it out together. Nobody offered me anything—that's the important point. So at the end of the apprenticeship, they had to come to a decision on whether to hire me or not. I was ready for it. I had done good work and had become really involved in the projects and was valuable to the department, I think, so they decided to hire me officially—but part-time because I was still in school. I did this for a while and then came to the decision to leave school to work here full-time when I was in my junior year.

What did you major in at school?

At Sarah Lawrence there aren't any real majors or grades; it's a little alternative. My concentration was in nineteenth-century European literature.

What did you plan to do while you were in college before the internship?

While I was at Sarah Lawrence I wanted to be an actor. That's all I wanted to do growing up. I thought that's what I wanted to do, but then I started to get interested in other things.

Did you have a big interest in film before you started at New Line?

No. I took a year off from college after my freshman year to fuck around because I wasn't doing much and was completely unmotivated. I just did some retail work. During this year off was when I got the idea of looking into the film business. **I wasn't sure I wanted to be in the film business until I was in the film business.** A week before I decided to quit school to do this it was a big question for me. There were still other things I wanted to pursue. It became a big draw though; I was given responsibility, people were listening to my ideas, and I was getting paid.

So they hired you full-time as a creative associate. What did you do?

I have to tell you that I've been doing basically the same things from day one to what I'm doing now. I've just continued to do them with more autonomy and on a higher level—with more authority. Now I can really start my own projects. I now have the ability to do my job better because I know more writers and I know better people. I've developed relationships, which is a large part of it. But I'm still reading scripts and deciding whether they work or not. There's several people reading them before I read them now, as opposed to me reading them right when they come in, which I used to do.

Everybody in this department is trying to find movies that work. We get them from agents, writers themselves that you have relationships with, producers that you have relationships with, directors, friends in the industry, anywhere.

So you have to read a lot?

Yes, a lot. During the week I'll read one or two scripts a night, and then we all have weekend reading. When a new script comes in it goes first to a free-lance reader who does a creative analysis as well as a summary of it. If the script has merit it will then be put on the weekend reading list, which a couple of people from the Creative Committee will read. Our Creative Committee is made up of creative executives on the East and West coasts which meets twice a week by conference phone. We'll meet on Thursday and divide up the scripts to read over the weekend, and then meet again on Monday morning to decide whether or not to proceed with certain projects.

What else does a normal day consist of?

A variety of activities. Undoubtedly you'll have projects at various stages of completion. You'll also spend a certain amount of time looking for new stuff. Once you have a certain reputation, people will be coming to you with new stuff, trying to pitch you on it in meetings or over the phone. It's keeping up with this and trying to continue to massage all those contacts so they'll give you good material.

There's also the projects that you have in development. New drafts of scripts are coming in which you have to do script notes on. You have to meet with the writers. You're putting together the creative team—attaching producers and directors and leading actors to your projects. We'll get involved in casting leading actors who will change the marketing profile of the project. If the movie is star-dependent, then we will have to bring stars to the table in order to get the company to agree to make it.

What's the best part about your job?

The best thing about my job is that I'm getting paid to do something creative that has an impact on culture—which is really the most exciting thing.

Good or bad impact?

That's up for grabs, I think it varies from film to film. I certainly have my own, I don't know if I'd say agenda, but certainly my own goals in mind for the kinds of films that I want to make, and the kinds of movies that I think propel society forward. I'm very aware of whether or not anything that I'm bringing to the table is doing that. **Sometimes projects have to be brought to the table that you feel have a negative effect, but that's a different story.**

I have to be aware of what's out there—what's working and what's not—and try to bridge the gap between projects that I think have integrity, which are creative and fresh, and things that fulfill a market niche—things that are going to please the audience. There's only a small percentage of moviegoers that are willing to take those kind of risks and go to see films that are not classically structured or films that have subversive themes to them. Antistructure films I think are the biggest turn-off to an audience. I think you can get away with a lot of subversive politics and quirky characters and unusual goings-on in a story if it is all framed in a very palatable classical structure. You can sneak a lot in. I'm always looking for those kinds of opportunities and for writers who can do that well.

What's annoying about the job, anything?

The politics of working for a large corporation. I don't know how much I should say. The schmoozing. That's how things get done and how decisions get made, and that's how people are persuaded. **It's not necessarily about content, but it is about schmoozing.**

You seem like a good salesman, a good talker.

Definitely the sales aspect is there. I don't necessarily think that's one of my strengths at all. I feel that my strengths in this job have to do with writing and editing. I think that's to my advantage. I have a good eye and I'm a good editor of material.

Listen, I'm looking for projects that I can get passionate about. That's what's really the best thing about this—something that I believe in on a lot of different levels. Something that speaks to me emotionally or politically, or, hopefully all of the above.

OK, say you have a great script, something you're passionate about—what's next?

In order to get the company (New Line) to buy something, you have to pitch it within the company. I have to sell it to the Creative Committee, then it has to be sold to the presidents of different departments: home video, foreign sales, domestic, theatrical. You know, you've got to get these people on board because these departments are the ones that are going to guarantee the money. And if it's an idea (a "pitch," meaning it's just a concept and outline with no script having been written yet), it's more difficult because there isn't a script that they can read and say, "Oh, this is what it is." You have to pitch them the idea, and that means selling your credibility, the writer's credibility and the viability of the idea as far as reaching an audience—which involves coming up with other films that are similar and that have worked—which is difficult when you're trying to do something that is really fresh. That's when you get people talking about, you know, *Terminator II* meets *Pretty Woman* and all that kind of industry double-speak.

How many projects do you presently have in development?

As far as projects in development right now, I have about eight at various stages. But just because something is in development certainly doesn't mean it's going to get made. Some aren't officially in development, in that they're not on our development report, which means the company hasn't spent any money on them. But I am personally developing them and waiting until they're ready to bring to the Committee.

So you're really developing them, as opposed to taking the hot spec script from an agent. (A spec script is an original, never-before-seen screenplay that an agent will send to a whole bunch of producers at once hoping for a bidding war and a million-dollar sale.)

If you limit yourself to waiting for an agent to send you a script that's ready to go, like a lot of development people do, you're really limiting yourself. It's a shame that a lot of creative execs do that. It's their job to bring in the best script. So their job consists of having relationships with agents mostly, and making sure that agents like them a hell of a lot so that they will send them the good projects. So they spend the bulk of their time schmoozing and lunching with agents. I'm not really good at this side of the business so I have to rely on my relationships with writers more.

There's often a lot of work to be done on speculation before I even bring a script to the Committee. It's not like I just get things in and show them. I have to nurture them myself so it makes for an appealing package when I present them to the Committee, otherwise it's very easy to say no. They want to say no. It's easier to say no. You don't have to spend any money when you say no. If you're going to get them to say yes, and if you're going to ask them to spend money (on developing a script, or doing a rewrite on a script), then you better have a damn good pitch and a lot of reasons lined up, creatively and financially, on why they should pick it. The success of my job depends upon my ability to put together a good package.

Why do you think you've kept advancing in the company?

I hope it's because of the work that I've done. **It's a political business; why people get hired, fired and promoted, I'd be a fool to say it's because of the work that they do.** There's a lot of other reasons why that happens. It's a great mystery. There are lots of personalities involved. We all do things for different reasons.

Why do you think some interns and apprentices aren't hired on full-time?

All I can say is what I look for, and that's talent. That involves a lot of things though. I look for someone who has really good ideas, good writing skills, good communication skills, is a really good spotter of talent, is really plugged into pop culture, has the ability to bring projects in, and knows what the audience wants. You have to be aware of all of that stuff. You have to be a sponge. You definitely have to have interests outside of the film industry. Definitely. There's nothing worse to me than people that have this narrow-minded perspective on film and filmmaking. That's why Hollywood ends up making so many films that are just about the film business.

So you don't look for someone who knows everything about every film?

I couldn't care less. I really don't think it matters. What impresses me is people that have a wide range of interests, a solid intellectual education and who have ideas of what to make films about. I think filmmakers and executives that have this narrow perspective make less interesting work—always rehashing old genres.

Do you have to have a cutthroat mentality to work in this business?

I think you have to have a certain amount of self-confidence. I don't think you have to be a killer. **That's not appealing to me— people who have that shark mentality. Although I can't say that that's not a good thing to have, because a lot of the people that make it are all about that.**

What should someone who wants to be a screenwriter do?

I think they should write a great spec script. I think if they are a director, they should do a great short film. It has to be a good story told well.

How would a writer get you to read their script?

They would have to know somebody that could give them a recommendation. Or if they had a reputable agent it would be no problem. They can't just send me the script. But I am always a sucker for a great cover letter. So if someone sends me a really well written cover letter and tells me a little about their project and it sounds interesting, then I'll respond.

What's a good way to get to be a creative executive?

Start as an assistant, an intern, a receptionist, a reader. There is no *one* way. Getting in with New Line, being an intern is the best way. You get to show your abilities, and it gives us a chance to get to know you.

Where are the film jobs? Are there many in New York, or do you have to be in Los Angeles?

It's almost impossible to get a job in the film business in New York. It's a really difficult thing. There's hardly any doors to knock on. Nobody's here anymore. Everybody continues to be moving to the West Coast. But there are wonderful people devoted to making films in New York, so I think it's possible, but it's not as easy.

How's the dating life for a film executive?

You have to be careful. **There are a lot of people that want to get to know you for a lot of different reasons, which can be a great ego boost at first.** But then you realize that these people aren't your friends, and stick with the people that are, and be really cautious. The glamour wears thin very quickly. There's a lot of politics. It's a tough industry. It can be very cutthroat. **You have to be slow to trust people. You've got to have your guard up at all time.**

What do you think of agents?

I don't know. I don't know why anybody would want to be an agent. **Just when I think all agents are scum, I'll meet one who's amazing; who has great taste and a lot of integrity and who doesn't lie.** I know some wonderful people that are agents, but I don't have a high opinion of most of them.

Is there a lot of stress in your job?

Yes. To make, to find, to produce, to get things in development, to have them make money and to be well received. The difficult thing—and the thing to consider when becoming a creative executive—is the fact that it has everything to do with popular culture, and it never ends. You have to find ways to shut it off for your own sanity. There's always a new song, a new book, a new TV show, a new actor. Any of these things can suggest something for a new movie.

What courses would you suggest someone interested in film take?

You have to have some understanding of what good writing is and have some sort of classical education. I think in order to be involved in the storymaking process at any step of the way, you have to be familiar with the great stories, because they're still coming around. That's where I think a good liberal arts education is crucial, and I can't believe people without exposure to the classics are involved with reading and giving writers notes. A background that has a little bit more wit than just studying and watching movies; certainly literature and history. No one in my department was a film major. Most of us were involved in theatre at one point, in either writing or acting. Most of us were English majors.

What is most surprising or shocking to you about working in this business?

The low amount of money for entry-level positions in this and any other creative field is shocking. Having a work-related social life and work-related friends is weird. The politics is shocking. Balancing different personalities. **Learning how to read people and play people just so that you can have a nice day; it doesn't happen naturally.** It's a very competitive industry. A lot of people are looking over their shoulders.

I've been fortunate to work with very nice people. I have to work with a lot of other people too. When you're in college, if there's someone you don't like, there's usually no reason you have to spend a lot of time with them. **This is a business where you inevitably have to spend a lot of time with a lot of people that you don't like.** That's a hard thing to get used to when you're twenty-one. That's what working for a large corporation means.

Is this a scummy business?

It can be. when I'm in L.A. I feel it much more—the insincerity, the phoniness, the lies, the stupidity. **You have to look before you walk, because you can step in shit. And there's a lot of it out there.**

Note: After this interview, I spotted Laurence's photo (a full-pager) in *Interview* magazine (August 1993) where it says that he's now in L.A. working for Robert Greenhut's Gotham Pictures as vice president of production.

EMILY GERSON-SAINES

Talent Agent, William Morris Agency, New York City

Twenty-seven years old

Hanging out with Emily and her assistant Gina in the William Morris Agency high-rise in Manhattan. "Diet Coke? Water?" Emily offers, as Gina opens the well-stocked refrigerator next to her chair and phone. The two make a good team and really seem to get on well. The chair, which is across from Emily's desk, is where Gina sits for most of an average morning. Here, she places calls and gets people on the phone, timing it perfectly so that by the time Emily gets off one call, her next one is waiting.

Gina will also answer incoming calls, the most important and urgent of which Emily will take. Usually there is at least one or two, but often three people on hold at any given time. Every call that comes in (around two hundred a day), Gina logs into the computer with the telephone number and time they called. This list is called the "phone sheet" (every agent refers to it like the Bible all day), which is revised and reprinted a few times a day. Every incoming call on that list must be returned that day, Emily informs me.

I watch a few minutes of this phone stuff and am readily impressed; both by Emily's grace and by Gina's friendly and cool professionalism. This was no show, for when trying to get this interview by phoning Emily, I received the same treatment by both of them, even before they knew I was a writer.

The reason I mention this phone business is because agents live on the phone. The heavy hand-held phones have been traded in for headsets, the kind you'd see on the Starship *Enterprise* or something. With no time to waste and no idle chatter being possible—two hundred calls a day—an agent must be careful not to offend anyone by being curt or quick. And in a business where egos are huge and fragile, and where an unreturned call is a statement, not a mistake, there's absolutely no room for error. Something you'll never hear twice from an agent's assistant is, "Oh, I forgot to tell you, Joe Schmoe called a bit ago."

How did you start out in the entertainment industry?

I was going to college at Northwestern University in Chicago (majoring in radio, television, and film), and there was a Chuck Norris movie that was filming in Chicago at the time. I did an internship on this movie and got the title of quote, unquote, assistant production coordinator. I really wasn't the assistant production coordinator—they make it sound really fancy. I was the Xerox woman so to speak. But I got to be around the set and help out with things like organizing locations. I got to see how a film was made by being on the set and doing anything that they asked.

The next thing I did was help out on a movie called *Nothing In Common*, which Garry Marshall was directing in Chicago starring Jackie Gleason. I was one of Garry's assistants on the set in Chicago.

Was this a paying job?

You know, I don't even remember. That's a nonissue and nobody should care about that with their first couple of jobs; do something else to make your money. I got Garry's tuna fish and avocado for lunch so he didn't have to eat off of craft services, and I carried his chair and his script.

So when I went out to L.A. people were really impressed because I had two professional film jobs to my credit. On my resume I wrote my positions the way they were titled, which sounded more important than they were. **Nothing's as glamourous as it seems, especially in a glamour industry.**

I wound up taking an assistant job at Creative Artists Agency (CAA) because I thought it would give me a good overview of everything. You could talk to writers, directors, actors, producers, studio people. This was a good source of contacts. When you're an assistant at a talent agency you talk to everybody on the phone, and, believe it or not, sometimes you're talking to people more than your boss. It's also a good place to be (a large agency) when you're starting out, because it's social, and you're going through the ranks with people who have now gone on to brilliant careers as producers and agents.

Then I moved back to New York to be with the man who is now my husband...and I knew nobody. You've got to call everybody you know that might be in a position to help you, besides making cold calls yourself directly. You never know. I went through the Ross Reports and called everybody that I possibly could. I got one very famous producer, David Brown, on the phone directly. His assistant just put me through for some reason, and he had me come in to meet him. He said, "Come on in, let's talk." He didn't know me from a hole in the wall. He wound up sending my resume around New York to various important people.

Another friend set me up on an interview with someone at International Creative Management (ICM) in New York, where I was offered a job as an assistant to an agent, which I took. I worked hard, with very long hours. **More often than not I worked until around nine at night. But just working very hard doesn't mean anything.**

So then how did you make the leap from being an assistant to being an agent?

I was working long hours, and I was one of the few people who was working long hours. Therefore, when Sam Cohn, who was running the office, needed something late at night he would come over and I would get him whatever he needed on the computer, or with anything. Therefore, he and I developed a relationship which was very instrumental for me, and I'm very grateful for it.

At ICM they used computers in which you could make your own programs, and I decided I would learn them. People would come to me when they needed something done on the computer. Not only did I know my boss's clients' availability (whether or not an actor would be possible for a role based on whether or not he had conflicting prior commitments), I knew other agent's clients availability. As soon as I saw that an agent was booking a client in a part, I would put it in a ledger, so everybody would ask *me* whether a client was available or not. **As an assistant you make yourself indispensable as much as you possibly can.**

This was calculated?

Oh yeah. But you don't want to be obnoxious or evil about it. **All you have to do is your job, and do it better than anybody else possibly can.** You never want to badmouth anybody. Let everybody have a chance to succeed. Just do your job and do it well. If I had a situation where I could do a little extra, I would do a little extra, because I thought it would make the difference.

I also talked to the agents about ideas—who I thought were good actors—and over time I think they respected my taste. They would listen to my suggestions about actors for certain parts, and then they gave me some small movies to work on. On my first project I booked two actors.

Around that time Agency for the Performing Arts (APA) was looking to hire an agent, and an actor's manager that I did business with suggested that they call me. ICM didn't have a job to offer me at that time, so I took the offer from APA because I didn't want to wait any longer to be an agent.

What was the adjustment like from being assistant to being an agent?

It's a pretty frightening thing from one day being an assistant to the next day being an agent. **It's like that scene in the movie** *Working Girl* **when I went in to work my first day. I walked over to the typewriter and someone had to say "No, that's your office."** It was very difficult getting used to having an assistant.

When you were starting out, you mentioned you had a few different job offers in entertainment. How did you decide which to take?

I go with my heart. I've taken jobs that weren't financially the best offers. I've wound up making more money by taking a job that initially offered less money, and a year down doubling my salary.

Did you always know that you wanted to be an agent?

No. When I took the job at the first agency (CAA), I took it because I thought I would enjoy it and that it would be a good overview. Actually, I didn't think that I would be an agent at all, but then I liked it—the fast pace and dealing with people. You get to deal a lot with people, and I love people.

How do you find your actors; your clients?

New York is very much a town where actors get developed. I would encourage anybody who is an actor, who is trained and serious about their craft, to come to New York first. This is where everybody gets their initial break into movies. I wind up going to every show-case I can or sending somebody. I take meetings with actors. I go to all the schools. I go to movies and plays all the time.

Is stealing other agents' clients part of being an agent?

I think that's why I like being a New York agent; I don't like steal-ing, I like developing. I'm very fortunate. For example, I just signed somebody, and dollars to doughnuts, in two years time he'll be a major motion picture star. I guarantee it. **And to me that's the most exciting thing—taking somebody with no credits and turning them into stars.** I've been lucky enough to do it a few times already.

Note: A month after this interview, this particular client booked the lead in a TV series.

That's a powerful position to be in; to make stars.

Our job is to get actors as many opportunities as we can. We open the door for them, position them properly, and get them into the room. If they don't deliver in the audition, then that's the end of it. I can't force someone to hire them. **Sometimes I think people give us too much credit. I can't make anybody hire someone.** I can simply open the door and lead them to the position where they can perform their craft to the best of their abilities.

What do you do when you come in to work?

The first thing I do is go through the "breakdowns," which list all the projects—film, TV, and theatre—and what roles are casting. Then, I'll send over pictures and resumes of my clients for a director, producer, and casting director's consideration. Then I call the casting director. I try to be very honest. I don't try and push the wrong people. I don't want my credibility to be lost. I need them to trust me. Frequently, I have already been in touch with the director or producer, having discussed my "name" talent. These calls I usually reserve until the end of the day since many of these people live in L.A.

Note: Flowers arrive from an actor who wanted to meet with Emily, but who had to cancel.

Is being an agent stressful?

I'm very lucky. I have a family—a husband, a son—another life. The problem with this business for most agents is that it's so consuming and there's always something that you can be doing; shows you could be seeing, scripts you could be reading.

What does it take to be a good agent?

I think one's success in this business in New York is from their taste. You have to have good taste. I think you have to be educated. I remember when I was in L.A., someone called an agent and wanted their client to do *The Cherry Orchard,* and the agent said, "Who wrote it?" My feeling is that if you want this job you should know who wrote *The Cherry Orchard.* (Chekhov.) I think you need to go to a tremendous amount of theater and film, and you have to watch TV. You need to cultivate your taste as much as you can through all of this. You need to be personable and know how to deal with people. You have to deal with people (actors) who on a daily basis are being rejected. You *do* have to be a sensitive person, and I think it's horrible when agents aren't. You also have to have a mind for negotiating and a stomach for it.

Why a "stomach" for it. Can it be nerve-wracking?

It's horrible. Sometimes you have to pass on an offer because the money is too low it's insulting to the actor. And you have to wait for them to come back with another offer. **It's hard. You have to figure out on a daily basis what somebody is worth.**

Is there anything that surprised or shocked you about this business?

What surprises me is that more people haven't figured this out; that you can do this for a living, because it's just so much fun. We have a great time every day. How many people can say that about their jobs? And it's not that there's little money in it—there is. If you're not in the entertainment industry though, you probably don't even know that this job exists.

Has this job helped your social life, or is it your social life, and how do you know who your friends are?

There are a lot of people that want to become friends with me or my husband because of what I do. Everybody knows an actor. Or they want to meet the famous people that come over. So much of my social life is mixed with business—plays, benefits, screenings, parties—that me and my husband try to have fun with it.

How many hours do you usually work a week?

Well right now it's pilot season, so for the last two weeks my assistant and I have been here until midnight every night. That's when L.A. is open until, and when you work in New York that's what you have to do. I have a lot of business in L.A. I do my New York business in the morning and I do my L.A. business later in the day. And if I'm not here working until midnight, I'm at home and usually on the phone. I also have a fax machine at home.

The people in L.A. always call at the end of the day to make their offers, so I'm up all night negotiating. **The day I gave birth to my son I was negotiating from my hospital bed.** I had a client who was being offered a TV series and he wanted me to be involved. So I had to do it from my bed. I had the baby at 8:30 AM and I was on the phone to L.A. that evening.

What would you recommend to someone getting out of school as far as getting a job goes?

When you get out of school, use every connection you can. If you don't have any connections, then figure out who does what you want to do. Find out every agency that's out there from the Ross Reports. And if it means that you're the receptionist initially, if you're smart, you'll figure out a way to get an assistant job when it opens because you're right there. You say, "I'd rather do that than answer the phones."

You know how much money I made on my first job? Two-hundred and fifty dollars a week. Who can live on that in a major metropolitan city? It's impossible, but you find a way. I went from paying $20,000 a year for an education to becoming a secretary. And if I'd had to start out as a receptionist, I would have. Even if you have to work for free. I worked a lot for free when I was first starting out, working on those movies.

Go in, answer the phones, type, get into the environment. And then you can talk to people about what they do. Slowly but surely you'll learn what they do. And when you're ready to do what they're doing, they'll let you if you're smart. But you have to be in the right place.

Is it hard going from the training program (see bonus mini-interview with agent trainee immediately following this interview) to being an assistant, to being an agent? What are your chances?

No one is saying to them they're definitely going to become an agent. It's up to them whether they're going to be made an agent. You create your own destiny. To figure out how to become an agent is probably one of the sure signs of whether or not you could be a good agent. **If you can figure out how to become an agent then you get to be one.** You have to figure out how to be indispensable to the company, and show signs of promise. No one just goes down the hall and says, "Oh, you're next in line, you're an agent." No. You've got to be aggressive about it, but, with finesse.

Does being a woman have any advantages or disadvantages in being an agent? Being an agent seems like such a macho guy thing.

My sex has never affected me adversely in any way. In this company it's amazing how forward thinking they are about women's issues—maternity leave and such.

Where do you see yourself in ten years? Could you go on from here to producing?

Absolutely. A lot of people have done it. It's a perfect launching pad to producing, because you deal with all the studio and network people. I've already had a few offers to produce movies, but I'm not interested in that right now.

Is it rewarding financially?

Yes, I'm thrilled. If somebody said to me that I could make this kind of living before I did it, I would have laughed. **I get to do exactly what I always dreamed of, and make more money than I ever thought possible. I love it.**

INTERVIEW WITH YOUNG GUY AT RECEPTION DESK AT WILLIAM MORRIS

Being a few minutes early for my appointment with Emily, I took the opportunity to interview the young twenty-one-ish guy in the suit and tie at the reception desk who was filling in while the receptionist ate lunch. Knowing a little about talent agencies going in, I figured he was in the infamous "training program," which is notorious for its long hours and little pay, and requires starting in the mailroom. He tells me that, yes, in fact, he is in the agent training program.

So, what do you do in the training program?

You start out in the mailroom, and then from there you become what's known as a "floater." Which means that you get to work in all the different departments of the agency (*talent*, meaning actors; *literary*, meaning TV and film writers; and *music*), which is very valuable and educational, because it gives you exposure to every department.

Is this a job you can get right out of college?

Yeah, this is my first job out of college. To get in the internship program you really need a college degree. Some people have had experience working in other areas of entertainment.

Have all the agents gone through the training program like you're doing?

Most of the agents started in the mailroom. The heads of the company now all started in the mailroom.

How long does it take from the mailroom to being an agent?

You go from the mailroom to an agent's desk as an assistant (around six months in the mailroom). When a desk opens up (when the agent's assistant leaves or gets promoted to agent) you apply for the position if it's in the department that you want to be in. After this, it takes around two to four years until you become an agent.

You have to reapply just to get out of the mailroom to become an assistant? Sounds competitive.

There's heavy competition to get an assistant job.

How's the money?

The money stinks, but it's worth it because the payoff in the long run can be good. It's a great business and it's exciting.

How many of the people drop out of the training program?

Around 75 percent after the first year. It's very difficult to become an agent. A very small percentage of the trainees and assistants will ever become agents. It's a long road and you've got to be really committed in order to make it. You've really got to pay your dues. When you work in the mailroom you really got to do the shit-work; everything from being a chauffeur—driving the big agents or clients around—to cleaning up after their meetings and running their personal errands. **It's almost like pledging to get into a fraternity. It's such a tight group and so few people can make it,**

you've got to prove how committed you are. It's a great place to learn though, and it gives you great exposure to the industry. It's good experience for getting into other branches of the entertainment industry.

What kind of person do you have to be to be an agent?

You have to be very persistent. You have to be kind of slick in a way. Not that you have to be sleazy, but in order to open up doors that might be closed to you, you have to be very political. **You don't need to be a genius or a bookworm to be an agent.** You have to be an outgoing, friendly, likeable person who communicates well with other people.

Agents don't have the greatest reputation do they?

The reputation of lawyers aren't so good either, but we're well respected and we're vital in the entertainment area because we handle every aspect of someone's career.

Do you get more dates?

Not yet, but I expect to. (Laughs.) You don't want to make any promises you can't keep though.

BECKY COLEMAN

Television commercial and music video producer, New York
   City

Thirty-two years old

A week or so after I do this interview with Becky at her apartment, she calls my machine and leaves the time and location of her next commercial shoot, you know, so I could see her at work. She says it won't be a terribly big or exciting shoot, but nevertheless, I'll get a sense of what she does. "Try to come between three PM and seven PM, there should be some cute model babes around at that time," she says.

Saturday, the next day, the day of the shoot. I show up at this small studio production space that's packed to the gills with lighting, camera stuff, and a cast of characters who look like they might have just been released from jail. Tattoos, cut-off shirts, ponytails, jeans— they look like a bunch of bikers. Not the actors, the crew. The stars of this A&W Root Beer commercial are a couple— a nice couple— neither of who appears to be under seventy years of age. Becky lied. It's three-thirty PM, just a motley crew and some old people under heavy lights doing take after take after take of:

> Wife to Husband: That's sounds pretty nice.
> Husband to Wife: Especially after sex.

and then:

> Husband to Wife: That sounds pretty nice.
> Wife to Husband: Especially after fooling around.

Try to imagine George and Barbara Bush (you know, the ex–first couple). Becky would repeatedly have to remind people that she needed "absolute silence on the set please. We're trying to catch these moments, so try not to laugh." Hard not to.

After the fiftieth take however, I was practically asleep, and others were losing steam. Becky had to keep the energy and pace up by shouting, "OK, let's go!" But things went OK. During one quick break from shooting (reloading film), when Becky, the director, and the cameraman were huddled talking, I overheard her say, "The lens changes were great. Real fast. I'm loving it." But it's New York, not Hollywood, so she didn't say "babe."

How did you end up in New York working in production?

I was raised on a horse farm in Iowa. When I graduated from high school I decided to come out and live with this step-aunt of mine in New Jersey. When I got here I made a lunch appointment with this woman who had been my sister's college roommate, and who dated my brother back in Iowa. She was out here working for this director. We had lunch and she said that the company was actually looking for a receptionist.

So I went back to her office, I applied, and they gave me the job.

I was making $200 a week. But it turned out to be, much to my surprise, one of the biggest companies in the country. They made one huge commercial after the other—Coca Cola, Kodak. And it was when commercials were all sixty-second spots. This director was really, really good.

What did you start out doing?

When I first started there I didn't know anything. I didn't know how to type. I didn't know anything. I was a disaster at phones. **Everyone wanted to fire me. Everyone treated me like shit. It took me a long time to learn anything.**

The first four years I worked for this one guy, I worked my ass off. I never worked so hard in my whole life. Never anything shorter than a twelve-hour day. We used to go like eighteen hours a day. And everybody became comrades, because this particular director was a maniac. He was real mean. Real, real, real mean. Everyone hated him and openly discussed how much we hated him. Clients would come in and they would go, "poor thing."

But it was good? I mean, you stayed for four years.

It was fabulous. I learned in a really good and thorough way. If you weren't absolutely top drawer, cream of the crop, you were out. It was really uncool not to be really thorough. It was a healthy competition of being really good. If you wanted to go home at eight PM, it was like, "Uh, pussy." It was like, "This is where we separate the men from the boys." We got into it. It was the only way to deal with it.

It was frowned upon when you left early. I got that right away. So even though I was making a pittance, I would go there two hours early and just type the dictionary or any document that was sitting around. Or even though I had nothing to do with a job—you know, all the grown-ups would be on this side of the room freaking out over some problem—I would just stay.

No one would give me any responsibility, but I was just there all the time until they left, and *then* I would leave. I would just stay there. I wanted a better job. I wanted to be one of them. I worked like a slave. I was a martyr too though, but it paid off for me. **Vanna White is not going to show up at your door with cash and prizes every day.**

Why wouldn't they give you any responsibility?

They were so afraid to give away the slightest bit of responsibility to anyone because they might fuck it up. So if you can't sharpen pencils well, no one's going to give you the next step. I literally would make sure that every single person there had sharp pencils and staples in their stapler. They never had to think about anything like that.

Did they tell you to do that?

No. You just have to look for ways. You do things before anyone ever asks you. It's a really good feeling to say, "It's already done." And then they start to pay attention to you. **People are afraid of excellence. They're threatened by someone who might take their job someday.** If you subtly make someone's life really easy, and then you go away for a minute, then they realize you've been doing all these things. The easier you make other people's lives, the more they'll like you and need you around.

So I guess they noticed.

I guess. Six months later I became this director's personal assistant. This meant everything from planning his wedding to keeping his schedule. Not dealing directly on the job (the making of the commercial), but just always being with him and doing personal things. "I need a stove. Make sure it gets out to my beachhouse." So I'd call the plumber, call the gas man, buy the stove. You know, just shit. Knowing where he was all the time and knowing everybody that he dealt with. **Seeing how many phone numbers I could memorize so I wouldn't have to look anything up, because if he had to wait too long for me to get anyone on the phone I would be out.** Every personal thing that went on in his life, I would make arrangements for. And then he started to let me coordinate jobs for him.

So that was the next step. What does the production coordinator do?

The producer tells you what to do and *you* actually make it happen. You coordinate everything from what the menu's going to be with the caterer to what time the trucks have to leave the barn to get to location on time. You hire the people: the electric department, the grip department, prop department, wardrobe, stylist, makeup artist. You've got to get them up there. How many cars do you need? Who's going to pick up the cars? You've got to make hotel arrangements and pay the hotel.

Making all these little details happen. Getting directions for everybody. Making sure the caterer knows what time to get there. Nothing can go wrong. If the caterer is fifteen minutes late, you're into an hour of penalty for seventy guys. That can be thousands of dollars. It's just a million little details that you're responsible for. It's a really hard job. It's just constant. It's hour and hours of nonstop work. **You don't stop for lunch. You don't stop to eat. You don't stop. You're hard pressed for time to go to the bathroom on a really busy day.**

So how does the process work—how does the agency decide what director to go with?

The client, for instance, is Budweiser. They go to the advertising agency. The advertising agency creates a campaign and will usually bid three different companies—three different directors they think are right for a job. They talk to the directors to see how they want to approach the job. The directors bid the job, submitting a price to the agency. Then the agency will award the job to a director. And directors have their favorite producers that they bring in.

The agencies don't have in-house directors?

No. They tried that about five years ago. Everybody started to panic because nobody knew what was going on with the industry. New York was falling apart. The big bucks were gone. I mean, when I first started, I would go out to L.A. for like three weeks and stay at the Beverly Hills Hotel when I was a *production assistant*. Big money all the time.

Also, companies back in the eighties used to be able to afford to keep staff producers. But times have changed a lot, and nobody can afford to keep fifteen or twenty people on staff. So, everybody's free-lance.

What will make the agency pick one director over another— is it just price?

That certainly has a lot to do with it. One director might say, "I can shoot this in two days," and somebody else might need three days because they have a different idea and it might take a little longer. One person might want to build a set, and the other might want to take it to a location, a real place.

To a place that's impossible to find, probably.

Exactly. We did a cereal commercial that wanted to have a guy running through a wheat field. But there were no wheat fields in the United States—it was like in the middle of winter. And it had to be shot, in the can, and on the air within a month. So you just get on the phone.

And that's your job as producer?

No. As producer you hire someone else to do that (the production coordinator.) You've got to make sure that it's really happening, though. You've got to fly someone there, make sure it's available, make sure it's not going to get *cut* in a week. You know, you get everybody out there, and they say, "Oh, we cut that field."

You just have to make sure everything is covered. Even for a little location on a street. You could get there and they could be doing major Con Ed work that day on your street. Did they paint a new line down the street that week, or do something that could totally change the look of what you wanted when you originally decided to shoot there?

You get asked to find some really crazy things. Most recently I had to find a battleship to shoot on. That was really difficult. We wound up having to shoot it in Italy. I researched Chile and like a million countries to find a battleship that would allow us to shoot there and that was right aesthetically.

What did you do?

OK, I need a battleship. I went to all the naval bases, they said no. The Navy said no flat out. Then I go to Puerto Rico's navy, or to a small country's navy, see if they'll go for it. They say no. Then you just start to call naval museums, the *Intrepid*. You start with one phone call and you take that until it's exhausted—until there are no more possibilities—and then you go to the next thing.

It just takes a lot of tenacity. I mean, you can do almost anything. **Before you tell someone no, that it doesn't exist, you better be right. Because someone else will find it and make you look like an asshole.**

Which inevitably will happen.

Right. I was doing a Kent cigarette job and I could not find the right location. We were looking for a beach, the perfect beach. Scoured the Caribbean, can't find it. Scoured everywhere, can't find it. Finally resorted to scouting by air. Spending thousands of dollars. Helicopters, airplanes, extraordinary lengths just to find this perfect beach. Dominican Republic, we finally find it. "Love it, love it, love it, OK, bring everybody down."

The next day everyone flies down. The caravan goes off to this location. We're driving through the jungle. We get there. There had a been a storm the night before. We'd finally gotten the agency, the director, everyone there—the beach is gone. It's gone. It had washed completely away. After spending thousands of dollars to find this beach, it was gone. It was like, "I swear to God it was here yesterday. I swear to God."

What happened?

They settled for something else. It always gets done.

So how do you go from coordinating to producing?

You just fall into it. You get in with a company and you coordinate (as a production coordinator) a million jobs. Then for some reason their favorite producer isn't available, so they give you the opportunity if the job is small or whatever. That's how you make the leap. And then at that point you have to decide that you're going to stop taking coordinating work so people are forced to relate to you as a producer.

How fast can someone go to being a producer from, say, a production assistant?

It took me a long time, longer than most people. Other people were better at schmoozing and bullshitting their way. It took me a good six years. Other people start, and are producing in two years.

So you can start doing it young?

It's a very youth-oriented business. I've seen a lot of really sad cases where people hit their late forties or early fifties and have just become "uncool." There's a lot of young people coming up and they (the older ones) just don't get hired anymore. It's really pretty awful.

How much money do you make producing?

Producers are making $700 a day now, as opposed to $350 for coordinators. Producers earn their money when the shit comes down and there's a serious problem. When you have to make a judgement call where the whole job is at stake. It's not like they work so hard all day. Coordinators work their ass off, but when the shit comes down they can always go to the producer and say, "What do I do?" They look to you to have the answers and to see all the potential things that can go wrong—which is anything.

Like what?

For instance, we were on the street in front of the Beacon Theatre (NYC) a couple of months ago shooting a commercial for Close-Up or someone. And because I've been in this business for a long time, I know that as long as you have a permit from the Mayor's

Office to be shooting, then you only have to be four feet away from the storefront. You are on public property and you have every right to be there. You might piss somebody off there. But if you don't have any equipment closer than four feet to their store, they can't force you to give them money. So people would try to shut us down. This guy said "I want two thousand dollars." And I told him, "That's called extortion, and I would be happy to call the police right now and have you arrested for trying to extort money from us." You can't be afraid to say that.

What's the worst shoot you've been on?

I've had a lot of those. (Laughs.) The worst shoot I ever did was in the Caribbean. All of my worst shoots have been in the Caribbean. People are like, "Oh great, you're going to the Caribbean." It's a nightmare to shoot there. Everything takes six days that would take one day here.

We did a job in St. Thomas for Continental Airlines where we had to build a set eighty feet under the water. The punchline of the commercial is, we see these two people, we don't know where they are, they kiss, and suddenly a fish swims by, and boom!—we reveal that we're underwater. The water's so crystal clear that we don't know where they are.

Well, the first problem was, how do we get their hair not to move and sway like it's under the water? We tried a million different things, nothing worked. So we just put it back in ponytails and made them look they they had really short hair.

Then the agency cast a woman with a perfect body. A beautiful, beautiful model that had never scuba-dived before. Mind you, she had to go eighty feet underwater, take off her breathing aparatus, and have it outside of frame. Now how smart was that? She's supposed to look comfortable kissing a guy eighty feet down and then a fish swims by? OK, we won't even talk about fish wrangling. Bringing in exotic fish and getting them to swim right in front of somebody? (She shakes her head in disbelief that they actually did it.)

Plus, there was a big danger factor on that job. We had like thirty divers underwater at one time. We had to get people to sign special waivers. People were running out of air. It was horrible. The actress didn't want to do it. She wouldn't sign the waiver. We finally got everything done, we shot, we wrapped. I said to the producer (Becky was production coordinator on this shoot), "We're in the Caribbean. You cannot send film back to the United States counter to counter. You must send it with a human being or it's not going to get there."

Well, nobody listened to me. It was too expensive. It would have cost $900 to send somone back with the film. So we sent it back counter to counter, meaning, we put it on the plane and it was supposed to get off at the other end where someone would pick it up. It never made it. This commercial was supposed to be on the air in like five days. They were going to cut (edit) the whole weekend. So the fact that the film was lost, the negative was lost, meant that we were not going to deliver this commercial. We were in big trouble.

We searched and searched and searched. We wanted to send our own people in to look for the box. They (the airline) said you can't do that. And I said, "Yes, there's got to be a way." And then they said, "Well, you've got to do this and this and this and this." **"OK, don't tell me there's no way we can do it. I'll do it, you watch me."**

I had special police hired to go with our production assistants to a fifteen-acre warehouse at JFK to scour it in the middle of the night with flashlights. I hired like five special police with special passes, went through this whole process to search for this box. It wasn't there.

I'm calling all over Pan Am. Calling, calling, calling. Can't get anybody with any power on the phone. Then I called this one special, supersonic number that I had gotten after like twenty-five phone calls. It just so happened that it was like, the CEO of Pan Am or something. His secretary had just left and he picked up his own phone. It was a one in a million thing. I told him the whole story: "This is going to devastate our company, we're going to shut our doors if we don't find this box." Well, he made a phone call and all of a sudden wheels started to turn faster than I had ever seen anything happen before.

It turns out—this is the god honest truth—it turns out that the guy at the warehouse we had been speaking to for the last three days to find this stuff, was using this one box to sit on. For three days he had been sitting on the box, *literally*, answering the phone and talking to us. I was practically throwing up. I had never been so scared in my whole life.

So when someone tells you, "No, you can't do that," you have to ignore them. It's always possible.

Everything's possible. It's real satisfying to know that you can get anything done. And it's really funny, because it's hard to relate that to your personal life. When I got married, I had four PAs (production assistants) at my wedding. I had four PAs just running around doing things for me. It's the only way I knew how to get things done. (Laughs.)

What do you do on the set?

You've brought all the elements together, it's up to the director now. That's why he's getting $8,000 for that day. Hopefully he's done his homework and truly has a vision about getting this off the paper and putting it on celluloid. Your job is just to keep an eye on things. See what's going on and make sure the agency is happy, that they're being treated well.

You're schmoozing and politicking and keeping an eye on the clock. You've got an assistant director there who's running the set. Moving the day from one scene to the next. That person has done a schedule to make sure that all the shots are laid out in a way that makes sense, so the day progresses in the most logical way.

Are the agency people on the set all the time?

All the time. That's a must. You need their approval on everything that you shoot.

Another part of your job is to keep the agency people away from the director, to let him do his job. The last thing a director wants is all the agency people hanging around camera, whispering in his ears. There's an old joke: "How many art directors does it take to change a lightbulb?" And the punchline is, "I don't know, what do you think?" No one seems to be able to make a decision. One person is allowed to go up and talk to the director from the agency group. You must make that clear, because if you don't, there will be ten people from the agency all telling him that they want something different and it will drive him crazy. "Let him do his job. That's why you're paying him $8,000 a day."

Does something always go wrong on a shoot?

No. I just finished one of the most pleasant jobs I've ever done, for Ivory Soap. It had the potential, though, for a real bad day. We were shooting at a woman's excruciatingly expensive mansion in Dobbs Ferry. Everything in her house was an antique. It took the prop department two hours just to prep the house so everyone could come in.

The first scene was a baby having her morning bath. And of course, it's the baby thing. It's Ivory Soap. It's a baby splashing and having a wonderful time in the bath. And with babies and animals you never know what's going to happen. A baby that is animated and giggly and laughing and fabulous in a casting session, can wake up cranky that morning and you're dead. So you have to have three back-up babies for every baby that you hire. But this baby was so adorable—laughing and splashing—and we got amazing footage.

How is producing music videos different from producing commercials?

Videos are much less arbirtary. There's a reason that you do stuff. With advertising, there may be an idea: "a woman in a nightclub wearing a red dress." Twenty meetings later this commercial has nothing to do with a red dress anymore, or a nightclub—now she's in a cornfield or something—but still somebody has a bee in their bonnet that "she must be wearing a red dress." But it no longer makes sense for her to be in a red dress. "Why is she wearing a red dress?" "Well, I don't know. Because she is." A lot of that goes on in commercials.

With music videos you just go with the flow. "OK, somebody just kicked us out of a location?" you just swing the camera around and start shooting something else. You know, it's real renegade.

You've done some rap videos, right? That must be different than shooting babies in bathtubs and shit.

These boys are a handful. I'm here to tell you. I did the "Down With the King," Run-D.M.C. music video. It had like 70 percent of the hip-hop community. Everyone was there doing cameos. Salt 'N' Pepa, LL Cool J, Kriss Kross. **We were shooting in a church in Harlem. We had to pad people down coming in. We collected a box of guns. One guy walked in strapped with Uzis, Glocks, everything.** We had a huge box tagged with guns.

They're gangsters. They're kids from the ghetto that have money suddenly. Thank god we were shooting in a church. A lot of personality conflicts, East meets West sort of thing. And here I am, I'm white, I'm blonde, I'm a woman. Some people would just tell me to go to fuck myself. That was a trip. That was an incredible opportunity.

Is producing more of a guy's thing?

There's many, many more women producers than men. It's so dominated by women it's incredible. There's a handful of men producers. Most of the directors I know like women producers better.

Why?

I don't know why. I think the business was wide open for anybody who could do the job. And if you're a woman and you're fun to look at, then that's even better. You know, it's men directors, "Gosh, why not have a woman around."

So, do you like it?

It's really satisfying and the money can be great. It can also be devastatingly scary, because as a free-lance person you can sit around for three months and not do anything. **You could be really hot for a couple of years, and then somebody might hear some story that gets distorted, or you've made a big mistake or something, and you're over. You're only as good as your last job.**

WORDS FROM ON HIGH:
Advice From the President of Troma Films on Breaking In

LLOYD KAUFMAN

President, Troma Films, New York City

Background check—Troma Films is a twenty-year-old New York–based independent film studio and has distributed the instant classics (by title alone) *Chopper Chicks in Zombietown*, *Class of Nuke 'Em High*, *The Toxic Avenger*, and *Surf Nazis Must Die*.

Is this a difficult industry to break in to?

It's an industry that is extremely closed. It's probably the most nepotistic industry in the world. It's probably the most racist and sexist. It's probably the industry that is most controlled by the smallest number of people. But other than those minor details, if you pleasure the right person it's a cinch to break in.

Twenty years ago there were many, many small movie companies flourishing and many entry-level job possibilities. Now you've got almost none; they're all dead. You've got five or six major multinational companies, and very few truly independent studios. And traditionally, it was those little independent studios that gave opportunities to the Martin Scorseses of the future.

Troma is a breeding ground for talent. In our film library we have two movies with Kevin Costner. How would he have started if it weren't for independent movies? And quite frankly, we want young new geniuses to use our company and our movies as a stepping stone to bigger and better things. Oliver Stone worked on some of our movies. The movie industry is unique in that once someone gets a beachhead or showcase for his/hers/its talent (or pleasures the right person), two days later he/she/it could suddenly catapult to being a million-dollar director.

So doing a small independent film is a good way to start.

Yes. You can learn it all and more. However, the independent film-maker is not respected among the bureaucrats in the general industry. You're respected more being some kind of a bookkeeper at Paramount than for writing and directing *Sgt. Kabukiman, N.Y.P.D.* You need not get the attention of those higher up who can say "yes" to you.

In the same way the Troma team creates our stars, like the Toxic Avenger, we are creating young executives, young directors, young writers, young directors of photography. There are people who start on our movies getting coffee, being messengers, who end up direct-ing second unit or as production manager. Imagine if you're nine-teen or twenty years old and you have a production manager credit on *The Toxic Avenger.* You put that on your resume, that's a hell of a thing. You can cake dance into a big-time studio job, the big shots will find you, and the bureaucrats will feel safe hiring you.

How many resumes do you get a week?

Hundreds a week. Many contain personal letters from people who grew up with Troma films—people not interested in working for just any company, but have specifically sought out Troma. This is a very hot industry right now and Troma is a brand name with a loyal following.

Any creative accounts of somebody trying to get a job with you?

Creative *accounts?* We certainly have had to come up against lots of creative *accountants* stealing from us....But you don't want to hear about that. Someone trying to get a Troma job...hmm...We had a guy working on Wall Street who used to send us Christmas cards. He used to send us weird, funny, crazy Christmas cards for two or three years, looking for work, and there *was* no work. Then one day some-thing opened up and we said, "Remember that guy who sent those weird cards? He must have a great sense of humor. Let's get him in. Let's have him fill the job."

He really wanted to be here, and we gave him a job. He's still with us, and his sense of humor—it's unfortunately more Troma-tic than ever! On Wall Street, this guy used to wear a tie every day. Now after a few years at Troma, he rides to work on a Harley, showing off his tattoo and pierced ear.

So that's the type of person who winds up getting a job.

When a job opens up it's usually the person who's extremely aggressive about wanting to work here. They're willing to work for very little; they just don't want to go away. And besides, a phony film school can cost him/her/it $20,000 per year, whereas Tromaville pays them...not much...enough.

We've got a young guy, a student, who's going to the Cannes Film Festival with us. He's paying his way. He's bringing his sleeping bag and we'll give him a floor to sleep on. He understands that the Cannes Film Festival is like a crash course in the movie business and the making of movies too. Everybody's there. He'll meet all sorts of people, from the heads of major Hollywood studios to underground filmmakers. That's because he'll be working alongside Toxie, Kabuki-man, and Tromie the Nuclear Rodent in the Troma offices at the Carlton Hotel at the epicenter of Cannes!

Is filmmaking, the actual work on a set, as crazy and demanding as you hear?

It is on a Troma set. A lot of people don't last more than two hours. We have people that come out of film school and they think they know everything. And we say, "OK, you can be an apprentice, or work in the prop department." And two hours later they flee. They can't stand it. They can't do it. We make them use their brains even when they are cleaning the crew's bathrooms.

Any advice for a young person wanting to break in?

You've got to forget about the money. Don't think in terms of "I'm working eight hours and therefore I should get paid for eight hours. If I work that extra hour I want money." The smart kid will say, "I'm going to forget about the money and do whatever I can to make *The Toxic Avenger Part IV* the best possible film."

If eighteen- to twenty-year-olds have got to have $500 a week, then they should become accountants or dentists or something useful. This isn't the business. This is not a business to make money. People assume they're going to come into this business and make their fortune, and it's not that kind of business. One must worship and adore movies.

Your impressions of working in film?

The thing I find about the movie industry is that 99 percent of the people are absolute scum. They're horrible people, they really are. Very nasty killer rabbits who hate movies. But the other 1 percent are really the greatest, most wonderful people in the world. They love movies—the art of movies and the business of the movies.

What about someone will make you hire them?

They've got to love movies. They've got to be enthusiastic. We want them to be able to write, to type letters, to speak intelligently on the phone—the basics of being a humanoid. And there aren't too many people like that, to tell you the truth.

We're looking for people who read a book occasionally, who have some kind of genuine interest in life, who are alive. It's very hard to describe it, but most people are not alive. They're doing what their friends tell them to do. They're living their lives because their friends tell them to live their lives that way. And they're afraid to live for themselves. As the Bard said, "to thine own self be true."

Are connections helpful?

Not with Troma. But certainly in the main industry it's very helpful. Half the industry is somebody's son or nephew or lover. And it's amazing, there are a lot of talented sons and lovers out there.

I'm turned on by people who love movies, who are movie nuts. Because then they can deal with the horrible business end of it. The lying and the ripoffs and the nastiness and the phoniness.

3

Advertising and Publicity

The 1980s merger madness seen in all industries did not exclude advertising agencies. Acquisitions and mergers doubled in advertising land in 1985 as compared to 1984, and is still the trend in the nineties. It's the perception of bigger being better that confers credibility and stability as well as providing international service. Presently, over 55 percent of worldwide advertising revenues are being generated by publicly reporting agencies. But if big and corporate is not your thing, don't fret. The fact remains that there are around 22,000 advertising establishments in the U.S., with the average firm employing about eleven people.

When you talk about the hot houses of creativity, the smaller, private companies generally garner the most attention. Chiat/Day in New York and L.A., Fallon McElliot in Minneapolis, and Wieden & Kennedy in Portland are good examples. And what it shows is that you don't have to be in New York or to a lesser extent, L.A., to do good advertising. As Mr. Fallon of Fallon McElliot says, "Imagination doesn't have any geographic limitations." (*The New York Times*, January 18, 1993.)

ECONOMICS

"The long-term outlook for the advertising industry is bright," according to the experts at Standard & Poors. While the five hundred largest agencies experienced minimal revenue gains in 1991 (2.9 percent), 1992 figures doubled that, and revenue gains for 1994 on are expected to be vigorous. This increase in revenue for the agencies, however, can largely be attributed to improved productivity and workforce reductions. These were basic, mandatory recession-survival measures taken by the agencies as a reaction to manufacturers' reluctance to advertise in a depressed economy.

Manufacturers know that in a recession that advertising becomes beside the point. You can say, "This product is better than that product," and give ten good reasons supporting that, but you're still not going to sell to a consumer who's not considering *any* brand. So what does a manufacturer do? He cuts his advertising budget, resulting in losses for advertising agencies and pink slips for advertising employees.

The worst seems to be over for the agencies though, so cheer up advertising wannabes. Two factors support this. One, corporate restructuring—that late eighties happening where companies laid off a lot of people, cooled off on their advertising, and took a deep breath before jumping into the pool again—is pretty much over. They're back in the pool. And two, the economy is expected to brighten up, making for more willing and confident consumers.

But these aren't the only factors at play that spell good news for the advertising industry. Since around 1990 there has been an explosion of new products to enter the market, all of which require advertising. More significant, however, is the dissolution of trade barriers in Western Europe and the quick spread of democracy in Eastern Europe, two events that have sent American advertising agencies running to set up operations there.

TOP GIGS

Creative

ART DIRECTORS AND COPYWRITERS

To say that the copywriter writes the ad and the art director designs it may have been the case 30 years ago, but not today. The two work together as a team, literally working in the same office a few feet from each other. Both are equally responsible for creating the concept of the ad, writing it, and designing it. In the end, of course, it will be up to the art director to make it look visually perfect and for the copywriter to make the final touches on the copy, but until then, both are doing the same thing—trying to come up with an ad the client will like and approve, that is at the same time fresh and creative.

ACCOUNT PLANNER (READ ROBIN DANIELSON INTERVIEW)

ACCOUNT MANAGER

The Account Manager acts as the middleman between the agency and the client. He or she takes the creative product produced by the creatives and presents it to the client. To quote Robin Danielson, "(Account managers are) the nerve center through which a lot of concerns are passed. They're screening. They're not letting the client know how panicked the creatives are. They're trying to project a facade of confidence. They're not letting the creatives know how negative the client is, because they don't want to dash hopes.

"They're dealing with their own management about the fact that the account isn't profitable or needs to be more profitable. They're responsible for how much time people are spending on stuff. They're dealing with the media people about where things are being placed and about what their deadlines are and whether or not those deadlines can be moved.

"They're just trying to keep the whole thing from falling apart. And the thing is, nobody ever thanks them for it, because it's like being a party planner: the only way you'd know what a party planner did would be if it didn't work. If it works then you have no concept."

Media

Note: A friend who recently left Foote Cone and Belding, to date, the largest (in account dollars) advertising agency in America, told me that the "media" positions that follow are not good entrees into the positions listed above. In fact, as an assistant media buyer, she was housed in an entirely different building than the creatives and account people.

RESEARCHER

You compile analytical reports of viewing and reading habits and provide support and statistics for the media planner who will determine the best media buys for a certain client and product. There's a lot of math and computer work with very little human interaction. Credit is taken for your work by others.

MEDIA PLANNER

The account manager will get the client to commit to a certain budget, to spend x amount on buying media space and time. The planner, based on information provided by researchers of the public's media consumption, determines the most effective medium/media to advertise a product in. What television shows, magazines, radio shows attract the demographics that the product is trying to sell to. You're looking at consumer behavior and are always on top of people's media habits. You're wined and dined by network people out to convince you that their shows are what your clients need.

MEDIA BUYER

The buyer negotiates the buy with each station for a client. He or she works closely with the client and planners before the buy is negotiated and operates as the middleman between the network and the client.

ROB SLOSBERG

Copywriter, Chiat/Day Advertising, New York

Twenty-seven years old

Background check—Chiat/Day was named "Agency of the Decade" for the eighties by *Advertising Age*. It's known for being a more cutting edge, "creative" agency. Two of its accounts are Reebok and Nissan, and it is probably most famous for its Energizer Bunny ("It keeps going and going...") and NYNEX Yellow Pages ads.

Michael and Elliot never worked at Chiat/Day. Advertising life represented in the TV show *"thirtysomething,"* in which everybody

knows your name and is constantly bumping into you, might exist in
TV land, or Philadelphia, but not here. Advertising life here exists on
five floors, each the size of a football field, and each indistinguish-
able from the next. Dozens of partitioned spaces are separated by
four-foot-high walls. There are no doors, only nameplates on the side
of your outer wall.

It's all part of the business philosophy, which includes no one
having a title other than "creative executive," and is the reason you
will find Jay Chiat's (a partner in the company) cubicle right next to
Joe Schmoe's. This is not to be confused with modesty, however.
These offices could not be more impressive, aesthetically or func-
tionally. A Macintosh and jet printer on every desk, and conference
rooms with the latest in electronics, as well as in designer leather
chairs. Though the setting and decor of *thirtysomething* was aban-
doned when creating this ad agency, the chic/relaxed personal
wardrobes of hot young execs were not.

How do you like advertising?

Getting paid money to sit around and say things like, "What
about a donkey sitting on a chair sipping an iced tea?" Or, "What
about a shot of an elephant's butt?" It's great. You just throw around
ideas all day long and you get paid for it. That's not a bad job.

Where did you go to college?

I graduated from U. Mass., Amherst, in 1986 with a journalism
major and mass communications minor.

Six months before graduating, and just like anyone else who's
twenty-one years old, I had no idea what I wanted to do with my life.
No idea. It was a very frustrating time. Very, very scary. I called a
couple of friends, and my cousin said, "Well, you can write, and
you're sort of a creative guy, why don't you go into advertising." And
I was like, "Oh, advertising."

My dad was in direct marketing at the time, and he had come up
through advertising. So I asked him how to get into advertising, and
he said you have to put a portfolio together (a "book" as it's called in
the advertising world)—a series of speculative ads. So I put a terrible

book together that at the time I thought were brilliant. They were just terrible, terrible. The body copy was well written, I just didn't know how to write a headline. (Laughs.)

How did you pick the products for your book, and, how many did you do?

I just randomly picked products. For a first job, a junior spec book should have anywhere from fifteen to twenty-five ads. There should be a few campaigns of different products. A campaign is three different ads of the same product with a tag-line or through-line that's consistent in each ad. And then also have a few one-shots.

So I went to my first interview and my dad said, "Don't get your hopes up because your book is real bad." I did the stupidest thing. I teach a class at the School of Visual Arts, and I tell people that are starting that when you go to your first interview, whatever you do, don't bring poems, short stories—anything you think is creative that has nothing to do with writing an ad. I tell everyone *not* to do this. Of course, then I didn't know any better, so of course I brought a short story.

So this guy is looking through my book, and this is at one of the worst agencies in the city, and he says, "Well, it's not very good." **He said, "By any chance do you have anything that shows that you can write?"** I said, "Well, I just happen to have...,"and I pulled out my short story. He read the whole thing right there and hired me.

What did you do at your first job?

My first account was Genesee Beer. I'm embarrassed to say what it was, but it's OK because they made me do it. It was done on bad video with bad lighting. **It looked like a bad Chia Pet commercial or something.** I had to tie an animal, through copy, to Genesee Beer. My first assignment was the cougar. So the copy was, "Hey, look at that cougar. Boy is he smooth...just like the taste of Genesee Beer." Or, "Look at that tarpon jump. There's nothing in the world like a tarpon...and there's nothing in the world like Genesee Beer."

It was bad.

The worst. So then I was laid off after eight months, even though I was working harder than anybody in that office.

Then I went to DMB&B and was there for eight months, and then was laid off again. When I was laid off that time I was thinking about quitting the business. I loved it and it was fun and I was having a blast, but I didn't know if I could take getting laid off anymore. It was frustrating.

My third job was at this small place that isn't around anymore. Then I got my big break at Scali, McCabe, Sloves where I had great clients. It took three years of hard work but it finally paid off. Then I went to Ogilvy & Mather where I was vice president, senior copywriter.

You say it took hard work. Anything else?

The best advice I ever had was from this guy who said, "I've got six words for you. "Your book, your book, your book." He said, "Take an advertising class at the School Of Visual Arts and make your book better. Nothing will get you better jobs and more money except for your book. Nothing else. Not personality, not good looks." **I was like, "Really, I won't be able to go in and be a good guy and move up?"**

How do you get interviews with people or get people to look at your book?

Everyone does it different ways. If you're a real advertising geek and you flip through award books (*The One Show* is an annual advertising awards book. Also read *Design and Art Direction* and *Communication Arts*) a lot of the same names keep coming up. A lot of people just call up the names of people they see in the book and say, "I saw your ad and love what you've done. I know you don't have any jobs up there, I don't want to get hired, I just want you to spend five minutes with me and look at my book." Sixty percent of the people will say, "Sure, come on in."

What good does that do you if there isn't a job available?

It does you good if you're good. If you're really good, they'll remember you. When a job six months later comes up for a junior copywriter, trust me, there aren't that many good young people just starting out. If you have a great book the person will remember you. Or they'll know someone at another agency who is looking for someone.

So if you have a good book it doesn't matter who you are, you'll get a job.

Absolutely. If you have a great book it doesn't matter if you dropped out of grade school and never took any formal education after that. The creative director here never finished college, but he's a very smart guy and does great advertising. They don't care who you are. Most would prefer a diverse background.

Is it ever too late to get into it? You know, is thirty too late?

Absolutely not. Come on. There's a great poster in the lobby of one of the School Of Visual Arts buildings that says, **"At thirty-five Paul Gauguin was a bank teller...It's never too late."** And it's true. I think at forty it's not too late. Because one thing that really helps you to be a great creative person is to have as much stimuli as possible to draw on. Go to different countries, work at different jobs. One of the better young copywriters here, I'm not exaggerating, had ten jobs before he got into advertising. He worked in a steel mill, as a road construction guy, he worked as a carpenter. You know, a real blue-collar type background.

So taking advertising as a major is...?

Stupid. No, there have been people who have taken advertising as a major and have made it into the business, but not many. It can't hurt, but it's good not to have such tunnel vision. You know, exploring different areas of life always helps in advertising. A lot of times it's just people that have done other majors, like philosophy and psychology.

How's the money starting out?

Starting out as a junior copywriter, which is what you start out at, is anywhere from $17,000 to $26,000. Then if you get some work produced, and you have a good book and a good reel, you can make a lot of money very fast in the business. You can go from $25,000 to $40,000 if your book has some produced ads. You have to show that you can produce work, and that you can sell ads to the client.

What accounts do you have here?

I work on the Reebok account. It's the only account I work on. Every so often I'll get pulled onto a different project. I just worked on the American Express account.

So you get some diversity from just one account. I imagine that could drive you crazy, working on one account all the time.

Not really. That's what is so great about this business. If you're not doing fun work, no account will ever make you love your job. If you're doing bad ads on Preparation H, bad ads on the Smoker's Patch, bad ads on the Tidy Bowl Man, and then another bad ad on Windex—it doesn't matter how diverse your accounts are, you're not having fun. If you're working on just Nike or Reebok, or just Volvo or BMW, you're pretty much set. All a copywriter and art director works for their whole career is to do more creative work. And if you're doing creative work then it's not tedious.

Are you saying you can't be creative with Preparation H or with the Smoker's Patch, or, you're not supposed to be creative?

These are accounts that because of the nature of the account, because of the kind of people that run the account, they will never buy creative work.

Are they wrong because of this? Should they take the fun, cutting-edge creative work?

Of course. Every creative person wants to believe that the most creative ad will sell the product best. **I want to sell Reeboks here.**

I don't just want to make my reel great and have people go, "Ooh, you made that cool commercial?" I want to sell shoes too. That's what we're in the business of doing. It's just that Reebok allows you to do more fun work. Those other accounts, they don't really want it. You could come to Marlboro with a hilarious ad—that's really funny, that will break through, that everyone will laugh at, and that might even sell cigarettes—but they're not going to buy it because they've got a successful campaign with a cowboy in it.

Have you ever had an instance where the client didn't like your idea because it was too crazy, too wild?

All the time. I worked at a big agency that had all sorts of conservative accounts. We showed work constantly to Marine Midland, Bounce, and Crest—wacky work, hilarious stuff—and there was absolutely no way they would accept it or approve it.

And you thought it was good though.

I thought it was great. (Laughs.)

Is that frustrating?

It's the most frustrating part of the business...by far. **Your client says, "How dare you show this to me. This is too funny. We can't run this. This is Preparation H! We have to talk about flaring hemorrhoidal tissues. We can't be talking about 'butts' and things like that."** It's frustrating because you finally get to a level where you have fun. You're laughing with your art director. You've finally come up with an ad, and you're both jumping around the office saying, "Yes we did it! We broke through the clutter, we came up with a brilliant idea. We're going to be famous, we're going to win awards." And then you go to the client and they don't share your enthusiasm. It's the most frustrating part of the business. Definitely.

What's wrong with them? Why don't they get it?

Sometimes they're boneheads. Sometimes they're smarter than you. Sometimes they know a lot better than you do, and a year later you say, "God, I was really stupid for even showing that ad. I'm so glad they killed it."

Are there any politics involved where you work, outside of the client-agency relationship?

Sure. Wherever there are people there are politics. There are places I've worked where a boss will ask you to work on a commercial, and you'll come up with something you think is great. You'll show him and he'll say, "I don't like it, it's not working for me." So you go back to the drawing board. And then two weeks later you find out that he made a presentation to the client and presented your idea with a slight twist on it to make it look like it was fresh, and put his own name on it. This happens to everybody in the business at least once, especially when you're just starting out.

Why do some products do great and some fail? Is it all advertising?

It's very complex. It's never just advertising. **David Ogilvy said, "The worst thing a bad product can have is good advertising."** That's because if it's a bad product and it has great advertising, people will go running to the store, they'll buy it, and say, "This is terrible." And you'll have entire America hating your product and you'll never dig yourself out of the hole again. So it's partly an advertising problem and it's partly a product problem.

Does that mean that the best advertising is truthful?

I've always felt a lot better about doing advertising that truly came out of the product, that really was honest. Those are the ones you feel best about. But there are times where you make a bigger deal of a benefit than should be made of it because you want to make it seem like a better product. Kind of like what Visa says (he does this in a funny, serious announcer-type voice): "And they don't take American Express." Very effective advertising, but it's total hyperbole. It's really bullshit because they say they don't take American Express at the Olympics. Well, they don't take Amex in like the souvenir stands right in the Olympic village.

Really? They make it sound like the whole town doesn't take Amex or something.

Exactly! You've said exactly what 99 percent of America is thinking, which is why it's an effective ad campaign. But it's very deceptive too, and it's unfair to American Express. American Express is taken all over in Barcelona.

Do you think it was wrong for Visa to do?

I guess **all's fair in love and war and advertising, because advertising is basically a war anyway.** American Express was killing them for a while and they had to do what they had to do. And it worked like gangbusters.

What time do you come in in the morning?

Most creative people come in around ten AM to ten-thirty AM and stay to seven PM or eight PM. Nobody in a good ad agency leaves at five PM. Last night there were about ten people here until four AM getting a presentation together for Reebok.

Sounds like it can be stressful. Is it?

It depends on the person and if you let it get to you. It can be very stressful. Your boss will say, "We need an ad by tomorrow. It needs to be running by next week. We need a mechanical by Thursday. We need to shoot the ad Wednesday. And it needs to be great. Since we're on that schedule, you need to show concepts to me in an hour." And you're like, "Huh?"

How do you come up with your ideas?

It's very hard to sit in a room by yourself and say, "I've got a great idea." How do you know it's a great idea until you bounce it off of someone? That's why the copywriter and art director work together, always. Both are in charge of coming up with the idea and the concept of the ad. Both talk about the visuals and both talk about the headlines. It's not old world advertising where the copywriter writes the words and the art director thinks of the visual. It's all very interactive, very synergistic between the copywriter and the art director.

Do your ideas come to you when you're not at work?

Absolutely. Absolutely and totally. Sometimes you're sitting there trying to do an ad and you'll think of it. Sometimes you're sitting there trying to do an ad and you won't have a clue. You'll just go through a hundred bad ideas, it will take you two days, and you won't have a thing. And then you're walking home or you're in the back of a cab or you're in the shower, and you get this great idea. This always happens because you can't turn it off. You can't walk into the elevator, the door closes and boom! your mind shuts it off. It doesn't work that way. You just keep thinking about it. You can't help it.

Does that drive you crazy?

The only time you're at peace is if you can turn it off, which you have to train yourself to do. You have to say, "I'm going to stop thinking about advertising right now." And that's difficult, but you can learn to do it. It's either that or I find when I'm close to peace is when I've come up with a decent idea, we've showed it to the client, and they've bought it.

But then you're worried that they're going to unbuy it, that they're going to call you and say, "Ah, we don't really like it." So you're going through anxiety then. Then you're picking directors and going through anxiety thinking, "Am I going to find the right director?" Then all through the production process as you're shooting it: Did you get the right shots? Did the director shoot it the right way? Color correcting: is the film going to come out looking right? Is the sound just right, the way I want it? Is the voice-over right? Is the music right? It's all anxiety. So I guess the only time you're at peace is when it's done the best that you could have done it. The commercial is done, and you're not thinking of any new commercials yet. You sit at your desk and go, "Ahhh." Then you're at peace.

You get involved in the production process and picking the director as well? You don't just write the ad?

It's your ad. Once you conceive it, you carry through with every aspect of the production process. You're there every step of the way. You look through directors' reels and pick a director. You talk to the director on the phone and tell him the way you want it shot. And the director gives you the ideas he has too. You go to the shoot and talk to the actors to make sure they're doing it right.

Once you're on the shoot it's the director, the copywriter, and the art director who have the most control. There's forty people there and those three people have the most say. It's your commercial. If it's not the way you saw it in your head you say, "No, no, no, that's not the way I saw it. Don't shoot it that way." You have that control. But a director might say, "I know you saw it that way, but watch the way I do this because I think I have a better idea." And a lot of times they're right. So there's a lot of input from the director, if not total. Sometimes you have a really crummy storyboard that's boring to look at, and the director will make your commercial for you.

So with the director you can't let your ego get in the way of the creative process.

Yeah. And it's hard sometimes, but you can't. It's hard because you say, "I know. It's my commercial. I see it in my head." It's hard to get past that and let the director do what he wants to do. That's where you get the famous and frequently used words on a commercial shoot: "We'll shoot it both ways."

Then after you shoot it you go into the color correct where you make the film exactly the color you want it. Then there's the music person you have to talk to. You'll say, "I want a jazzy feel," or a sound effect added in, and they'll come back with something.

What's the most fun part of your job?

Getting an ad approved that you think's fun, and seeing it through production. It's a creative process all the way through; from writing it, picking the director, to choosing the music. It's fun to make all these decisions. It's as good as a mini-movie up there. It's a faster reward. You do a commercial and three months later it's on the air.

What's the low point of advertising?

It's people posturing to get the right offices. It's people stealing ideas. It's creative heads being afraid for their jobs. It's people getting mad at you for taking their assignment away when in actuality it was fair. Someone complaining they don't get as high a salary as some other guy or girl.

It's very, very competitive because it's so unlike any other business. You have this thing that you can touch called your book and your reel; it's tangible. It shows exactly how good you are. This ad, this ad, this TV spot, this TV spot—that's you. You can say, "This is my book, this is exactly how much you should pay me." In other jobs it's this bullshit that you can't really touch. This is something that you can touch, so it becomes very competitive. **If you do a great ad, you're increasing your salary. If you steal someone else's great ad, you're stealing their salary.**

Also, I think the low point of advertising is after getting really, really excited about it, saying, "This is the most fun business, I love it, it's great," and then you wake up in the morning and you say, "It's just an ad." You know what I mean? Everyone in advertising has gotten that feeling at least once in their life, if not once a day.

It's also a very unstable business. Say Reebok decided to pull their account and go to another agency because of something political up at Reebok, or because they didn't like something here, or because they got in a fight with Jay Chiat. There's forty people here working on Reebok alone. That's forty jobs. That's a fact of the business. It's very unstable.

What kind of person should consider advertising?

Someone that has got a diverse background, that's been through different experiences and feels that they know a lot of a little bit. Everyone I've ever known that's good has known a little bit about a lot of things. I think I'm no genius in any one given area, but I think I know a pretty good amount about a lot of different areas in life. Also, I think you should read a lot, and you should be able to write a paragraph. You should know how to write, because when it comes down to it you're going to be writing that body copy.

People think that advertising is all about being wacky and wild and out there. It's not. It's about having great ideas. If you have great ideas, that means you'll have a great book—which means you'll be a great copywriter.

Do you personally ever have a philosophical problem with advertising. For instance, selling people stuff they don't need?

Yeah. Absolutely. It depends on the person. **Some people can just go nine to five and not even give a second thought about selling somebody a douche.** But other people really feel like they have to give back to the business in other ways. I have lots of pro-bono stuff. We're doing this project now called Witness. It's a program that helps to distribute media technologies like fax machines and video cameras to third world countries that don't have them, to help them expose injustices and atrocities in their countries—kind of like Tiananmen Square.

This question can really get to some people to the point where they have to leave the business. People say, "What am I doing here? I'd rather be writing a novel or selling a stupid screenplay." But advertising is also a beneficial part of society. It's a cog in the wheel of society. It sells products. It's part of the economy. It stimulates economic growth. There are some good things to advertising. You would never know about a lot of products if there wasn't advertising for them. It can be and should be very informative sometimes. It's like a form of literature. You're expanding someone's mind by telling them about something. That sounds a little philosophical but....

So you're informing them about something rather than trying to convince them to buy something they don't want.

There's a great old ad for advertising itself that says, "Contrary to what people think, advertising won't sell you something you don't need," and it has a lady with shaving cream on her face. It's a great ad because it's so true. **You can't make someone buy something they don't want.** Are we all zombies walking around in a trance (imitating a zombie): "Ah, ah, now what? Oh, there's a commercial for Massengill douche. Oh, I'll go buy a douche." I hate when people say that. I mean, if you don't want a product, you're not going to buy it. It's so silly.

Are there any other preconceived notions that people have about advertising that aren't true?

No one puts women's breasts in ice cubes. Nobody puts penises in Spaghettios ads. Subliminal seduction is bullshit. It's not true. If I could change everyone's view just on that one point it would be good because everyone thinks that we're plodding weasels, and we're not. We're just people trying to make an honest living, trying to sell products.

ROBIN DANIELSON

President/Director of Account Planning, Mad Dogs & Englishmen, New York City

Thirty years old

Background check—Mad Dogs and Englishmen is a New York–based boutique agency that has won more than sixty awards. Its accounts include *The Economist*, Parsons School Of Design, and *The Village Voice*.

There I am after five minutes, on the floor in the kitchen area of this huge office/loft with a massive Labrador lying on top of me. The founder of Mad Dogs—Nick, the Englishman—is crashed out on the frameless futon with the other dog. It is a Saturday, after all.

"Hi, Charlie? Sorry I'm late," Robin says, as she strolls in.

"No, that's fine. Hi." I say from under the dog. Quickly, Robin notices the progress that Nick has made on an ad that they've been working on, as Nick springs to life and they start discussing the ad. Me, I'm still under the dog.

Footsteps. The dog jumps off me and runs to Nick's wife, Sharon, who's rounding the corner. Great, now I'm the only one on the floor, looking like an idiot. "You must be the writer."

"Yes, hi. The dog, he was lying on me, that's why I was, ah, on the floor." I look to Nick and Robin for a confirmation of my story, but they're too busy looking at the copy of an ad on the computer screen that reads, "You're looking at my thighs, aren't you?"

I have coffee and a chat with Sharon and wait for Robin to take her attention away from the computer screen.

So what does all this have to say about advertising? That it doesn't have to be big and corporate, stuffy and Madison Avenue? That the work never ends? That it's people's passion? Yes.

What were you planning to do when you graduated? Where did you go to school?

I was an art major at Yale. When I graduated I hadn't thought much about getting a job because my parents are hippies and they wanted me to be an artist. I got out and realized, ahhhh, I got to work. So I waitressed and racked my brains as to what I might like to do.

What made you think of advertising?

I had always been one of those kids who remembered every ad. I didn't watch the shows much, I watched the ads. I talked back to the ads. I fought with the ads. There was a Skippy ad, "Ounce for ounce Skippy has as much protein as fresh tuna fish." And I'd go, "But you would never put as many ounces of peanut butter on a sandwich as you would of tuna fish." You know, it would be disgusting. So it's a completely specious claim.

So I took a couple of classes in advertising at the School Of Visual Arts and I met a guy who suggested that I meet a friend of his who had started a two-person agency. I was the first hire. So I went in and I answered the phones and I typed things and I met with media reps and wrote some ads and art directed a couple of ads and put together pitches—and I was completely burned out. They used me. I mean, they really used and abused me. I would open the agency in the morning and close it at night. And I was like, "Why am I doing all the work here?" I was such a martyr. So I left and thought, "Well, screw that, advertising, uh-uh-uh."

So I went to temporary agencies and stuff thinking of publishing, the magazine business maybe. But then I got called by an ad agency and I told the people, "You know, I don't want to do advertising anymore." But the job offered me more money than the rest of the jobs. It was receptionist work, but it was also being an assistant to the three partners in another start-up (ad agency). It was about twelve people.

So, quickly I stopped doing secretarial stuff and started doing secondary research: writing proposals and points of view of things, analyzing information. For instance, I would put together reports on the car market.

In both jobs you went from doing secretarial stuff to doing real things pretty quickly. Were you real ambitious?

It was more a matter of managing my management. In the first job where it was just two guys, it was intensely emotional all the time, and a lot of my job was helping them function. Not doing work necessarily, but being a bit of a therapist to them I guess. Telling them things were OK or saying, "Well, if you look at it *this* way it's not so bad." Or saying, "I'm so proud of you, you did a great job."

And I think I carried that habit into the next job, just in terms of noticing what people were doing and saying, "That's really interesting," or "How did that go?" And they talked to me about stuff because I seemed interested. **It wasn't like I was ambitious, because I really didn't give a rat's ass. It was more that I was nice.** I was smart and I was nice and I was really efficient. And they felt like they could trust me. If there was a day when I was out, they really noticed that things were different.

So then what happened?

Then my first boss called me and told me that he and his partner—who I hadn't got along with—split up and that he wanted me to come back, but to be an account planner. What he wanted to do was do a three-person creative team, with the writer, art director, and planner working on the creative. And I made him grovel and apologize for being such an asshole to me, and once he'd done that I went back.

Then a little while after that he got asked to go to a big agency to start a planning department, so he took me with him. And then that agency got split into another agency, and by that time, you know, I was basically a planner. I'd learned my chops. Then they fired my boss and I quit in protest, and fortunately got a job very quickly at Chiat/Day/Mojo, and was there for three years as an account planner.

I had never heard of account planning before. How is it different from account management?

It's new. There are lots of account managers, there aren't very many account planners. It's the new thing. Account planning was brought to America by Chiat/Day. And when Chiat/Day was named "Agency of the Decade" at the end of the eighties, a lot of agencies thought, "Well, what's different about them? It's planning. Let's get some planners."

And what does a planner do?

The gist of it is that you get and have a knowledge about how consumers interact with the category, the product, and advertising. And based on that information you have a point of view about what the advertising should be about.

Say we needed to do a newspaper campaign for a new ship for Royal Caribbean. I would go on the ship—I took three cruises during that period of time—and write reports about it for management so that they understood it. Writing a report about why it was good or bad or different, who the kinds of people on the ship were, what were they like, and comparing it to competitors.

I did focus groups with travel agents. Talking to travel agents all over the country about how they sell cruises and what they think of the industry and blah, blah, blah. I would administer a tracking study of advertising effectiveness. I would sit with the account people and do the brief. There would always be a brief written *before* the work was done about what the advertising was going to be about. Like who we were talking to, what are we trying to do, and what were we trying to say?

The brief. That sounds important. What's that about?

The planner writes the brief—the thing that says who's the target audience, what is the advertising supposed to be doing, and what's the advertising about? For instance, on an account like Reebok you might have six ads running at the same time: a TV campaign, a print ad for a trade book, a print ad for a runners book, a sales video for the tennis category, etc. The planner decides what each of those ads is going to be about.

Break the brief down for me.

First off, who are we talking to?—the target audience. It would be like setting you up on a blind date and saying, "Well, let me tell you about this girl. For one thing, she hates Indian food, so an Indian restaurant is out. She's really gorgeous and what she really likes is theatre." You know, just giving some stuff about this group of people that somebody can work with.

Two, what is the advertising trying to do? Is it improving the image of something? Is it making the phone ring? Is it changing somebody's mind about something? Is it reinforcing an opinion about something?

So you sit with the client and discuss what the ads are going to be about. Clients are proud of their brand. They're proud of what they do and they want somehow to convey *everything* that's wonderful about themselves. And communications don't work that way; you don't have that much of somebody's time. A client will say, "Isn't this great?" But to an impatient person who's flipping through a magazine, it doesn't matter. It's just not important.

You have to manage their expectations. So if the client says, "No, no, no, I want it to be about this," the planner will say, "Well, if you want it to be about that, the ads you're going to get are going to be like this. That's not what you want. What you need is for it to be about *this*, because then the ads you're going to get are going to be kind of like *this*."

I would then take my brief to creative and they would either say OK or they'd say, "Uh-uh, I can't do this; I don't think this is right."

Would they ever look at the brief and research and go, "Why, fuck it, I just want to do this fun, irreverent ad instead"?

Yeah, I've had disagreements with people about whether the ad was supposed to educate the people about the benefits of something, or make them think that something was cool. And I've often run into situations with creatives where they would prefer to make something cool, but usually because they did think that that would work, to make it cool.

Does cool sell?

It depends a lot on the target audience. Say you're talking about runners, people who run fifty miles a week. People who run fifty miles a week tend to be almost like anorexics; they're control freaks, they're obsessives. They write down their bowel movements. They count what they eat. That's what kind of person you're talking to. And when they look at a shoe ad, they're information hungry.

So say the client wants an informational ad and the consumer wants an informational ad and the creative just wants to do something really cool? You've got to give them (the creatives, i.e., the copywriter and art director) some empathy for the person you're talking to. It's like, "You're not selling yourself shoes, you're selling shoes to *this* person."

That's interesting, your job being to make them empathize with the buyer.

I feel that it's my job as a planner to do that. If the people who made the advertising (the creatives) had some real genuine affection for the people that they're talking to, that would be great. It's generally a group of extremely egotistical young men, and the system makes them that way. **Because in order to get work sold in a**

bullpen environment, it's the person who says "I've got the biggest dick," that's the guy who wins.

A lot of times the work is relatively equal, so the stuff that gets through is very often from somebody who is willing to say, "I am king of the fucking world." Therefore, **successful creatives are trained to be assholes.** So, to try to make that person have some genuine affection for a maniacal runner or for a Poughkeepsie housewife, or for a black teenage girl...you have to like them.

Actually, that's been a lot of my planning background: trying to help men understand how to talk to women. (Laughs.)

We had to do an ad for a nutritional program in primarily what we would call the "diet population of America," which is the vast population of women who have been on diets, or are on diets—basically, your average woman. But the ad was being written by two guys. And the subject of food and dieting and body image for women is a very different subject than it is for men. I'm telling the guys, the creatives, "women are fucked up. You know, we're all a little bit neurotic about food. We all want to lose a little weight. We all hold out great hopes that something will work, and we're sick of being fucked with in advertising."

And the thing that they couldn't understand was the "women are fucked up part." They kept gravitating back towards things that would be perfectly fine for a man, but were really insulting to a woman. Like, there was a headline that said, "When one hand is holding the TV remote, is the other hand holding the Dipsy Doodles?" You know, it's like saying, "Are you a fat slob?" **You can say to a guy, "Are you a fat slob?" But you cannot say to a woman, "Are you a fat slob?" because they're too fucking insecure.**

I couldn't make them get it, so we did a small focus group of women. The writers did a whole bunch of lines that we could show the women, most of them basically saying, "Are you a fat slob?" And in a brief, I had written that women are a bit defensive about their weight, i.e., "You're looking at my thighs aren't you?" The writers observed the focus group, they listened, they got it. That line really worked. So that's what a planner does—help the creatives understand what it is that they're trying to do, and who they're trying to talk to.

The psychology of selling.

It's like psychoanalysis. It's periodically doing a meeting where somebody who sounds really fucking smart—because half of the planners in this country have English accents so they sound really smart—tells you about your brand and your customer, and the client gets into it. Planners do a psychological profile of what's going on, and clients find that fascinating, because it's all about them.

Do you like your job?

I love my job. When I was young, somebody once said, "If you could have any job you want what would it be?" And I said, "I would like to be paid to notice things." I always thought that was what I was really good at. Going around and going, "That's cool!" Or, "Look at that! Isn't that neat the way that that's doing that?" Or, "Look at this, this is really stupid!" I really loved doing that, and I got a job doing that. That's pretty fucking amazing.

How does that happen in a daily way?

I was on the phone with a potential client, someone who works for a silk company, and she asks me, "What's going to happen when silk is dead?" And I said, "Silk isn't going to die. It's just taking off now that people are beginning to know that it's not so fragile." Now why do I know that? No fucking reason at all, except that I'm a dilettante. But immediately, she's like, "Ooh, connection. This person understands something about my business."

And then she says, "We want to do something that would be for kids that would be on MTV." And I say, "Not a good idea, because your bread and butter is men, men who are going to be watching that along with kids. If you're out there in public, on television, saying that you're a kids' company, it's going to undermine your men's franchise." And that's just not an in-depth knowledge of anything. It's just this little dilettante information. It's just that you're kind of interested in culture—that you know what's going on in culture.

So it's knowing a little bit about everything.

The thing about planning is there is an expectation of intellectual prowess. You're supposed to be smart. You get paid to be smart. I liked that I was paid to be smart. But if you're female and you're really verbal and you have strong opinions, you almost inevitably get pegged as being shrill and bitchy. People do accuse me of those things. It's funny, they didn't until I got to a certain level. I knew I'd arrived at Chiat/Day shortly after they made me a VP when rumors started to fly around that I was a lesbian.

So as a woman you have to tone it down?

When you're working with creatives, and when you're working with clients, inevitably you have to try to figure out a way to make them think that it's their idea. **Particularly if you're female.** To try to take them to a point of view without getting into an ego conflict. With an ego conflict you're fucked.

I hated being in a situation with creatives where I couldn't say, "That sucks." Because in order to actually have an effect on the work, I had to maintain their interest in my opinion. When they became disinterested in my opinion I fell out of the loop. And that's the problem with account planning; it's not actually necessary—it's value added. People have been doing fine without it for years and years and years.

It's "value added?"

You know, creatives do the work, the account people take it to the client, and the client either likes it or doesn't, the account person either fights for it or doesn't, creatives can fight for it or not, it gets changed or not, and then it runs. Adding this element of somebody who has a responsibility for knowing about how the consumer dynamics work is pure added value. So if you get people pissed off at you, you just fall out of the loop. They stop informing you of what's going on.

Female planners tend much more to guide people, to be wily. Male planners sort of put themselves up on a pedestal as being the gurus of thought, you know, the really, really, really smart guys.

So why are so many agencies adding planners if it's not really necessary?

It's like, the client's paying the agency a lot of money for a creative product. The creative product may or may not be working, and there are a lot of forces outside of people's control on that. So if the agency can provide the client *another* service, besides the creative product, that makes the client like the agency and look to the agency for help. Then you're ahead of the game. Planning winds up doing just that.

I think the reason it's been so attractive is that it's a very good new business tool. It makes for much better presentations; that's basically what it comes down to. If you have research, that's great, but it's just information. The difference between planning and research is that planning isn't as interested in the information as it is in what you do with that information.

How about account managers. What do they do?

Now that I have to do the job (at Mad Dog) I have a much greater appreciation of it. They're the nerve center through which a lot of concerns are passed. They're screening. They're not letting the client know how panicked the creatives are. They're trying to project a facade of confidence. They're not letting the creatives know how negative the client is, because they don't want to dash hopes.

They're dealing with production. They're having the print production person in their office saying it can't be done for the money, and dealing with their ego and trying to get them to go back and do it for less. They're dealing with their own management about the fact that the account isn't profitable or needs to be more profitable. They're responsible for how much time people are spending on stuff. They're dealing with the media people about where things are being placed and about what their deadlines are and whether or not those deadlines can be moved.

They're just trying to keep the whole thing from falling apart. And the thing is, nobody ever thanks them for it, because it's like being a party planner; the only way you'd know what a party planner did would be if it didn't work. If it works then you have no concept.

Sounds high pressured. Is advertising in general?

Yeah, it's very high pressured. **It's like doing makeovers. People think that advertising can work miracles, and it can't**. It's only one part of the marketing mix. I mean, if you've got a shitty product, a lousy distribution system, a crappy sales force, and if you've got unrealistic goals, then you're fucked. But people in that situation will think that advertising can help, and it can't. So it's high pressured because it's hoped that you will be a rainmaker.

It's also a committee-working environment: there's lots of people who have to do different things. There's a lot of handoffs down the line, so there's a lot of ways that things can go wrong. Any weak link in the chain can fuck everything up. You know, you can have great writing, great art direction, and a lousy director and it's going to be a lousy ad. You can have great writing, great art direction, a great director, and a lousy cameraman and it's going to be a lousy ad. You can have everything be great and the media (where the ad is placed) be bad and nobody's going to see it, it's not going to work, and it's going to suck.

And then there's deadlines. It attracts a bunch of politically correct dilettantes who aren't very good with deadlines, who wait until the last minute. So it's a constant churning of stomach acid.

These dilettantes that are bad with deadlines, do they belong in advertising?

The people who do get into advertising shouldn't be in advertising for the most part. People get into advertising because they don't know what else to do and they think it will be a hoot. It's a business that attracts dilettantes. **It's a business that attracts people who don't want to be lawyers; people who are marginally creative, reasonably persuasive, and don't really want to work.** And they wind up in advertising because they see ads and they go, "Well I can do that." And the problem with most advertising is that it sounds like most advertising. If you have an interest in solving problems, go into advertising.

Even copywriting?

That's what that's about too. It's about creative problem-solving. It's like, "I've got to talk to these people, I've got to tell them this, and I've got to do it with this much space." The other reason to be a copywriter is because you're interested in show business, because you want to put on a show. If you were one of those kids that really wanted people to look at you, then advertising is a perfectly appropriate thing to do as well. But if you want to be an artist—if you want to express yourself—then for god's sake be an artist, don't go into advertising. A lot of times with creatives you're saying, "People aren't going to read this and think, 'What a great ad Joe did.' They're going to read it and go 'What an interesting ad from Ford.' It's not your name on it."

Is that a problem? Do they wind up frustrated?

They wind up actually being pretty good at it, because they write to their peers, and their peers like what they write. So they wind up being good at it, they wind up making more and more money, and then they become filled with self-loathing. And eventually they become bitter, twisted, rich people who drink too much. (Laughs.)

Someone interested in advertising, should they study it in college? Is it an advantage?

It's not necessarily an advantage, it really isn't. For the most part there is a real assumption on the part of the people who are interviewing you that the fact that you went to ad school means that you're a total idiot. You've got to be a fucking wonk to love advertising. **Loving advertising is not going to mean that you do good advertising.**

People that I've interviewed that majored in advertising, they've got to get over that. What would have made them weird enough? It's a blatant illustration that they don't have a common touch, that they're not normal, and that they probably weren't smart enough to actually study something cool. For a planner, I'd much rather talk to somebody who studied art history or psychology or communications

or journalism. Communications is another one that's a little dicey, as
is marketing. Besides which, who teaches advertising? And what the
fuck are they doing? They couldn't be any good, so what are these
people learning?

*I remember when I was in college, I never really considered
advertising because I thought it was evil—selling things to people they don't want or need.*

**People say, "Advertising sells people things they don't
need." They rarely say, "Advertising sells *me* things I don't
need." It's your own fucking responsibility, frankly, to decide
what you need**—whether you want Nikes or Reeboks. And if you
don't like the ads for something, don't buy the fucking stuff, you
know?

Absolutely.

CLAIRE RASKIND

Director of Publicity, Skouras Pictures, Los Angeles

Twenty-eight years old

Background check—Skouras Pictures is an L.A.–based pro-
    duction and distribution film company whose films include:
    My Life As a Dog, Blood Simple, Watch It and *Joey
    Breaker.*

I'm in love with Claire Raskind, OK? I get the feeling though,
that everyone else is too. Or maybe it's just her job to be adored, I
don't know. After our interview, she took me to the opening party of
Miramax's film *Strictly Ballroom,* a nice little Hollywood affair (little?—yeah, right) you'd think was thrown in her honor.

We walk in and are assaulted (well, sort of assaulted). Kiss, kisses
on cheek, cheeks, one after the other after the other. Unbelievable. I
wanted to walk around a little, see the room. But for the first hour
we never made it past the doorway, the room came to us. (I liked it
though. I felt kind of important. "Who's the guy with Claire?") But I

don't think I could ever date Claire, if she'd have me, 'cause I'd be jealous as hell. So, guys and gals, only date a publicist if you're really sure of yourself and your relationship. Oh yeah, and some career advice, only become a publicist if you have absolutely no wallflower tendencies, and a boy/girlfriend that doesn't get jealous.

What did you do after you graduated?

I went to graduate school at Pepperdine for psychology for a year, but decided I wanted to do something that was a little lighter. I always loved film so that was the next thing.

How did you go about it?

First of all, I thought, What do psychology and film have in common? Well, the marketing side of film can be pretty manipulative. So I got my first job in the creative advertising department at Orion answering phones and doing a lot of computer stuff.

How was that?

I liked advertising, but I was always watching the publicity people. I thought, Oh, how exciting, they get to attend premieres and screenings. It seemed so glamourous—working with the camera crews and walking around with the talent and filmmakers, going to screenings at night, and being invited to things.

So how did you move over to publicity?

I knew that the assistant to the VP of publicity was leaving, that she was actually getting fired. So I went to her (the VP) and she gave me a chance.

Why?

I was always kind of the smoother. I can't explain it, but I guess my demeanor was really even. People would complain about other people, and I kind of would just smooth things out, even though I was just a secretary to somebody. It's weird, you have power to do that. You can create a better environment. Even though I think a movie is important, and it's important to make money because it's paying your paycheck, it's still a movie. You're there because you're supposed to be having fun.

Right. Let's not take ourselves too seriously.

I remember one time the president of Orion walked up to my cubicle and handed me his jacket. And I said, "Oh do you want me to hang this up?" And he said, "No, I want you to sew a button on for me." And I was like, you know, it's that moment where you can either go, "I'm not going to do that," or you can just swallow your pride for a minute. He wasn't doing it to degrade me, he had a meeting and he needed a button on his jacket. He has enough pressure. He's running the company. It's a lot of pressure.

Now another time, **an executive came up to my desk, handed me his lit cigarette, and said, "Can you put this out for me?" And I said to him, "No, I don't smoke. I can't."** And he was furious. He basically hated me the whole rest of the time I worked there.

Alright, what's the scoop, what do publicists do?

Anything to do with the media that's not advertising is your responsibility. I mean, you can buy a radio spot, and you have to pay for that, but you can also get someone interviewed live on Howard Stern, which is free. So it's someone's responsibility to call up the producer of "The Howard Stern Show" and say, "I've got this movie, why don't you see it." So then you set a screening for the Howard Stern staff. They see it, they like it, you ask them, "Would you be interested in interviewing someone?" Maybe they identified with someone in the movie and say, "Yeah, I'd like to interview Gene Hackman. He's kind of funny and he's had a good, strong career. It'd be fun to have him. Yeah, let's do it."

So then it's your responsibility to call Gene Hackman's publicist, who handles all his press requests, find out when he's available, and make sure he gets there. You have to handle everything. You have to make sure they're getting the accommodations they want. **Are they afraid of heights? Well then, put them on the first floor. Do they like Perrier? Well then, make sure their refrigerator in**

their hotel room is filled with it. Just really catering to these people so that they have no excuse but to do what you want them to do—to pump your project, your movie.

That's a little manipulative, isn't it?

You have to make them happy. Successful actors are usually pretty busy people, and you're not paying them to go on "The Howard Stern Show"— they're using their own time. I mean, it's obviously exposure for them, but you want to make it the best possible situation it could be.

You have to know your people. You have to know where they're coming from so you can make the interview the best possible thing. I remember when I worked at PMK (a major Hollywood PR agency), one of Jodie Foster's requests was "Make sure you tell the journalist before I meet with them not to talk about the Hinckley case."

I also worked with this A-list celebrity (Sorry, can't name him) who lives with this other A-list celebrity. *Now* he's very public about being with this actress, but years back when he was less well known he didn't want to be public about it; he didn't want to use that to advance his career. But we didn't really know that. So he was doing an interview with some magazine and they were really diving in and asking him about his relationship with her, which didn't have anything to do with him or his film, and he got really pissed off and the interview was shitty because of it.

It works the same way with the press person too. I've run into situations where the actor likes to do things really early in the morning. So you set up something for 9:30 AM, you call the journalist, and they're like, "I sleep till noon every day." The journalist isn't going to be as accepting in an interview when he has to be somewhere at 9:30 AM. It sounds like really trivial things, but if you don't put it together well, it can really be a disaster.

So you're trying to set the scene for the best possible interview. Do you also have to teach them how to do a good interview?

Usually what happens with newcomers is they're so anxious to do well that they're nervous in an interview. That is the worst, especially when it's an on-camera interview, because if you're not confident with yourself it shows. Most actors are pretty polished because they're actors, and they can turn it on and turn it off in an interview. But when you're new and just starting publicity, there's no script, you know? You're being asked questions that you didn't know they would ask. So a lot of times what I do with new talent is I'll do a mock interview with them. I'll sit down with them and do an exchange.

To get them over their nervousness, or what?

One thing I find all the time with actors that are just starting to do publicity is they won't expand on a question. An interviewer's job is to spark you so you'll keep talking, like you're doing with me; you're just giving little bits and I keep going and keep going. But a lot of actors will answer, "Yes, that happened," and that's it. Come on, we want to hear about you, that's why we're here. So you have to tell them that, you have to draw them out.

Why do you go on interviews with actors? I was doing an interview once and this person's publicist insisted on being there, which I thought was silly.

These interviews are business, they aren't just friendship. On *Hell Raiser III*, the lead actor was going to be interviewed. I could tell he was a little nervous so I said, "I'm going to come along." And exactly what I thought would happen, happened. He was extremely clammy and would not open up. So every once in a while I'd go, "Oh, what about that project that you talked to me about the other day, when are you starting that again?" Or, "Remember how you hurt your arm on the set, wasn't that funny how that happened?" And he said, "Oh, yeah," and then he felt real comfortable and went into this whole spiel on how he broke his arm on the set. **I was getting things talked about and leading the interview the way I wanted it to go. You want to have control over what image people are getting of your film.**

How else do you control that?

You know how you'll see on "Entertainment Tonight," "Opening this week is *Mermaids*," and they show a clip? Well, that clip they show, is it going to be a happy clip, or is it going to be depressing? Is it going to be a family arguing, or is it going to be a family playing? I mean, that's going to be how people perceive that movie. And when that person's watching TV, if they like what they see maybe they'll go to the movie. Maybe they won't, but if they're really turned off by what they see, there's no way they're going.

We're doing a movie right now that has a character in it who's terminally ill. The person's a great actor, but I'm not going to show clips of him being terminally ill, lying in bed eating his dinner in a bed tray. No. Someone's going to see that and just be totally turned off by the movie and not want to go. **I'm going to push the woman who has big tits. That's completely sexist, but it's true.**

And a lot of times if the movie's not very good and there's a pretty girl in it, I know exactly what journalist to call that wants to interview pretty girls. All I know is that I have to send a photo and they'll do it. Or on another side of that, I'll know if there's a gay journalist that likes cute, young boys. I mean, that's fine, it's the same thing. I'll send him a picture, and he'll be all over it. He'll be on the phone calling and saying, "I want to interview him."

Whatever it takes to get them interested in writing an article about your film.

Free-lance writers get paid per word. So when you pitch to these writers, you have to give them an angle, and a lot of times there really isn't an angle. So you try to kind of coerce them into an angle that maybe wasn't quite as obvious. Maybe it's a production story, like what happened during the making of the movie. Or how did they make this movie for such little money? You tell the free-lancer, "What a great story, you're going to be able to sell this (to a magazine). Anybody who's interested in inside Hollywood, this is a great story." And so they bite or they don't.

Another thing I do too: you know when you see an ad and there's advance quotes from critics, there's quotes in ads? The publicity people are responsible for that. You have to call the journalist and say,

"We're making our print ads for this movie and we know you liked it, will you give us a quote?" And the quotes can be really deceiving because someone can say, "It was a very enthralling film, but I wouldn't recommend it to anyone," and all you see printed in the paper is, "It's a very enthralling film."

Do they ever get mad at you?

No. Well, something like that they would. I mean, if you have any ethics you would check with the person, but a lot times you don't. If you need a quote, if you really need a quote, you know, just do it. But they need you too. When *Batman Returns* is opening and they want to interview Michael Keaton, and you represent Michael Keaton, they need you. It doesn't really matter if you've fucked them over.

There's been articles in several magazines about PR agencies and how someone (from a magazine) will call (an actor's publicity agent) and say, "I want Robert De Niro for the cover." And they'll go, "Fine, if you want Robert De Niro for the cover you have to do an article on the inside (of the magazine) on Elizabeth Perkins and Lolita Davidovich who are also both our clients." And a lot of journalists get really upset with that bargaining. But you know what? You have that power. It's very manipulative.

What would Robert De Niro feel about his PR firm, to which he's paying a lot of money, bargaining like that with his name?

He'd probably be bummed. He'd probably be really bummed. That's if it's his *personal* publicity agency. But if I'm a film company and I'm doing that, he can't say anything. I mean, I'm representing a product, *he's* not paying me.

And also, the reverse of that is if a journalist writes a bad article about someone like Christian Slater, who you could see as having a bit of an attitude. So they write this horrible article about Christian Slater, and then the next time the journalist calls and wants to do an interview with someone represented at that PR firm, the PR firm says, **"We don't work with you anymore. We don't need you. You fucked us on that interview."**

So you're not going to find writers who are going to be willing to write controversial, or interesting articles.

The ones that do don't get as much cooperation when they request an interview. I mean, it's a given.

When is it not war? What's a good moment in all this?

It's so exciting when you have an actor in a movie, and they're *kind* of well known, but not a household name by any means, and you get them on "The Tonight Show." You go home, you put your feet up, it's 11:30 and you turn on Channel 4, and they're sitting there talking because *you* coerced that booker or that producer on that show to go to your screening. You bugged them, you kept calling. They didn't want to come. They had ten other screenings that week, but you got them in. They saw *your* movie.

How do you get stars to go to your premieres?

The publicist at the studio calls the personal publicists and faxes all the PR agencies that represent talent, and says, "Invite your clients." And if it's a really big Hollywood premiere, like *Batman* or something, they say, "Invite only your A-list clients."

That's another job of the publicists. It's like, **Robert Redford's coming to the premiere? How am I going to get him in here without him getting mobbed?** OK, I'm going to have someone down in the garage that's going to meet his car—it's not going to be a limo, because everyone will know he's in it—and bring him up through the back elevator.

We did the premiere for a Miramax movie, *Hear My Song*. I'm outside the theatre, they're setting up the red carpet, I'm telling them, "Put lights here, put a station here"—it's this whole big production. And this guy comes up to me and says, "Are you running things here?" and I go, "Yes, I am." And he says, "Hi, I'm Jim. I'm Madonna's personal bodyguard. She's coming tonight."

Not only is that a blessing for me, because those photos that the paparazzi take that say, "Madonna attending the premiere of *Hear My Song*," people think, "Fuck, it must be a good movie if

Madonna's coming out for it." But the point is, I'm petrified. I had to make sure she got in there safely, and that I had someone reserving her seat. Make sure she was escorted down this aisle. Have a security guard watching from over here. And when the last scene came on, the person sitting next to her would be tapped on the shoulder who would tell her that it's time to get up and leave. It was this whole thing. But she made the evening for us.

Why did she show?

She knows Harvey and Bob (the owners of Miramax at the time) because they released her movie *Truth Or Dare*. **We faxed an invite to her office and said, "If there's any way you can make it, we'd love you to come." We didn't hear back. Madonna doesn't need to RSVP.**

What do you hate about your job?

What I hate about my job is that your job is never done. There's always more breaks you can be getting. That's definitely what I hate about it. And that you're supposed to be the know-it-all. You're supposed to know where the best restaurants in Malibu are because Joe Blow actor lives in Malibu and he doesn't want to drive further than five minutes from his house for an interview.

And that's a major pain in my spine all day. It's just another thing I have to worry about. I've had countless times when you rent a car for an actress, they're coming to town and they say, "No, we don't want a limo to pick us up from the airport, we'd just rather have a rent-a-car." A rent-a-car. They're not saying that. They're telling you, "I want a Miata; it has to be black, with electric windows." Then it's like babysitting. I feel like I have bigger things to look at, like the scheme of how the film's going to make money—the big picture—rather than worrying about if someone has Perrier and ice in their room.

How else can they be a pain in the spine? Or ass for that matter.

I remember at PMK, a client was wanted for a photo shoot for a major magazine like *Harper's* or *Elle* or something. She was not an

A-list, she was a B-list. She was very lucky to get this layout. And when I called her to schedule the photo shoot she said, "You know what Claire, I'll do it, but I have a manicure scheduled for that day so if you want me to do it you have to send a manicurist to the location of the photo shoot so as not to screw up my schedule." This woman is lucky that she got this piece. The only reason she got it—which she still doesn't know to this day—is because an A-list dropped out and we happened to represent her also, and I pitched her.

Did you do it, did you send the manicurist?

Yeah. (Laughs.) I did it. And I still have the article to this day and her nails look great in that picture. (Laughs.)

I was working with a very well known A-list celebrity in promoting an exercise video that just came out. We went to this seminar and did this press conference about watching what you eat. And then on the way back from the interview, I was in the car with them and they said, "Let's go to McDonalds. I'm dying for a Big Mac." And you're saying, what am I doing? This person just blatantly lied. They eat like a pig, but their metabolism is zero, so they look great even though they're in their forties. And **you're sitting in the car and looking at your job going, "What am I doing. Why am I doing this?"** The stories are countless.

Why do actors hire personal publicists? Don't the studios and film companies provide for publicity?

I work for a film company (as opposed to being a personal publicist at an agency like PMK aforementioned). When I'm pitching a film to somebody, I may not be pitching a certain actor, even though he may be great in the film. My bias isn't him, it's about the movie—about getting people into the movie. So **that's why people hire a personal publicist; so they have someone rooting for them all the time.**

Someone like Cher needs a publicist because she gets so many requests to appear here, to do this magazine, to do this interview, host this special benefit, and all this special stuff. She just needs someone to weed out the requests. But then again, if you're an up-and-coming actor and you hire a personal publicist, then that person is on the phone every day pitching to press about how hot you are, and you've got this project coming up and this project. You'll get noticed a lot sooner.

Let's get back to your career. Why did you leave Orion?

Mike Medavoy leaves Orion and everything changes. My boss who's been there for sixteen years gets fired and I'm told that I'm going to be promoted to a publicist, finally, after three years. I don't know what to do, I feel kind of torn because this woman that I got so close to, who taught me everything, has just been kicked out on the streets.

They told my boss in one room that she was getting fired and told me in the other room that I was getting promoted, and I just thought the whole thing really sucked basically. They had just kicked my boss out on the street who had been doing a great job there for sixteen years. How did I know they weren't going to do the same thing to me after they learned how everything was done?

So I left and I worked for this producer on the post production of *Mermaids* for three months and just hated it. I really missed the publicity end of it. So I quit. And then, what do I do? I have to pay my rent, right? So I go to a temp agency. So I went from almost being up to where I wanted to be, to going to a temp agency.

Then I got completely obsessive. I took my Rolodex and I went through and I wrote a letter to everybody, even if I thought we never really clicked. When you're working on different films like I did at Orion for three years, you meet a lot of people. I thought, someone must know of a job opening in publicity. After three weeks of looking I got hired at PMK as a junior publicist because the woman there knew me when I was at Orion and we had enjoyed working together.

How did you go from PMK to Miramax?

When I was there (PMK) I worked on a film for Miramax. It was a very small film but I think we did a lot on it. When Miramax was looking for a publicist, they thought of me. So I went to Miramax as a publicist, finally, full-fledged.

Then Skouras called me and said, "We're completely revamping and we want to make you director of national publicity, would you come in and talk to us about it?" It's pretty much sink or swim now. I mean, our movies are opening the end of March, and whether they do good or not, it's me generating whatever publicity there is.

And how's it going?

Great. Right now the phones aren't crazy because our movies aren't opening for another two months, so I have time to do quality pitching to people. Not even quality pitching, just getting on the phone with a journalist and saying, "Hey, are you and so-and-so still together?" You know, just schmoozing and keeping up my contacts. Because that's why Skouras hired me. **It's not what I do, it's who I know. When you're a publicist your Rolodex is your life.**

Note: Claire recently left Skouras and is now head of marketing for an international film and television production and distribution company.

WORDS FROM ON HIGH:
Advice From the Director of Personnel at Chiat/Day Advertising on Breaking In

EVE LUPERT

Director of Personnel, Chiat/Day Advertising, New York

Background check—See Rob Slosberg interview.

What qualities will get an applicant hired?

Someone that is just *this* side of being arrogant and being really confident. So you've got to have somebody who's confident and not arrogant.

I'm looking for somebody who's energetic, who is bright, who's enthusiastic, and who can think. If I ask them what's their favorite ad, and they say the Energizer Bunny. And I say "Why?" If they can't answer that then they don't think.

After we interview someone we always ask each other, "Can they think outside the box? Can they get out there and look at it a new way?" We have a new company slogan: "Innovate or die. Death is not an option."

How many resumes do you get?

In the Spring I get more, probably fifty a week. The rest of the year I probably get like thirty a week.

What do you do with them?

I look at all of them. With the college students I'll read the cover letter first. If the cover letter is any good at all I'll put it in one stack. And if the cover letter isn't good, I don't even look at the resume.

What are you looking for in a cover letter?

I'm looking for complete sentences that aren't run-ons. I'm looking for somebody who's writing to Chiat/Day and not sending the same letter over and over again.

So I'm looking for somebody who reads the trades and can say something intelligent about the company. Such as, "Gee you just got this account, that must be very exciting." We're not talking about comparative research, but somebody who's just aware of the marketplace.

How about wit in a cover letter?

It helps. Absolutely. But you don't have to be terrifically clever, because it's hard to figure out what kind of creative thing to say but not sound stupid.

A lot of the cover letters are very boring, they're form letters. They'll say, "I believe that my skills can match those in your company." And then they don't say what their skills are and why they think they would match the company.

What else?

If my *name* is misspelled (She shakes her head. Forget it). That sounds really egotistical, but it shows they don't pay attention to details. They can call the desk and get the spelling of any name.

Does that happen a lot?

All the time. And they misspell the company's name.

Do you look for college—where they went to school—is that a consideration?

A little bit, but not much. And I don't look for advertising degrees at all. In fact, I'm less likely to hire somebody with an advertising degree. I'm not talking about creatives (copywriters and art directors) particularly, because they really do need to go someplace and learn how to put their book together and learn the craft.

How do you go about hiring?

If we're talking about entry level, I look through the recent letters. If you really want to be in a place, it doesn't hurt to send a letter every three months, because for all I know you've gotten a job. I *do* keep resumes, but I look at ones that seem to have promise from the last couple of months. You can even send the same letter, just change it a little bit.

What do you look for on the resume?

I look at activities. I look at travel. That can tell me if someone has an interest in the world. So if someone's part of the Shakespeare Book Club and has travelled to Italy and has worked for a sculptor, that's somebody that's intriguing to me—someone that I want to have here.

How about someone's GPA?

I don't care. I don't even look at it.

Connections?

I will always see someone who's got a connection as a courtesy, whether or not I have an opening. It certainly helps.

Do you use recruiters for entry level?

I do use recruiters for entry level, because they can screen for you. I'll use recruiters for receptionists or anything. Answering the phones is an entry-level job here. I can get an MBA to answer the phones here.

Do you use recruiters for creatives (copywriters and art directors) also?

Creatives are done through the creative department. They hire them by looking at their books. They can make an appointment to drop off their book with somebody or they can go through a recruiter.

How about for account managers?

To be an account manager you'll either start as an account assistant or receptionist, it just depends on what happens to be open at the time. If I have an account assistant position open, the first thing that we do is look at the receptionist. Are they ready? Are they interested in this position? You see how they're doing. And they can interview for the job. If there isn't anybody (a receptionist) appropriate, then I'll go to a recruiter, and I'll look at resumes. And the requirement will probably be that they've had an internship.

So doing an internship is a good idea.

Yes. But I'll tell you something though. I just hired somebody who is great and wonderful, and he didn't have an internship. But what he did have was two years in Teach For America. I was so impressed with that. That's the kind of person that I want to have here. It's very impressive.

How about the interview?

I really make an effort to make somebody very, very comfortable in an interview. Later on (however), some people, just by their nature will be more frightening. Someone (an interviewer) will approach things differently. He'll terrify them, and we'll see how they do there.

I think one thing everyone needs to remember in an interview is that—and this is really important—I want you to be the right person. Every personnel manager *wants* you to be the right person. Because then they can get through the interview process and go on with the rest of their job. So they're on your side.

Is there something you'll ask them, something different?

I ask them what they have achieved recently that they're proudest of. Even if you're right out of college, you should have one thing that you've done that you're really proud of.

If I can get somebody to engage in a conversation and exchange ideas with me, they're on the right track. You've got to be able to engage in ideas, because that's what we do for a living. We don't manufacture stuff. We create and realize ideas.

I'll ask them their favorite book. I'll ask them their favorite movie. They need to live in the world. This is a high-stress business. And if this (advertising) is your whole life, it becomes much harder to cope with it. Because if you have a bad day here, then your life is bad. Also, unless you see what's happening in the world, you can't do good work. So I look for people who really live on the planet.

Are follow-up calls a good idea?

It doesn't help me. We have electronic mail, unfortunately, which means that everyone who calls gets through. I can't call them all back unfortunately, because I get too many calls. However, I will admit that I've picked up the phone and said, "Well, come in and see me this afternoon, because I happen to have an opening—a job just became available."

But if you call every two weeks—*that* hurts.

Do you do typing tests?

No. But we do ask if they can type.

Any interesting accounts of someone trying to get a job here?

Surprisingly few. You'd think so.

Age requirements?

I want the best and brightest people here. That's my *only* requirement.

How about dress. Should guys wear a tie?

Absolutely. If they don't, I think they're a fool. You want to appear as a professional.

How about some style?

Yeah, absolutely. Have some style, that's fine. Women who will wear a piece of crazy jewelry on a very conservative suit. Yeah, I love that, that's great.

Any last advice for someone interested in getting into advertising?

If you're looking for security, run away. Run away right now. Go get a job in a funeral home. You know there's always going to be work there. You need to be prepared for being migrant workers in this industry. Clients leave. Clients' budgets shrink. It depends on what's happening in the economy. We're one of the first people to feel it when the economy gets bad, because clients are going to start to lower their advertising budgets before they let people go. And when they lower their budgets that affects us very deeply and very strongly. I've spent a day letting people go. I've spent all day doing that.

How about when they start. Are there any common misconceptions young people have about the work world?

People come here and expect a classroom, and need to have their report card. And they're not going to get it. Somebody said to me the other day, "You know what, this salary doesn't motivate me." And I pointed out, "It's not our job to motivate you. Our job is to produce great advertising. It's your job to motivate you. And if you can't figure out how to do it then you're in the wrong place. I'll encourage you and support you, but you've got to be the one who's motivated to do it."

4

Fashion

To an outsider, the fashion industry might seem like it is in total flux, always changing. And they'd be right. To encourage people to keep buying, retailers, manufacturers, and designers must embrace the seasonal change of colors, fabrics, skirt lengths, etc.

This constant change, however, is not so much about new designers constantly crashing the scene as much as it is about a bunch of big-name companies constantly redefining what's fashionable and what's in. Therefore, an industry that relies so much on change is in fact very stable, controlled by manufacturing, retail, and design giants whose bottom line is around $1.3 trillion a year.

The rise of the supermodel and that which it represents—elitism, high fashion, glamour—is not the core of the fashion world and its job base. Model wear (you know, the clothes models model) is just a small segment of the fashion industry. The reason models are millionaire celebrities is because high-end designers depend on them more and more to sell their clothes in a highly competitive and shrinking high-glamour market. The industry has shifted away from this towards manfacturers, secondary lines (such as DKNY, Emporio Armani, CK Calvin Klein, A-Line by Anne Klein, etc.), and no-frills retailing.

ECONOMICS

After seeing net sales increase by 50 percent in the years 1986-1989, publicly traded apparel companies found that in 1990, when twenty-somethings stepped up to the plate, the umpire called it quits, the fat lady sang, and the companies barely kept pace with inflation. Meaning, job growth came to a screeching halt. Sorry.

However, the apparel companies that not only survived but have flourished in the nineties have been the more basic brand-name companies. Levi Strauss & Co., Fruit of the Loom, and Liz Claiborne—makers of affordable women's wear—have been three of the top five most profitable public companies. Meanwhile, the secondary lines, such as the ones listed above, have become the financial foundations for those designers.

On the retail side, giants such as May Department Stores, Macy's and The Limited made out like bandits in the hard-luck year of 1991. Shortly after, Macy's and Federated-Allied (which owns Bloomingdales, A&S, and others) filed Chapter 11. One retail sector that has been steadily growing, however, is the discount stores. T.J. Maxx, Filene's Basement, Ross, and Marshalls, among others, comprise nearly 50 percent of all retail sales.

TOP GIGS

Retail

BUYER (SEE LAURIE WEDEMEYER INTERVIEW)
MERCHANDISING SPECIALIST
   The merchandising specialist works for the designer in the stores. They make sure clothes are displayed appropriately and with good positioning. The job involves lots of travel. They wear the clothes and serve as a walking advertisement. They may work as a specialist on the selling floor, working the Liz Claiborne product in a Macy's or a Bloomingdale's.

Designers and Labels

MERCHANDISER

Merchandisers work for fashion firms from The Gap to Giorgio Armani to Nike. They travel around the world to see what's next style-wise to make sure the company is in step with what's out there in order to fashion their line according to the trends. They're like researchers for the designers, helping them to conceive the line. They'll hunt down different fabrics and choose colors, presenting these choices to the designers to choose from. Merchandisers decide how many units of each pattern should be made—blouses, skirts, jackets—and from which fabric. They decide, along with the production director (see below), where to have the garments made and are responsible for determining the price points for each item.

PRODUCTION DIRECTOR

This person works closely with the merchandisers and designers, deciding where is the best and most cost-effective place to make the garments. They are in constant touch with the factories to make sure they complete manufacturing on time. They'll also take care of the shipping and handling and deliveries. Production is the watchguard over many seemingly unimportant details. What kind of shoulder pad should be used in a certain jacket. What kind of fabric should be used on a certain blouse. Whether or not a garment gets a lining and what kind of button it gets.

So, as you can see, the designer in some companies often acts as a kind of editor over a design team. They'll have the team put it all together, then they'll come in at the last minute and say, "OK, what have you got, show me. I like this, I like this, I don't like that." From there, a sample of each item will be made for the models who parade down a runway.

SALES REPS

A sales rep for the designer takes orders from the store buyers of pieces they want to put in their stores. Basically, they help the buyers plan their business, suggesting the appropriate garments for their market. Sales people work in the showroom, where the line is on permanent display for buyers to come in and check out, or for magazine editors as well. Some sales people will also travel around the country to trade shows for buyers and press alike.

PUBLICIST

Some designers have their own public relations departments, some hire outside firms, and at some smaller design houses the sales person will take on this capacity. PR people's primary responsibility is to deal with the press. They get them to the shows and to the showroom so they can take a close look at the collection. They pitch ideas to the editors saying how they can incorporate these clothes in the magazine/newspaper or for a specific story. They provide information on what stores carry the line, the prices, and they arrange for samples to be available for photo shoots and stuff.

Related Industries

FASHION SHOW PRODUCER/SPECIAL EVENTS PLANNER

Fashion shows are basically a forum for a designer to present to the retailers who buy the product—the buyers—and to the press what their vision is for that season. It is a forum that the world's photographers come to; therefore, selected clothes will end up in newspapers across the world. Since it is a very expensive and important tool in making a designer's name known to a wider public, independent producers are often called upon to put these together. They arrange for the building of elaborate sets, hire the models, and figure out the seating, the last of which is, from what I hear, a nightmarish episode of political musical chairs.

FASHION EDITOR (SEE FARRAH GREENBERG INTERVIEW)

FARRAH GREENBERG

Fashion Editor, *Elle* magazine, New York City

Twenty-six years old

You don't mind that Farrah is late for your appointment. The lobby of *Elle* magazine is a nice place to wait if you're a young single guy that likes young, fashionable, pretty women—because you'll see plenty of them.

"Is it all women?"

"Yeah, it's pretty much all women. I like it. It's like a big sorority. When I first started as an assistant I thought it sucked that there were no men. I was just out of college and I wanted to meet people and it was just girls. And the guys that were there weren't straight. I don't care now.

What type of person works here, or should work here?

Someone that can start at a really low salary, like $18,000 a year.

The money isn't great?

It's the glamour, it's not the money, because you don't make any. But when I think I don't have to wear a suit every day to work, and I don't have to sit at my desk—I'm out every day at different appointments—I guess that's the tradeoff.

What did you think you wanted to do when you graduated?

When I graduated from USC I knew I wanted to work for a magazine. All my summer jobs had been geared towards fashion. I did one internship in Paris for a designer. One summer I worked for my aunt's PR firm. She does fashion PR and she represents Comme des Garçons, Jil Sander, and others. And then one summer I worked for ABC casting as an intern, which had nothing to do with fashion.

Then when I graduated, my aunt knows a lot of people in the industry, and she introduced me to a senior fashion editor at *Glamour* magazine. She agreed to meet me as a favor to my aunt, even though there wasn't a job available. So I went up there. We were chatting. I didn't even pull out my resume, and before I knew it she said, "I think you would be perfect for the job." And I said "What job?" She said she needed an assistant. Then four weeks later she went to *Vogue* to work, but I stayed at *Glamour* and worked for the new senior fashion editor.

What did you do?

A lot of schlepping. It was very boring, but everyone has to pay their dues in this industry. Sending clothes back and forth from the designers. Getting coffee. The editor goes out in the market (to the showrooms) and pulls the clothes for the stories that they're working on. Then they usually come back and tell their assistant to send a messenger to, say, Calvin Klein. Then from there on out the assistant is the liaison between Calvin Klein and the fashion editor.

The editor will say, "Get me these six pieces," so the assistant will call the Calvin Klein PR people and say, "I want these six pieces." And a lot of times Calvin Klein, or whoever, will say that you can't have them because a lot of other magazines want them, or they're at fashion shows, or they have to sell the clothes to the buyers. There's just one or two sets of samples. So then you have to maneuver some sort of deal like, "We'll take four of those pieces today and send back three tomorrow." That's what the assistant tries to do.

When you're at Condé Nast as an assistant, you're really an assistant. You get coffee, you clean the closet, you get the editors their money (petty cash). Basically, it was just being a messenger.

So how did you break out?

During that year I would volunteer to assist one of the stylists when they needed help, because it interested me more. This means assisting on the shoots: booking hair and makeup, finding locations, getting the clothes there, unpacking, ironing, sewing. Just dealing with everything that's involved in a shoot. So when an assistant stylist position became available, this stylist hired me because she knew I could do it.

So as an assistant stylist I would go on all the shoots. Say we were flying down to Barbados for a week in February. I would prepare a budget with hotels, airfare, car rental, food, miscellaneous. I'd make all the travel arrangements and accommodations. I would book the hair and makeup people. Once the stylist had picked all the clothes and jewelry I would take pictures of it so that everyone in the office had a file of it, and then I would pack it. I would have all the tickets and all the money for the trip, and would make sure that everyone got to the airport. This included all the models, hair and makeup people, the photographer. Then I'd take care of customs if we had to go through.

On a day shoot we would wake up at five AM. We'd do hair and makeup and then shoot a little bit. I would try to find some houses and things to shoot around. Say if we wanted to shoot in front of a particular house, I would go up and negotiate: "Can we shoot here? We'll give you a hundred dollars," or whatever. Sometimes the stylist would give me a picture in a magazine and say, "I don't know where this location is, can you figure it out?" So it's being resourceful and figuring things out.

As an assistant stylist you need to be really organized, quick-thinking, and able to handle stress, because there's a lot of stress. It was more like a producing kind of job. I thought it was great. I loved travelling. I loved everyone I worked with. It was always fun.

So I did this for a year and then was promoted to associate fashion editor.

How did you get that?

Glamour needed someone to style and pull the clothes together for these smaller pictures in the front of the magazine—"how to" and article pictures. So my boss said, "You can do that." I did this along with my other job as assistant stylist, and I started getting antsy, you know, I was still schlepping and packing suitcases.

Then a friend of mine who had come here (*Elle*) to work called and said they were looking for a market editor, and would I be interested. At that point I was tired of schlepping suitcases. I wanted a promotion. So I came over and I was hired. I've been here for a year and two months.

It's really who you know. When I hear about a position—say Calvin Klein is looking for someone—I'll call a friend that I know from the industry and say, "I know you're not happy. Calvin KIein's looking, you should call over there." **(With my assistant,) my friend said, "My cousin has a friend who wants to get into the industry, will you meet her?" So I just hired her.** Some people get it on their own, but a lot of people know people.

So what do you do now?

I'm one of the fashion editors here. What I do is cover the American and the French designer market. We come up with story ideas and then we go out and cover the market—go to the designers' showrooms—and try to find clothes that fit the stories. And we also pull slides and pictures to go along with what the writers have written for the feature article. Besides that, when we're out in the market we keep the PR up between the magazine and the designers.

What's a normal day like?

We work from ten AM to six PM. This morning I had four appointments at showrooms. I went to Chanel and Anne Klein, Anne Klein II, and A-Line.

What did you do at Chanel?

There's a whole closet full of clothes, and I went through and pulled like seven or eight pieces for these stories we're working on. Then I went to Anne Klein and looked through this book—because a lot of the clothes are gone from the show—and picked outfits that I wanted. Then I went to A-Line (a lower division of Anne Klein) and picked some things out. Then I went upstairs to Anne Klein II and pulled some clothes. Then I came back and looked through slides of some clothes to pull for a story—slides from different places I'm not going to run up to. I returned some phone calls, and on a regular day I'd go back out to the market at around three PM.

What made you pick Anne Klein and Chanel?

From the shows that I saw, they had things that would work for this story.

How do you come up with stories?

It's done differently at different places. At *Glamour* there are meetings for the stories and for the clothes. Here, it's not really so much a meeting as much as it is, "Oh, by the way I'm going to do this story." It's much more casual here.

How many stories are you responsible for per issue?

Each magazine is different. Here each month we could shoot five or six stories, or we could shoot ten or twelve, and then they just have them for whichever issue they want. They can save it or put it in now. At *Glamour* it was just four stories every month. Here it's just a different system.

Is writing any part of this job? You know, you're a fashion editor.

There's no writing. There are writers who just write.

What stories are you working on now? (It's the beginning of May)

For the August or September issue we're doing a gray flannel and a brown leather story. And then we're doing a winter off-white story, like sweaters and leggings. So now we have to go out and find these things to make a story happen.

Why did you pick the flannel and the off-white; are you setting the trends or are designers setting the trends?

For these particular stories a stylist and I were talking and they said, "What do you think is out there?" And I said there's a lot of gray flannel and a lot of brown leather. So we said, "Let's do that."

Do designers woo you so you include them in your stories?

The PR people for the companies with big names don't have to really woo you, but they are nice to you. But **some of the smaller companies will try to woo you: "Let me take you to lunch." And at Christmas time everyone sends you gifts or donates to a charity in your name.** That's really the only wooing.

I get phone calls all the time from people saying, "My name is so-and-so and I have a line I'd like to show you." There's so many people, I try to call them back, but you know, if they don't have a show-room or if they're not represented by a PR firm, it's very hard to go see everybody. The best thing for a new designer to do is send pictures, because there are so many bad things out there. There's only so much time in a day. If I like something I can always go to the place the picture came from.

So if someone can get you to their showroom, and if you like their clothes, then you're in a position to give them free exposure and credibility by including them in **Elle.**

People might think that, but I don't think it's true. When we have a lot of clothes in (from the designers) and we're looking through them we'll say, "Here, use this and this and this," to the stylist, and they'll say no. I mean, it's the stylist's decision in the end what clothes they want to shoot. We bring all the clothes in, and the stylist puts it all together for the story. So if they don't want to use it they don't have to. But then again we can say, "Well, they're an advertiser," and then they would use it.

What's that all about?

Well, **advertisers give you a lot of money, so you try to give them some attention.**

Do you have to?

You try to because they're important. They are what keeps the magazine financially going. But you can't guarantee anything.

Do the advertisers ever get mad if they're not included in a story they think they should be?

Some people get mad, but they don't deal with us as much as the advertising department. Then the advertising department will say, "Listen, we have to get a credit (put them in the magazine) for so-and-so." And we'll say to the stylist, "Come on, this is so-and-so, we have to use them." And they'll try. I mean, **we all know it's about money, and that we have to keep everyone happy, so we try.**

Do you ever wonder how much control you have over what you're going to cover because of the pressure of putting your advertisers in the magazine?

No, because you want to. Because they're giving you money, you want to do something for them.

When you were an assistant were you nervous about moving up—to one day being an editor?

When I was first hired at *Glamour* (a Condé Nast magazine), my boss said to me, "The best thing you can do is start at Condé Nast as an assistant, get trained there, and then leave. Go somewhere else as an associate and then come back." Because supposedly, Condé Nast trains really well, and other people will take an assistant from Condé Nast and make them an associate. Whereas Condé Nast would not really take an assistant and move them up, but it can happen.

What would you have to do? How would you have to be to get promoted?

I think you have to have your own personal style—the way you dress. You have to have a good eye for fashion. **You have to be able to deal with a lot of people that you don't want to always deal with.** I think it's also important to be organized, creative, and intelligent.

Why do you think you got your original promotion?

It was probably merit, and because my boss and I had a good relationship. **It really all depends on your boss what's going to happen to you.** You could do a hell of a job and he or she might not like you for some reason. You can keep your job, but you're just going to stay where you are.

Have you ever seen that?

Oh yeah. I adore my assistant but my boss doesn't. I would send her on appointments when I can't go somewhere, but my boss doesn't want me to because she doesn't like her.

So she probably won't advance here.

Yeah, but maybe she will somewhere else. Anyway, it's hard to become an editor because there are so many people that want to do it. Everyone feels that you really have to pay your dues before you can be one.

Do you see any social value at all in what you do?

I don't think fashion has a social value in the sense of doing something good for the world. But if someone sits down for an hour and looks at the pictures and reads the articles and relaxes and enjoys themself, then that's an accomplishment.

What about the social life?

There are a lot of parties and stuff.

Why do fashion magazines put clothes in there that nobody is going to buy and that nobody can afford?

A lot of it is just for the beauty of the picture. We won't say, "Who's going to buy that?" The idea is that you can see what's on the page and copy it in a different way, and for cheaper. Some magazines have price points where they set a limit, but here we don't. Here it's more about the picture and how it looks—the fantasy of it. They want you to take the fashion and recreate it yourself if you can't afford $5,000.

Is the job stressful at all?

It can be. Say we're shooting five different stories in two days. Last Thursday they came in and said, "We're shooting a cover on Friday," so we're scrambling all day to get clothes together in a day. October and March are the busiest months because that's when the collections are. October and November is when they show Spring. March is when they show Fall in Paris and Milan. And then April they show Fall in New York, and that's really busy. It can be stressful when you have to find things for a story that aren't really out there. The stylist will say, "I want this," and your job is to find it. Sometimes they'll want to do a story and they haven't been in the market to see that there isn't much of that particular item out there.

What do you like most about your job?

The freedom. That I *can* come and go as I please. Here if I don't have anything to do I can get up and leave and not feel guilty. And, that you meet a lot of people along the way. You're not sitting at your desk doing numbers.

This is a good job for someone who likes to be creative. It's a job that isn't filled with problems. **Sometimes people think the world is going to end, and it's really just fashion, you know, it's not brain surgery. It's just skirts and blouses.**

LAURIE WEDEMEYER

Buyer (at a major, I mean *huge* department store)

Twenty-five years old

Fashion. For an industry that one could dismiss as being vain and superficial, it sure takes itself seriously. So much so that every single person I knew or was referred to, either at design houses or retail stores, informed me that they were not allowed to talk to press of any kind. That's why I wasn't allowed to name Laurie's company in this interview, but trust me, it's a biggy.

A guy I *grew up with* who designs stuff for either Calvin Klein or Ralph Lauren, I can't remember which, refused to do an interview with me. He told me that he thought it had to do with not ruining the perception people have that Calvin, Ralph, Donna, et al., have of designing every single thing that they produce. Which of course they do not. OK, fine, whatever. But why won't the retail stores allow their employees to talk? Why do they have policies of silence? They're not designing, they're just selling. God only knows. I guess it all comes down to this simple yet elusive factor: image, and the fear of tarnishing it.

How did you end up at here?

They had a recruiting session at Stanford. I went through three rounds of interviews. They're actually pretty intense sessions. Then they flew me down to L.A. with a couple of other people to interview at the store.

Did you have to be a certain major to get this job?

No. I doubled in communication and design. Other people in my training class majored in English to art history to economics. Any major is OK, although I think they tend to lean towards the liberal arts.

Why do you think you got the job?

I think they're looking for a certain image. Their image is very professional, clean-cut. It's a fashion industry, but they don't want you to be too wild and crazy—it's still a corporate company. They like somebody, I think, who's very outgoing. I mean, in order to be successful in this job you have to be able to hold your own in conversation, in fact, hold your own in an argument.

For the most part, the people that they choose are very similar to one another. **They're not just looking for assistant buyers, they're looking for people to be part of their club, their team, their company.** It's a lot more helpful to the company to have a lot of people that like each other and hang out together.

But I think the biggest factor is the enthusiasm more than anything. They really like people that take initiative, that are hot shots. People that are self-confident, not cocky necessarily, but believe that they're qualified and that this company would want them for the job.

What did you start off doing as an assistant buyer?

Lots of drudge work a lot of the time. In the very beginning I was the coffee maker and the order inputter and the phone anwerer. You've got to realize that it's not going to be the greatest thing to be an assistant buyer; it's a lot of hard work. And you feel, especially if you graduate from a good university, or whatever, you feel like, "Somebody ought to give me responsibility," so you can show you know what you're doing. **You want to be king of the world, and you're at the bottom again.** So it's important to realize that it's not going to last forever, but it's a matter of paying your dues however long it takes.

What would a normal day be like for you as an assistant buyer?

Well, basically the first thing you do is pull up sales to see what they were the day before, against what you had planned and what you did last year. Then I would start checking shipping: pulling up every purchase order for the month that we were expecting to receive and see what status it was in—whether it had been received or not. Every day of the month you're either pulling up on the computer to see if it has been received, or you're on the phone with the vendor finding out when it's going to ship or if it's been shipped.

So a lot of the job is tracking your new inventory.

Tracking merchandise, right. And even after it's received, it's the assistant buyer's responsibility to see that it gets out of the warehouse and into the store. That is their responsibility completely—to keep the buyer updated as to the status of the merchandise at all times. When you have something advertised, then it becomes very crucial. We do our advertising three months in advance if it's a direct-mail colored-photograph catalogue. We decide three months in advance, based on orders that we placed, what's going to be in the catalogue and on the floors for the sale date, and if you don't have it in the stores...(I think the impression is, you're °@#!ed.)

It can be stressful because the company that I work for, the people are very hard-core and serious and they expect a lot out of everybody, including brand-new assistants. You know, you have to really bust down and do your job and do it right and be responsible.

As an assistant buyer, was it guaranteed that you would become a buyer?

No. I started out in a class of twenty-six in the buyer's training program, and at this point there's about ten of us left, and five of us are buyers.

If you want to go forward in the company, it's important not to just sit and wait for them to come for you. I was under the impression that somebody, someday, would knock on my door and say, "You're a buyer."

So how did you do it?

I knocked on *their* door and I asked for the position. **Basically, every time I changed positions within the company it's been because I asked for the job.** After a year and a half, I felt I was ready to be a buyer. And it was evident that nobody necessarily saw me that way, because they hadn't needed to. So I just started out asking my boss if I could interview for jobs, and asking his boss. They were very supportive along the way. I just went up the ranks and said, "I'd like to interview for a buying job. I feel I'm ready—this is why." I prepared a whole new resume. It was just like going for another job interview. It is. It's not a given. Every new position, you have to interview for it, even though it's the same company. I gave a resume to my boss's boss's boss, who didn't necessarily know my background. And I didn't get the first job I asked for either.

You had to be aggressive?

Oh, definitely. But I did it in a professional manner. I went up the ranks. I didn't go directly to the head of the department and say, "I want to be promoted." I went to my boss, got his support, I went to his boss, got her support and went on, all the way up to the top. And I really think that if it hadn't been for me asking for it, it wouldn't have happened. I think that taking the initiative was impressive to them.

So, what are your responsibilities as buyer?

I'm responsible for everything. From buying the merchandise, having the correct assortment, making sure the stores are stocked at the correct level. If they start selling something faster than I planned them to, I have to get them more merchandise.

The buyer buys the merchandise and is also responsible for distributing it in thirty-seven stores. You have to keep the stores in balance in terms of making sure they have enough merchandise even after you've received it. Managing the markdowns. It's up to the buyer and the assistant buyer together to keep track of the markdowns, and if they're getting out of hand, you change your sale. So I'm in charge of what goes on sale.

What's that about?

If I don't put enough things on sale for a big event the company won't make any money, it won't generate any sales. But if I put too much on sale then I'm going to have a whole lot of markdowns that my company can't afford.

So you're directly involved with the profitability of the company?

Bottom line, when it comes to the end of the year, I'm responsible for the margin, the profitability. I'm responsible for taking the markdowns, and if I take too many then that's my fault. If I don't take enough and I don't get the sales, that's also my fault. If something isn't shipped on time, that's my fault. Even though the vendor is the one not shipping it, it's still on my shoulders responsibility-wise. To see that it gets to the floor is also my responsibility.

I'm also responsible for the advertising. I decide what's going to be advertised, and at what price it's going to be advertised for. Then I'm in charge of reviewing all the ad copy to make sure that the prices are still the same, and if they're not I'm going to get in trouble for it.

I'm also responsible at the end of the year for the shortage, the missing paper work, my expenses. Bottom line, how much money does my area generate. That all goes into my review.

Sounds like too much responsibility. When do we get to the fun part? Travelling. How often do you travel and what do you do?

I travel to New York about once a month and stay a week each visit. I go around to various showrooms—each line has their own showroom. I make appointments with people that I'm currently doing business with and then other people that I may in the future want to do business with. That's the glamourous end of it, I think— travelling and being in a big city and going to visit the different lines. Each line has their own personality and they usually do their showroom very extravagantly, depending on the line obviously. And they're trying to impress me as a buyer. They want me to buy and they want to make me comfortable and happy. They offer me whatever I want to drink and eat or what have you.

Take you out to dinner?

Being taken out to dinner, out to lunch, out to Broadway plays, and all that kind of stuff. It's great. You feel like you're in the real world. A big part of the job is building relationships—establishing partnerships that it takes to have a business. That's an advantage working for a big corporate company—you're very important to everybody out there. They want to do business with you because you're a large account. And you're also tied to the rest of the corporation all over the country. So if they don't make one faction happy, they run the risk of losing everybody else.

Is that one of the best parts, going to the showrooms?

I really get into going to the showrooms and picking out the merchandise and feeling like, "I know what's happening out in the fashion world," and that the color that I like is going to be the one that sells. Not necessarily what I personally like, but I know what sells. **And also it's a power position being a buyer. They're asking me to come in and look at their line. It feels good to go in there and feel important.**

Also, it's a hobby of mine to know, like, what skirt lengths are in today. I just enjoy putting things together and seeing how they look. You have to really like looking at clothes. Some buying jobs maybe aren't that way, but I think certainly in women's clothing you have to enjoy that aspect of it, or at least feel that you're good at it.

You want to hear about the bad parts?

Yeah.

The hours can be ridiculous. The stress levels are unbelievable. Especially in a company structured like the one I work for. A lot is expected of you, and a lot of time is expected of you. It's not the norm to go home at a decent hour. I usually roll out around seven PM on a good day. Two weeks ago during import meetings I was working until ten PM every night while we were in New York. Eight o'clock in the morning sharp until ten at night. It's very stressful. They really put a lot of job responsibility on each person. When you get to be in a position like this you take responsibility and you care about what happens, because if for nothing else, if something goes wrong, you're going to get yelled at.

When you were an assistant buyer did you have any idea that it was going to be this stressful?

No. People tell you that, but no, I didn't. It's a very fast-paced industry and you have to be able to react at a moment's notice. For my import program I buy a year in advance. But through my domestic resources I'll buy anywhere from three months in advance to a *week* before I want it shipped, depending on my needs, my stock levels, and how much money I need to generate.

So is that the worst part, the pressure?

The thing I like least about my job is probably the pressure. There are also a lot of rules and regulations; it's a very structured kind of job. And it tends to be more numbers oriented and more report reading and calculating and estimating numbers than actually looking at clothes. Number crunching. What percentage of navy blue did you buy in that particular order? I have to figure that out. How many shorts did you buy all last summer, and what price were they? We do a lot of comparing to the previous year, so it's a lot of calculating.

Was there anything that shocked you about being in the real world or this business in particular?

Yeah. I didn't expect it to be so politically charged. I'd say the hardest part of my job so far has been trying to decide what the politics of the company are. **A lot of what happens to you with your career has less to do with your ability to do the job than with your ability to be political.** How to act within different situations. Know who to talk to, know what to say, know what not to say, know how to dress. You know, a lot of that is a big part of it. You don't want to offend the wrong people.

The thing about this industry is that it's very close-knit, very small in a way. The players remain the same. And you never know who you know that might become somebody important. When I started here there was a man who was the vice president over the division that I was in. Now this guy who was my boss, that I had formed a relationship with and who liked me, is now the president of a $500-million company and very important in the industry. So if I ever decide to leave here, he's an important contact and someone I can always count on for a recommendation. You never want to burn any bridges.

It was also shocking to find out that I wasn't important at first. You know, the whole thing about getting out of college. I thought I was pretty hot when I graduated, it was kind of shocking to see that I wasn't.

WORDS FROM ON HIGH:
Advice From the Vice President of Personnel at Liz Claiborne on Breaking In

KATHRYN CONNORS

Vice President of Personnel Liz Claiborne

Background check—Designs and manufactures women's and
    men's clothing, accessories and cosmetics. Among the five
    largest apparel firms and one which consistantly garners
    one of the highest return on sales. Offices in Manhattan and
    New Jersey.

How do you go about hiring?

Five years ago we started a program which we call CIM, Careers In Management, for which we recruit off the college campuses.

Is it competitive?

Very competitive. We take about twenty people into the training program each year. When we hire these people, for the next eighteen months they're ours—they don't belong to a particular division yet. They belong to Human Resources for the duration of their training. It's three month rotations. They do a stint in a front-end position like marketing, merchandising and sales, things that everybody finds exciting. But since it's not always exciting, they also work in a back-end job like customs, traffic, shipping, distribution, and finance. And then they spend six months in retail, actually selling in the Liz Claiborne stores. So they see the product cycle from the early conceptualization of it through the production and distribution, and then they physically touch it with a customer.

Why do you have this program?

It enables them to see what everybody does. I think part of the problem on the college campus is they only learn subject matter. And the real world—unlike what their marketing, merchandising, or design class may have taught them—is so diametrically opposed, that when they get into it they either don't like it, don't feel challenged by it, it isn't what they thought it would be, and we lose them.

We also have a program called AET, Account Executive Training, under the premise that there are people who *know* they want to be in sales (in the showroom).

What kind of grades do you need to get into CIM?

We have generally said 3.5 with some mitigating circumstances, but we'll never take anybody under 3.0.

What schools?

We have found through the years that the best schools for us are Harvard, Dartmouth, Columbia, Syracuse, Georgetown, Boston College—and then the local schools—NYU, Fordham, Seton Hall, and Rutgers. What we have found with these schools is that many of them come from families who have lived in the Northeast, so they have a concept of what it's like to live here.

How many drop out from the program?

For our CIM program over the past five years we've have an over 90 percent retention rate of people. We recruit for the long haul, so when we cut our data we look to find out what schools are best for us and what geographic location is best for us.

Are you looking for any specific majors?

We're not looking for majors necessarily. Liberal arts is as good as economics is as good as finance, because we're really training them. So as long as they're bright, creative, motivated, passionate, and want to work in this industry, we don't even care what their major is. Same with MBAs. We're not after MBAs. If you have one it's not going to negate you from the program, but it's not going to give you any special credence over anyone else.

How many applicants do you get for the CIM program?

I suspect we probably get around five hundred a month.

How do you weed them out?

First it's done on campus. We choose around three candidates from each college who in our opinion are terrific. These candidates are then invited at our expense to come back here where they're put through a series of interviews with the various divisional presidents. These people have a checklist of things they're going to ask them. Then they all get together and say, "I loved this one, this one's not going to make it." And then based on the votes that come from the management team, we select the twenty of them.

Who makes it?

You have the basic criteria from the standpoint of grade-point average. You're also looking for people who have a passion for the apparel business. They would *kill* to work here. We don't want the person that says, "Well I could work in computers, or I could work in oil and gas, you know, I really don't know where I want to be." We want people that really want to work in this business.

This business is crazy. And there's no question in my mind that you *have* to love it, because you're going to be working at it fourteen to sixteen hours a day. You're going to be asked to do everything from sweep the floors to rack the line, and you can't have somebody that says, "It's not my job." As I tell them, "That's very interesting because I haven't been able to figure out what *isn't* my job." If my boss asks me to do it it becomes my job. Whatever *it* happens to be. So you look for somebody that doesn't have an elitist attitude— somebody who's willing to do the mundane, stupid little jobs. Someone that has a passion for the business and that has a high energy level. Someone who is not looking for a nine to five.

Any creative ways people have taken to get a job here?

We've gotten everything from chocolate telephones with their phone number on it saying, "Please call, I'm great and I really want to work in this industry," to balloons saying, "I'm really terrific for apparel." You open up the box and their resume floats out of it.

Did they get an interview?

Oh, absolutely. I'm not sure they got a job, but they *sure* got an interview.

What do you look for during an interview?

We're looking for people that know about the company. What I normally do, and I don't think it's atypical of most of the interviewers, is I ask all my questions and then I'll say to them, "Do have any questions for me?" If the first thing they say to me is, "What does Liz Claiborne do?" I say, no. Not that I don't deal with them. I'll tell them. But that is the end of that person. Now, the person that comes in and says, "That green man's T-shirt that you had on the floor in the group called Nautical Express just really didn't fit with that group. Now if *I* had been doing it, I would have made it long-sleeve, or short-sleeve, or whatever...." You say, "That's the person that knows this business. *That's* the person that's going to be successful. That's the one that took the time to go to the store to look at the product, to formulate an opinion, to have something intelligent to say." And even if your opinion is wrong, we don't care; as long as you have one.

I oftentimes will ask them, "What do you think is the greatest problem facing the world today, or facing your campus?" just to kind of see where their head is at. If they say, "The teachers are lousy and nobody understands me," you say, "I don't know if that's the person we want working here."

What else do you look for?

We look for participation in team activities. This company is formulated on teamwork; we're a team. We don't reward individuals. Our feeling is: players score but teams win.

How about unsolicited resumes—what do you do with them?

We don't do a whole lot with them.

Cold calls?

They don't work. We're very good at screening. (Laughs.)

How about dress?

If somebody comes in in a Liz Claiborne outfit, I think it sets a tone. It's a good idea. If you're going to see the person who produces that product or has a pride in that product, and there you are wearing it, I think it predisposes them versus coming in in another designer's outfit. I think if nothing else it sets the stage, it creates a nice atmosphere. Now, if somebody looks fabulous and came in in Donna Karan, would we fail to hire them? Absolutely not—we're not that stupid.

Common mistakes on resumes?

Misspellings are something that will absolutely throw you out. We've had people misspell the company's name. You see it all the time. People misspell my name all the time. Attention to detail is so key in this business.

Any mistakes young people may make regarding moving up the ladder?

I think patience is a virtue. I think young people come into the workforce and think that in six months they ought to be promoted, and it may take two years, it may take five years. It's not, "I exist, therefore you're going to figure out what to do with me." This is not something that is *bestowed* on you, where somebody is going to knock on your door and say, "Isn't this a wonderful job, wouldn't you love this?" And I think in their heads that's exactly what they're thinking: "I work hard, and I'm a good worker, and I'm on time all of the time." I hear this all the time. Well, we don't expect people to come in late. Good, I'm glad they come in on time—if not we'd probably be disciplining them. Or, "I have a college degree." Well, so does everybody around you.

Can you tell if someone is right based on an interview?

Yes. It just sort of *leaps* across the desk at you. I'm always amazed at the enthusiasm level of some of these people. People who say, "I'd *kill* to work in this industry. I'll do anything. Make me the receptionist, I'll do anything, just hire me." That's the person I want.

If somebody's main thrust is, "How often am I reviewed, and what's the percentage of my increase, and when can I expect to be promoted?" then forget it.

People will actually ask those questions?

Oh, yes. I think somebody *tells* them that those are good questions to ask because it's amazing how routinely they're asked. That's not the person we're looking for. The person we're looking for is the person that would *kill* to work for this company.

5

Television

The fear that network programming will be a dinosaur due to the emergence of cable, pay-per-view, VCRs, and all those other threats, real or imagined, seems not to be the case. As Veronis, Suhler & Associates says, "The worst is over for the networks in terms of competition for viewers." Most homes already have cable and VCRs, so there can't be too much growth there. And pay-per-view has basically failed to catch on, due to high prices and stupid programming (fights and heavy metal concerts—yes; 120 hours of Olympics—no).

And when they say, "The worst is over," you know the networks are saying "Thank god." It's been pretty brutal for them in that eyeball market. Considering that they ruled until the late seventies with a viewer share of nearly 90 percent, which then dropped to 60 percent in 1991, you can well imagine what "restructuring" meant to them—they couldn't print pink slips fast enough.

ECONOMICS

Over the next five years network advertising is expected to grow at a 6.2 percent compound annual rate, considerably higher than the 1986-1991 growth of 2.5 percent. This is very good news for the television industry and very good news for employees and job hunters. The more advertising bucks being pumped in, the more the networks are expected to allocate towards the production of new shows from independent production companies. They are also expected to spend more money on in-house production, which they're beginning to do more of these days due to recent relaxed restrictions governing the percentage of programming the networks can produce.

HOW THE BUSINESS WORKS

Local Stations

You've got your local television stations everywhere, from Gary, Indiana, to Tupelo, Mississippi. Creative programming doesn't really exist at these places. Instead you have news, sports, and public affairs shows that you can either write, host, direct, or produce on a local level. Are they "hot jobs"? Sure. You're just swimming in smaller ponds with fewer sharks and probably less headaches; however, you have a chance to take on more responsibility, generally at an earlier age. But if you want to do something other than news— you know, the glamour world of TV—then you've really got to be either in L.A., and to a much lesser extent, New York.

The Networks Vs. Independent Production Companies

When considering getting a job in TV, one might quite understandably think right away, "the networks." Certainly there are lots of jobs at the networks, from publicity to advertising to marketing and programming, but they are not the hothouses of creativity. Very few of the shows you see on a network are things that they actually have created or produced. The majority of shows, from "Seinfeld" to "Roseanne" to "The Simpsons" are produced by independent production companies who basically rent their shows to the networks. And for prices you cannot fathom.

DEVELOPMENT

Yes, the networks have "development" departments that do what the title suggests—develop programming. But development at a network differs from development at an independent production company like Carsey-Werner ("The Cosby Show"; "Roseanne"). Devel-

opment for the latter is dreaming up a show and writing a pilot about
an overweight, wise-ass housewife named Roseanne. While development at the former is sorta like, "Yeah, sounds good, here's $750,000;
go make a pilot."

Working on staff at an independent production company like
Carsey-Werner or Castle Rock Television, the main emphasis is on
finding and creating new shows, i.e., development. A production
company might option a script from a writer, or will say, "Hey, let's
try to do a show with that comedian Jerry Seinfeld." They will then
take a script or concept into the network and pitch it, hoping to get
money from them to produce a pilot. Say the network or studio gives
the company x amount of money to produce the pilot. It is then, for
the most part, the responsibility of the production company to make
it. They will hire the actors and director (subsequent to network
approval), the cameraman, rent the studio, build the set, edit it, and
so on.

They'll shoot a pilot and the networks will show it to test audi-
ences to see if the average person likes it or not. If so, it may get
"picked up"—meaning, the network will give the production company an "order" to shoot a bunch of shows.

PRODUCTION

The production company then hires a whole separate staff to produce that specific show. They'll hire writers, production managers
and coordinators, crew people, and a slew of assistants—all of whom
work on a free-lance basis, for as long as the show runs. There's less
job security working on a particular show than there is if you are on
staff at a production company. But you generally make more money.

TOP GIGS

So if you want to find and create shows (development) get in with a
production company answering the phones or doing whatever. Volunteer to do script coverage, go out and see plays, and write up a
short analysis on that and eventually you'll move up the development
food chain—from being a reader, story editor, development executive on up.

If you want to write, become a writer's assistant on a show. If you want to produce or work on the set, get a job as a production assistant, doing all the crap that nobody else wants to do.

If you want to sell all this stuff to the public, figuring out what people should see and when, get a job at a network in marketing, programming, or advertising.

As a bonus, here's a list of top gigs on "Late Night With David Letterman" as told by Spike Feresten:

> Researchers research who's going to be on the show. Say Anthony Hopkins is going to be on the show, you have people researching any recent magazine article about him. Maybe finding his yearbook, finding out everything there is to know about this guy as if you were writing his biography to pick the juiciest questions so Dave can ask them.
> The talent department pursues cool guests to have on the show, like someone who looks like a hog and is being honored for it in Michigan.
> The segment producers are pretty much the heads in charge of the guests. They work with the guests finding out what they want to talk about. They ask questions and see if they have any cool or funny stories. All this work goes into the meeting with the head producer. They'll say, "OK, I found the guy who's being honored because he looks like a hog, and I've got a list of questions to ask Anthony Hopkins." The producer will then bring this stuff to Dave, and Dave will say OK or no.

SPIKE FERESTEN

Writer, "Late Night With David Letterman," New York City

Twenty-seven years old

Author's Note: Interview was done before David went to CBS, taking Spike with him. Sporting a T-shirt, jeans, and sneakers, Spike's your typical guy from suburbia, surprisingly unpretentious considering the people he hangs out with on a daily basis. He was the kid in high school who was always looking for the next prank or thing to blow up. Things he once got in trouble for doing, he now gets paid to dream up—like having Biff, the stage manager, drive a golf cart through a wall of champagne glasses, for instance.

We meet in his office in the GE building. A nice size room with a large window that looks out to a courtyard. Various newspapers are scattered on the floor, and above his desk a bulletin board exhibits snapshots of Spike with Elle Macpherson and Spike with Dwight Gooden.

During the interview, a couple of the writers periodically interrupted us, simply to check on the progress of things, they said, but really to try to embarrass and humiliate Spike and make him lose it in front of me, his biographer. They're tougher on each other than Dave is on his guests.

How did you start out here?

While I was bartending in Boston and going to Berklee College of Music, I met this cocktail waitress, Harriet, who became a friend of mine. She had an old boyfriend who worked on "Letterman," who apparently still liked her. And she sort of used that relationship to get me in on an intern level on "Saturday Night Live."

In what department?

I worked in graphics with this cocktail waitress's boyfriend. He did the graphics for "Saturday Night Live" and for "Letterman." He did the bumpers and props and all the photos for Weekend Update. I was his runner—finding photos—you know, a real gofer-type job.

What was your routine?

I was commuting at the time from Boston. What I would do was bartend double shifts Monday and Tuesday in Boston to pay the rent, and on Wednesday morning I'd fly to New York. There were really cheap rates at the time for students. I'd stay with friends or relatives in Long Island, whoever would put me up for the week. I'd work Wednesday through Saturday. On Saturday night after the show taped live, I'd go to the cast party for an hour, and then take a 3:00 AM train back to Boston and sleep all day Sunday. I did this from January to June. It was exciting. **It took a lot out of me and I almost got an ulcer, but it was a lot of fun.**

And you weren't getting paid?

No. I was working for free. But it was great. These are shows I would watch when I was a kid. My dad would wake me and say, "Hey, you got to see this, this is a great show." It was really the only show I watched on TV. I really didn't watch TV at all.

What did you think you were going to do when you were in high school? Did you ever think of being a writer?

I was going to be a rock star. (Laughs.) No, not at all. I still don't really consider myself a writer. At that point it would have been like a dream, being a writer on "Late Night." I never looked at it realistically like, "OK, I should go to school here to get this done." It was sort of just on a lark, "Hey, I can intern on the show. This is the closest I'm going to come." So I did it.

How did you go from being an intern on "Saturday Night Live" to being a writer on "Late Night?"

That fall, after the internship on "Saturday Night Live," they asked me to be a receptionist. A paying job.

So I'm answering phones on the front desk of "Saturday Night Live," and right next to me is Dennis Miller's office. I started writing jokes for Dennis just thinking, "Hey, wouldn't it be great to get a joke on national television; that would be sort of fun." So pretty much when I'm not answering phones I'm writing jokes. And it turned out that I started getting a lot of jokes on Weekend Update, which Dennis hosted. I still wasn't getting paid for it, but I started making a small name for myself around the office.

Was that difficult, getting jokes on the air?

You don't have to be that bright to write jokes if you start doing it every week, and read newspapers every day. No one really wanted to write for Dennis. The real writers on the show were too busy with their sketches every week. Weekend Update was an afterthought. So just being there I could see that it wasn't happening. I could see Dennis's frustration and therefore an opening. I had the advantage over everybody. I wasn't doing anything but sitting there taking messages and putting people's mail in their boxes. I had hours and hours to read newspapers and concentrate in a small area.

After the season was over a spin-off show called "Night Music" was being started, which David Sanborn was going to host. They thought this was the perfect show for me because I had a music background, and originally the show was supposed to be half music and half comedy. I was brought on as an assistant to the writers, but still getting to write, which the union didn't know about.

Then the producers decided not to have any comedy on the show. It was like having Yakov Smirnoff opening for Pink Floyd or something—it never worked. So they cut the writing staff down to one writer the first season. Then the following season they just made me the one writer to write wrap-around stuff, write stuff for David, and do short films with a handicam on the show. Little one-minute bumper films. Granted they weren't the funniest things in the world, it was just a good way to slip in. After two seasons "Night Music" was cancelled.

And this led to "Letterman"?

So what led to this show was, I had written a submission and sent it to the head writer, Steve O'Donnell, which I don't know if he ever read or not.

What's a submission?

Six or seven pages of comedy. Opening remarks for David and things you think would be suited for the show. So then these two writers that used to write for "Letterman"—and had brought me out to L.A. for a couple of months to help out on a pilot they were making—called Steve to tell him about me. Steve had already seen my submission, and at the time I was also playing softball with the "Letterman" people. So **I really think it was my softball skills that got me the job, because I'm a really good softball player. I threw Dave out in a double play, so he said "OK, this kid is pretty good, let's hire him."**

So then Steve asked me to do another submission, which I did. And then I was hired. And it's been the highlight of my life so far. (Delivered deadpan. Serious or not, I can't tell.)

How many writers are there on this show?

I think there's nine or ten of us right now.

How long have you writing on the show now?

A year and seven months.

I'm a big fan of the show.

I am too. I'm a big fan.

What can you do next having worked on this show?

Circus work. Cleaning up after the elephants. (Laughs.) I can only comment on what people have done before me. Everybody that used to occupy these offices pretty much went out to California and got deals with Fox. Just about everybody who's been writing on the show now is in California either producing their own shows or writing.

What shows?

"In Living Color," "The Simpsons," "Fresh Prince of Bel Air," "Married...With Children." Being on this show is like getting your education in writing and then you can move on to the big money and better opportunities. As far as I'm concerned though, it's not really about the money; it's sort of something you can believe in and write on. And this show is one of the only shows I ever watched and laughed at and thought, this is something I'd really be interested in working on. So that's what I'd like to work on to—what will be the next "Late Night" or the next "Simpsons" or the next revolutionary comedy show.

How many days a week do you work? What's your day like?

Five days a week. I usually come in around ten AM. **Every morning Dave (Letterman) comes by with pastries and fruit juices.**

I think it's kind of really nice, although sometimes I never touch them. Then everything's pretty much scheduled out. It's not written down anywhere, but it's sort of just understood.

From ten AM to noon I write opening remarks.

You do that alone or with others?

Alone, in my office. I read my newspapers and read what's going on today, looking for promising joke areas—like Bill Clinton not inhaling pot.

So you have to be informed?

Dave likes topical jokes. He likes to comment on what's happening at the last second, which is fun, which keeps him fresh. And it also gives you an opportunity to comment on things that are happening right now, instead of weeks down the line.

Do you guys have any sort of political agenda?

No, it's wherever the jokes are, and whoever is really putting their foot in their mouth or just doing something dumb.

Then we work on Act One pieces which is what Dave does after he does his opening remarks and says, "Hi Paul, how was your weekend? Good." That's when he does an Act One piece. Whether it's a phone call across the way to Meg, or a sound effects quiz, or celebrity tax tips.

Is this all written together with the other writers?

Everyone goes to their own office, writes, and turns in a page to the head writer. The head writer goes to Dave, and Dave goes, "Yes, no, yes, no." From that you'll get maybe fifteen jokes, which are put together for rehearsal at two-thirty PM, and then it'll be whittled down to nine.

At two PM all the writers get together for a "Top Ten" meeting. We'll come up with ten, maybe fifteen "Top-Ten List" ideas—anything from topical to something odd. We do this for around fifteen minutes and also discuss what's going on on tomorrow's show, and really, the whole week.

At two-thirty PM it's rehearsal, which is pretty much just Dave and the head writer and the production staff. We can sit here and watch it from our TVs to see what's going on. During this time you work on the fun stuff—the stuff you really like to work on—and the longer pieces you've been working on for a few days for something down the line.

Then at around three PM a writer's assistant comes around with the "Top-Ten List" subject that Dave or the head writer has picked. I'll then work on this for around forty-five minutes and come up with ten to twenty possible list suggestions. At four PM we all get together and read what we've come up with. We laugh or we don't laugh, and think of more if we need them. At four-thirty PM the head writer goes to Dave with around twenty choices which he checks off, "yes, no, yes." And then at five-thirty PM we shoot. From there on in we watch the show from our offices or maybe go down to the studio if you want to see who's on, or see a band play.

Do you stay late?

Sometimes we're stuck. Sometimes we don't have a piece for the next day. Sometimes we don't have an Act Two at all. Sometimes we don't have an Act One or an Act Five, which means we don't have tomorrow's show. Which means we're going to be sitting after the show, all of us in a meeting, coming up with ideas for Dave. **But that's part of being a writer. You stay late, you work hard, and then you get weekends off. (Laughs.) It's the desk job of comedy writing and it's pretty neat.** And then you get twelve or thirteen weeks of vacation every year, and they're all paid.

You get all that time off?

Sure. We're not shooting this week, so a couple of us decided to fly out to the biosphere in Arizona to look at it, and sort of just play golf and drink tequila. It's hot out there, like ninety degrees, and they have a desert and a biosphere and they have lots of good tequila. So we're gonna drive around Arizona and kill time.

So, is your social life Hollywoodish?

No, I prefer to play with my cat.

Is there any pressure involved in the job?

Yeah sure, a certain amount. But it's sort of spread out between all the writers because we're all, for the most part, working on the same stuff. There's pressure as a group, but it's nice because it helps you to get motivated to do a piece.

Will Letterman ever get mad if his jokes or if an Act One piece doesn't get a laugh?

Dave sometimes lets his dismay with the staff be known, but nothing that we're not guilty of. Nothing like what he could do. He's a good guy. He's a good guy to work for. He's there. You can talk to him if you need to talk to him.

How would you recommend someone get a job as a writer on "Late Night" or "Saturday Night Live"?

Enroll in Berklee College of Music and play good softball. (Laughs.) There are a variety of ways to do it. Ultimately, I think it's almost like winning the lottery—it's just really lucky. The most direct way to do it would be to write a submission out of school, after graduating college, or whenever. Whenever you feel you are writing stuff that would be good for the show. Just write up a submission and send it to Steve O'Donnell, our head writer. He reads a lot of stuff.

He'll actually read it?

Yeah, he does his best. He's got a lot of people sending him stuff. He tries to go through as much stuff as he can. **I've seen him read submissions from housewives from Michigan and Iowa and laugh and actually send them back a critique.**

Do you need to have any past writing credits?

No. A couple of guys were stand-up comedians. We have a woman who was writing at a newspaper in Salem, MA, who was corresponding with Dave and submitting jokes. We have a guy who was

writing for an ad agency in Virginia who was just submitting opening
remarks that Dave liked. There's also a lot of guys like me that came
in on an internship, who submitted stuff after they got to know
everybody and threw stuff on the head writer's desk.

What should somebody study?

Personally, I think a nice liberal arts education, and then getting
in here on the internship is probably your best bet. I'd say study a little of everything. You're talking about writing comedy. There are
times when we're writing pretty much about everything, from Pil-
grims to Mesozoic times. And then we're writing about what happened yesterday.

The cool thing about our staff is that there are a lot of different
backgrounds. You've got someone with a musical background and a
weird suburban life—which would be myself. You've got guys who
studied engineering who are just complete bookworms. You've got
guys that have law degrees. **There are writers here who are very
good magazine writers, and then there are people like me
who sort of just goof off.** It's a nice mix. Together we have a nice,
full range of references. We just hired someone who was an engineer
at Bell Labs who has a Ph.D. in Physics.

How did he get a job here?

He decided he wanted to give up researching laser telephones or
something and decided, "Hey, I want to write lame jokes about Ted
Kennedy's pants." So he quit Bell and put in a submission here and
got a job. There's a worthwhile endeavor. **He could have bene-
fited society with some sort of lifesaving telephone device,
and now he's just here writing about the *Thighmaster*.** Whatever makes you happy.

Can anyone do the internship?

I think you have to be getting college credit for the internship.
That way NBC can not pay you and still have you work forty hours a
week. They're not going to help you get a job to support yourself

while you're here, or a place to stay, but they'll give you the opportunity to work with people. I can point to most of the staff—Morty the producer worked in the mailroom when he was a kid. Half the writers were interns.

Not all interns get jobs out of their internship though. Any advice on how to?

Just don't be an idiot. We had a couple of interns stealing shirts. Just do a good job and get along with people and show you're not just doing this to get free T-shirts and dates with models. When you're there in the internship you've got to know where to make the right moves—it's your call. You can't just come in the first day and go, "Here, I've got jokes," because they're gonna look down on you for that. There's nothing wrong with being ambitious, but it's got to be the right place at the right time, and make the right move at the right time. Because everybody pretty much wants to be a writer that's here.

You'd be really surprised what some interns would do. You have to understand what your position is. **When I was an intern I was like, "Whatever you want me to do, go ahead and ask me. I'm going to do it. I'm not going to be an idiot.** You want me to get coffee, I'll get coffee. You need me to get this photo, I'm not gonna come back til I have this photo." You'd be surprised. I've heard interns say, "I'm not gonna do that." And then years later this person is suddenly up for a job on this show, and someone says, "Oh yeah, she was your intern, she used you as a recommendation." And you're like, "No, tell her to go fuck herself." (Laughs.) I don't know. I wouldn't really do that.

Don't make a nuisance of yourself, but at the same time, if you have an idea or have some jokes or something, don't be afraid to push it through. It can't hurt to show it to someone. **Just find a way of not being a pain in the ass and still getting your ideas in.**

So you're saying nobody's just going to hand you a job, you have to sort of create it?

They might if you're Warren Littlefield's daughter. (He's the head of programming at NBC.)

Are your friends from high school or college surprised that you wound up as a writer for "Letterman?"

A lot of my friends from college say, "Weren't you the guy who was goofing off?" You know, I was the guy blowing things up in the backyard, staying out late, and not doing my homework. And now I'm here getting paid to think the exact same way. What can Dave blow up now or, hey, what can Biff drive his golf cart through? **These are the things I did and got in trouble for, and now I get paid for it.**

Is there anything about this job that you don't like?

Being in close proximity to Willard Scott I guess, or Gene Shalit's mustache.

Do people treat you differently when you tell them what you do, you know, like all of a sudden they're really nice to you?

No. No one cares I think. It's almost like the opposite. Once I was pulled over for speeding and the guy says, "What do you do?" And I said that I worked for NBC. Then he says, "Who do you work for at NBC?" And I tell him I'm a writer. He asks for who, and I tell him David Letterman. "No wonder his jokes suck," he says.

What's the oddest or strangest thing that's happened to you on the show?

It's always so odd anyway. I mean, sitting in a room with Jerry Brown (presidential candidate), watching Willard Scott toss his toupee from the sunroof, or standing in the bullpen with Dwight Gooden.

How's the money?

Let's say it's close to just under what the President gets paid.

It's good?

Yes, it's very good.

I have nothing more to say to you, do you have any more questions? (Laughs.)

No.

Good.

JEREMY SPIEGEL

Segment Producer, "A Current Affair," New York City

Twenty-one years old

I met with Jeremy at the Fox Building in New York in the "A Current Affair" wing. You're amazed anything gets done here. Organized chaos, or just chaos, how do they do it? Newspapers and video tapes are in seemingly random piles on desks, shelves, and on the floor. *National Enquirer* articles are taped to walls and to the sides of desks. The sets of "Mary Tyler Moore" and "Murphy Brown" were not modelled after this "news magazine" show.

How did you wind up at "A Current Affair"?

I had sent my resume all over the place for internships—ABC, NBC, CBS, WOR—and then called to follow up on them. Generally, what I got from each place was, "We'll call you if we're interested." Which from a couple of places was a rejection letter a couple of weeks later. I called Fox to follow up on my resume.

For what show?

I didn't know. I said in my cover letter that I was willing to do anything. I told them I was interested in broadcasting and if they wanted to put me in the mailroom I didn't care, just give me something, I want to break in. I got the personnel director on the phone and told her I wanted an interview. I felt that I interviewed very strongly and I needed to get in and meet these people in person.

So I came in for the interview, we talked for an hour, I interviewed with the producer the next day, and they offered me the job.

So I worked as an intern the whole summer here, May through August, and worked really hard.

What were the hours?

Fifteen to twenty hours a day, five days a week. I was here constantly. I lived here. I worked around the clock.

For no pay?

For no pay. **I made five dollars a day for transportation and it cost me ten dollars. I lost money by working here.**

What did you do as an intern?

I'd come in in the morning and separate all the newspapers into the way we used them to look for stories. Doing phone duty, getting people coffee, running scripts upstairs, getting tapes copied, running tapes up and down to the studio. Anything and everything. Running personal errands. Anything.

Then, midway through the summer I started to push myself. I have no problem getting people coffee, but I really wanted to milk it for all it was worth. I pushed and got myself into setting up stories, which is an actual position here, and partly what I do now. Calling all the people in the story and getting them to come on, and doing research and all that. So as an intern I started doing that.

How did that happen?

I said, "Hey, can I start working on some stories?" At first they were hesitant. They're not going to let an intern do this. But they trusted me and they let me do a couple. And I worked very hard and I did it.

You would actually find the stories you'd put on the air?

Oh, yeah. I would find the stories, then I'd set them up. Basically, what I'm doing now I started to do while I was an intern. Then at the end of the summer they asked me to drop out of school to work here full-time.

What do you do now as a segment producer? You come in in the morning and do what?

I come in with coffee, sit at my desk, and go through today's local papers. I mean, every day is different. That's what I love about this job—there's never a day that goes by that's the same. Some days I'll come in and sit there and do nothing. I'll read newspapers all day and clip articles and hand them in to the news desk. Some days I'll be on the phone the second I walk in because we're shooting a story the next day, and I've got to make sure everything's set up and ready to go.

How do you get your stories?

A lot of the stories we get from newspapers. As you can see, everything in this office is newspapers. We have a subscription to a hundred-something papers, weekend papers, magazines. You'll see an article on something and you'll say, "That's interesting." And we'll do some research on it and find the angle on it—something about it to do a story on.

What does setting up a story entail?

If the story is viable we have to decide what players we want in the story for our show. There could be twenty people involved in the story, but obviously we can't fit twenty into it. Then you have to find the angle and a spokesperson for it. Sometimes it will be a psychologist. I just did a couple of segments with Dr. Joyce Brothers commenting on a story that we did called, "Men That Kill Their Wives." She commented on the cases to discuss what was common about them, what was different, and what women can watch out for. How they know their husband is going to murder them. How not to get murdered by your husband.

It takes a little investigative skill when you call the people involved in the story. Sometimes it's using our little—which I won't disclose to you on this tape—news sneaky ways of finding things. Finding someone's address, their phone number, their relationship to someone.

I'm like a salesman sometimes. **I mean, to be a producer on a TV show like this you have to be a salesman, you have to be a researcher, a writer, an artist, an accountant.** You have to be all these things at once to be able to get a segment on the air, because you're responsible for the whole thing. I'm leaving for Oklahoma next week to do a story, so I had to spend an hour and a half the other day doing a budget on what costs I'm expecting: hiring a free-lance camera crew for two days, hotel, airlines, hiring actors to do a dramatization, little extras, props. Whatever it takes, I've got to be able to budget the whole thing.

You mentioned being a salesman. What do you mean?

You want to hear me be a salesman? (He picks up the phone to demonstrate.) "Hi, this is Jeremy Spiegel from 'A Current Affair.' We took an interest in your story. It's very compelling and I think it would be something to bring to national attention—we're a nationally syndicated show. What's happened to you, this shouldn't happen to people. You must be outraged that something like this could happen. How do you feel about it? What do your friends think?"

OK, what have you just done?

Two things. I've tried to find out in my mind—it's almost like an interview—if we want this person on our show. If they are dull or have nothing to say, we don't want to see them, because who's going to want to watch them? I have to decide on the phone if they're worth our time on camera. Not only are they worth our time—that they're going to be an intriguing and interesting interview that is going to round out our segment and tell us what we need to know— **I have to convince them that they have a reason to come on "A Current Affair." We don't have a great reputation. Some people say "sleazy" or whatever. I've been hung up on so many times I feel like I'm a telemarketer.** "No thank you." "Don't call me." "Leave me alone!" Some people are dying to come on the show though.

I also work with reporters as the liaison, coordinating everything while they are out on the road. The news desk will tell one of our reporters to, say, after this assignment fly directly to California for their next story. "Talk to Jeremy about it," they'll say. "He'll set it up for you." So he'll call me and say, "What's going on?" I'll fax him an article or summary of what the story is and then I'll say, "You're going to be in L.A. on Monday. OK, what time can you start? One o'clock? OK, I'm going to set up so-and-so on Monday, so-and-so (people to be interviewed) on Tuesday, shoot B roll (extra, miscellaneous footage) on Wednesday." So then I have to call everyone in the story and make sure they're still willing to participate.

I'm also responsible for getting in footage from local news stations. Say some guy kills his wife. We weren't there at the time, so the news station will furnish us with videotape of the guy being brought downtown.

Do you shoot everything on location where things actually happened?

A lot of times we do our dramatizations in New York as opposed to on the road. We've shot plenty of reenactments at my parents' house in New Jersey. On one instance the reporter was on the road and she called me and said, "We need a dramatization for a segment I need to cut on Thursday and I don't have time to shoot it. Go and shoot it. **I need a stripper carrying balloons with a gun in her hand.**" So I went out and found an actress—we have a file cabinet of headshots—that looks the part. I rented and bought the props, got a camera crew out to my house, and shot the different angles that the reporter wanted. I then gave this to her to cut into her segment.

How did you learn to do this—get the proper angles and shots?

A lot of what I'd do when I was an intern was stay after hours, because a lot of people work at night cutting segments. I'd work the phones until eight PM and then go back to the edit room and stay until three AM just to watch and ask questions and see how they put a show together. That's how I learned.

How do other people get jobs here?

When I was hired I was told I was the first intern they've hired in like six years. They don't usually hire interns. A lot of people start out as trainees here. It's a six-month traineeship, and if they want to bring you on staff as a production assistant they will, but it doesn't happen often. The staff stays the same for a long time.

Do you have to be young and right out of college to get a job here?

No. I'm the youngest one here. There's a guy that's just starting out here as a trainee that's twenty-eight. He was a writer for a newspaper for a couple of years.

Is there a specific major someone should take to prepare for this job?

I don't think any major really means anything. When they were deciding whether or not to hire me full-time, our executive producer had left and we had an interim producer. So they went and said, "We want to put Jeremy on full-time. Is that OK?" And he said, "What's he, one of those journalism majors?" He didn't want some journalism graduate that thought they could come and apply it here. He wanted someone that was well-rounded that just seems that they've got something there. Do something that interests you and that's going to make you a well-rounded person. The media is about everything.

You said they rarely hire their interns. Why do you think you were hired?

I was just talking about this with my boss tonight. She just did a lecture to kids about how to get your first job in media, and she said that she mentioned me. **She said, "The reason I hired you was because you made yourself available for anything that was asked of you. You were never too above anything that was asked of you.** When you were an intern, the other interns were like 'I'm not getting coffee, that's not what I'm here for. I'm not answering phones, I'm not running a tape downtown.'"

She said what I did that impressed her and other people was that

it didn't matter what the task, that I would take on anything if someone needed it done—without ever being told sometimes. That's
major around here. You can't wait to be told what to do—not in this
business. I would overhear someone say "Shit, where's the tape for
the promo?" And without anyone saying anything I would run downstairs to pick it up because I had seen it earlier that morning. People
don't have time to worry about anyone else. You've got to worry about
what you're doing, because you've got so much work to do. **When
we're in sweeps and we're in production and we've got a show
to put on every day, it's crazy. People running into each other,
screaming at each other, throwing things at each other.**

You've got to know what's needed of you. And even if it's not
expected of you, you've got to be willing to do that too. There was a
time when they threw me in a car at eleven PM and said, "Go to the
airport and meet this reporter before they go out on the road."
Being an intern is a foot in the door. You've got to take advantage of
the opportunity, because there's a stack of resumes every place I
went for an interview.

**But, you can't come in here with the attitude that you're
going to only do what they allow you to do. You've got to
drive yourself to do more.**

Any examples of office politics?

I recently got my own desk. I was sharing a desk before, but then
this desk became available downstairs. There's this person above me
(by rank) and she's got her own desk, but now I've got a nicer desk.
I've got a really nice L-desk and she's got this little cubicle. So, she
said to somebody, "Why did he get a big desk downstairs?" And my
friend who knows me well said, "Because he asked for it and pushed
to get it." No one said, "Jeremy we'd like to give you your own desk."
I saw that the person there had left and nobody else claimed it, so I
took it. They're never going to say "Here, here's a nicer desk."

Sounds pretty competitive.

It's pretty testy and stressed out. The slightest thing can set
someone off— it doesn't matter what it is. Someone came in here

the other day at noon—she wasn't feeling well—and the girl that sits next to her that had been here since eight AM was like, "Noon? You're strolling in here at noon?" And the other girl was like, "Oh, I don't feel good." So the other girl said, "Fuck you! I don't feel good either. Why don't you get in here at eight AM and stop bogging me down with your problems." That's the way it is around here. People here can be pretty insecure. **Everyone's afraid they're going to lose their job, that someone's better than them, or making more money than them, or is more popular than them.** It's like a total ego thing in this show. I think it's TV in general, because I know people in news (Fox) and it's the same thing.

Does it bother you at all that this is such a sensationalist show?

It's entertainment. We don't profess to be a news show. We are a magazine show. There are certain days when I don't want to call another cop and ask him about a brutal murder that resulted from a love triangle. However, whether it's sensationalism or not, I'm here to do my job for what this show wants. **This is a highly successful show. It's not my job to decide whether or not this show is adding anything to society.** My opinion is, we have 25 million viewers. It's adding something to them if they watch us every night. They're being entertained. I don't care if it educates them or if it does the same thing for them as "60 Minutes" does. We don't try to be "60 Minutes." If we did then we wouldn't be on the air.

I'm not just here for "A Current Affair," I'm here for me. Regardless of what this show is about, I'm learning skills here that I can use on any other show. You know, if I were to go over to "60 Minutes" to work, I'm going to know how to take a camera crew out and do an interview, and know how to shoot something and know what techniques I have to do every step of the way to get a segment on the air. How to edit it. How to shoot something to edit. What you have to shoot in the field to get what you need. How to write it. How to interview people. How to decide what's important in the story. How to meet deadlines. It's not what it's about, it's the way I do it.

Any time for social life, or is this it?

This job is my life, absolutely. My close friends are here now. **If you're going to work in this you've got to be willing to compromise every single thing that you have. Your friendships and relationships and your free time.**

JOHN VERRILLI

Managing Editor, Fox News, New York City

Thirty years old

I knew I wanted to do a TV news interview, but I didn't know who did what, and therefore who to include in the book. So I called up my friend who works on the news desk at Fox and asked if I could visit her at work. You know, to check out the "work environment." Work environment, forget about it. These people are all crazy. It's like a hundred of them in one room, yelling.

I took cover kneeling behind the assignment desk next to my friend. Things had actually calmed since earlier, I was told. This morning a top Exxon executive was reported missing. Dragged from his car near his driveway, weeks later he would be found dead.

The challenge right now was to get a reporter out to that driveway in the suburbs. Apparently, having made a few wrong turns or something, the reporter still wasn't at the scene. With air time in less than one hour, and considering set-up time, it would be close.

John was still. Wasn't saying a thing. "Who's that guy?" I asked my friend. "The managing editor," she says. A little young to be the boss I thought. "What's he doing?" I ask. "Praying, maybe?" The Tom Landry of the news team, cool and quiet. I found my interview victim.

A week later we do the interview at John's place in the city. No chance of doing the interview at the station, too crazy. Like clockwork, he flips on the tube to Fox and goes into the room to check his answering machine, just in case anything happened on his five-minute walk home from work.

After a couple of false starts—phone call interruptions from the station—we get into the groove. Oh, by the way, the reporter wound up making it to the driveway on time.

Where did you go to school and what did you major in?

I graduated from Lafayette College in '84 and majored in history. Most of my college career I didn't know what I wanted to do. Basically, I was just there to learn. That was where my head was at at the time.

Were you worried about graduating, you know, what you were going to do?

Yeah, I was a little bit. Probably not as much as a lot of others. I didn't even go through the college recruiting process. I was not really concerned with finding a job right away. I took the summer off and went up to Nantucket and then travelled for about a year—and was *definitely* not worried about finding a job at that point.

I wasn't so anal about, "I've got to get a job now, I've got to do this now or my life is not going to be on the right track." I gained a huge wealth of experience just going across the country. Sleeping out every night. Just being independent.

Then I got back home after my trip and started doing a job search. I went to the local library. I said, "Well, I'm going to get a job in journalism. Let's see, where do I start?" So I got the books out that list all the different television stations, radio stations, and newspapers on the East Coast. I made a huge list and then figured, "Well, everyone that works in newspapers always says they want to be in television, so I'll start in television and see what happens." I sent like a hundred letters and resumes out to every organization on the East Coast. I also did all the big stations in New York, channels 2, 4 ,7, 9, 11, 5.

You sent them to Personnel?

No. Don't do that. Especially in television, because Personnel doesn't hire anybody except trainees and interns. The actual hiring is done by executive producers, news directors, and managing editors like myself. I sent them to the news directors.

So I sent them all out, and two weeks later I get a call from Channel 5. I mean, this never happens. **Never in my career, as a**

boss now, have I looked at a resume and said, "Oh, I'll give this guy a call." It doesn't happen.

But it happened for you.

It's actually a very funny story how it happened. I got a call from the news director's secretary, who is now a producer on Channel 5. She would get all the resumes and cover letters and never give them to her boss, because *she* wanted the job of production assistant herself, so she hoarded them. But she felt guilty, and figured every now and then she had to give her boss a resume—figured he was *expecting* them. She decided to give him *my* resume because I had put on the bottom of it that I had studied in Florence. It turns out that the news director loved Italy, had gone there several times, loved Italian food, is just a real Italian lover. So she thought this guy will have something to talk about with me.

Two weeks later I get a call. I go in for the interview and talk with this guy for about fifteen minutes, and all we talk about is Italy. I guess they were thinking about firing someone. So they fired them the next day and called me and said, "Can you start next Monday?"

A funny thing is, when I got the job I didn't ask how much it was, just figuring that at a New York television station you're going to make at least 20 to $25,000 to start. I came in and they tell me, "Oh yeah, you make $12,000 your first year." I almost died when they told me that. But with overtime my first year I think I made around $16,000.

What do they make now?

Not much more. If you're there longer you can make as much as $300 a week. You seriously have to pay your dues. The nature of the business is it's so competitive—there's so many people out there who want to get involved in this—that they can afford to pay that little. Because if you don't do it, somebody else will.

What were some of the things that you did as production assistant?

You're responsible for little menial things like changing ribbons. But you also get to cut tapes, which is a great job. You cut voice-overs into sound bites. We have a deal with CNN where we use their material and they use ours. You would monitor their shows and tell the producer, "This is good and this is good."

I took it upon myself not just to do the basics and say, "This press conference ran at this time, this is the log, here, you figure out the sound bites." I would always come up with suggested sound bites. I'd say, "This is good, we should use this," or "Take a look at this."

Why would they listen to you?

If you take an active interest in news and you know what's going on, **people will always trust you to take responsibility—if you're good. And once they trust you, the more responsibility you get.**

My break was, the producer of the ten o'clock news became a friend of mine, more like my mentor. He began to trust me. I'd say to him, "There's a really good package that ran on CNN, I think you should take a look at it," and he'd look at it and use it sometimes. As a producer you're in charge of basically coordinating everything for the show, so you need people that you can count on. And this producer learned to count on me. So I took advantage of it and really worked hard. And I think he recognized that and gave me a shot to do other stuff.

Like what?

After a year and a half of being a production assistant, I came in on my own time, on the weekends, to write. The next step from being a production assistant is to become a writer. So I would come in on the weekends and do that on my own.

They weren't paying you for it?

Well, at first they weren't paying me. After a while when they started using my stuff they said, "OK, we'll pay you." And eventually they made me a writer on the weekends.

What does a writer do?

You basically write everything that the anchor reads. The anchors don't write their own copy too much. It's usually done by a writer. You also write the voice-overs. Anything that's not a package, which a reporter does, is done by a writer. So the lead-ins to reporter's packages, you write. You write the "opening" and the "goodnight." You write teases. A tease being, when you're about to come to a commercial saying, "Coming up next...."

So I was writing for about four months on the weekends, and I got an amazing break. Because I had gotten involved very much as a production assistant and knew how to do a lot of different things, this producer I mentioned gave me a huge break and said, "I want you to be my copy editor for the ten o'clock news."

Wouldn't you usually go from full time writer to that?

Yeah. So two years into it I was copy editing. I said, "Sure." I couldn't say no, but I was shitting in my pants. I was so scared. I was now copy editing writers' material who had been there seven or eight years.

Were people pissed off that you sailed right by them?

Yeah, people were openly angry. They were definitely going to make me prove myself, none more so than John Roland, the anchor. Because for him, the copy editor is the point man. You have the final look at the copy before it goes on the air. And if something is wrong with the copy, *he* looks bad because he's reading it. People at home don't understand that it's the copy editor and a writer who put this together, and that the anchor is just reading it.

So he didn't trust me at first at all. **Whenever there was a mistake, John Roland would turn around during a commercial and let me have it. I mean, ream me out.** In front of everyone. And he did it so often, it was scary. During show time it was like, "Oh no, is it going to happen today?"

Were you making a lot of mistakes?

I was a kid. I was twenty-four years old and his reputation was in my hands, so to speak. He's a bully by nature. He likes to have some-one to punch. A lot of people do who are in power. I was the perfect target. I was this new kid that thinks he's hot shit coming in here being copy editor. And he's like, "I'll show you something."

Eventually things worked out and it was fine. I found that I had to just stand my ground. **If you stand your ground people start to respect you. If you let them stomp all over you, they'll stomp all over you,** and this was the case with him. Now we're friends and everything is hunky dory, so to speak.

What does a copy editor do?

As a copy editor you're approving what the writers write. The pro-ducer does a rundown and says, "I want to put all these stories in the show." Then the copy editor assigns writers to each story. You have to make sure that they get the story done in time. You look at the story for content and style and grammar, and make sure it's not too long.

You have an hour show and a set number of stories. The pro-ducer will say, "Listen, I can only have this story be twenty seconds." It's very difficult sometimes to write exactly in time, twenty seconds. So I'd look at it and say, "It's too long," or, "You missed a certain ele-ment of the story." So as an editor you also have to go through all the wire copy of the day so you're familiar with each story. So you know what the emphasis should be in the story, what parts are important, and what parts are not.

So I did this for about a year and then was offered the weekend producing job, which I did for a good year and a half. It goes in that progression: writer, copy editor, weekend producer, producer.

What does the producer do?

You decide what your lead story is going to be, the rundown of the show, what anchor will read which story, how long you want each story to be. You're in charge of working with reporters. You have free-lance crews that go around and shoot stories, and you take tape from them. You put all this information together and put together a show. You have to rely on yourself a lot.

Was that scary at all?

Yeah, and it's still scary now. Now as managing editor I'm in charge of what stories are going to be covered, and pretty much run the newsroom as far as trying to get the stories covered. And it's a very competitive market. As managing editor you watch the other stations—we have monitors in the newsroom that play all the other stations—to see what's covered, how they cover it, and if they got an exclusive interview or something. **There's a lot of pressure not to miss something. It's still frightening every day when I come home and turn on Channel 5 at 10:00 PM and see what I missed.**

What's a normal day for you as managing editor?

I get in to work at around seven-fifteen AM. The first thing I do is listen to the news radio to find out if there's any breaking news overnight. I read all the newspapers: the *Daily News*, the *New York Post*, *New York Newsday*, *Wall Street Journal*, *New York Times*, *USA Today*, and *The Washington Post*. I try to read those fairly thoroughly each morning from around seven-thirty to eleven-thirty AM.

How do you decide what stories to cover?

It's just news judgement basically. If it's a story that affects children, if it's a story that involves celebrities, if it's a story that involves racial tensions, riots. When you hear that a black guy was beaten up by a group of Hasidic students, and the mayor comes out with the police commissioner and talks about this new racial incident in Crown Heights—you're all over it. Because you know it's going to be a big story, it's high interest.

How do you hear about these kinds of stories?

The assignment editors listen to police radio, EMS radio, fire radio, the transmissions between police to police and fire to fire. If you hear EMS rushing several units out to this school in Flushing, Queens, because they say they have many kids who need attention, you call up EMS and find out why.

And people call in too?

Sure. Some people are news junkies: they like to be a tipster. So you get calls from people all day long. Every now and then you'll get a good story out of one of these tips. Someone calls and says, "Listen, I was on a corner and I just shot (videotaped) cops beating up this black guy and kicking him, and I have this home videotape of it." And you'll go, "Oh yeah? Well, let me see it." And they'll bring in the videotape and you'll have a good exclusive.

Do you have to be aggressive to get stories?

Oh yeah. **You have to be a magician on the phone to get an interview with people that don't want to talk to you a lot of times.** You have to convince them to talk to you, and get them to talk to you *now*, because you only have a crew now. You have to be aggressive on how to come up with angles to stories, and once you've come up with that angle, how to make that reality on tape. Which means finding the person to talk to and getting them to say the right thing that you're looking for them to say. And get it before anyone else gets it. Get it first. Get it fast.

What do you mean finding the right person to talk to?

That's where the creative part is. Say you have this great idea for a story and you know what you want to do, but you can't get anyone on camera to say it. So it's important to have a good Rolodex, and to know a lot of people out there who are proficient at speaking in sound bites. Someone who can put two sentences together in front of television—unlike Admiral Stockdale. (Laughs.)

Give me an example.

Mary Jo Buttafuoco is coming back from L.A. where she was in a hospital because they found an infection where she had a bullet in her head. We didn't just want to do a story of, you know, "Here she is, she's back home." We wanted to find a doctor to talk about the dangers of the infection of having a bullet in your head—"Can this mean death?"—that kind of thing. So I would say to the assignment editor, "Listen, I want to find a doctor." And so the assignment editor would start calling different hospitals and say, "We're looking for a doctor to talk about such and such," and they'll set up a time for the story. And that's basically what we do all day. We set up stories for reporters.

What's the most challenging part of your job?

The most challenging part is the pressure of trying to be right on the stories you cover. You have to make decisions. And once you decide, it's difficult three hours in the day to change gears and say, "Whoops, I made a mistake, I want to do something else."

How do you defend or explain the growth of sensationalism in news?

The news is sensationalistic and that's probably not going to change, because you look at ratings every day. News directors across the country are trying to determine what is going to get that good rating. **Everything is based on ratings. Journalism was never *supposed* to be based on ratings. You never even looked at ratings.** You'd cover what was important news, not what people want to see. Now, people are concerned about what is going to sell. And so you have stories about Woody Allen, about Madonna, about celebrities, because people are interested in them. People want to know about Amy Fisher, this little girl in the suburbs who all of a sudden becomes a prostitute and shoots her lover's wife. It's obviously *made* for television, and it *becomes* television.

Do you ever catch yourself? Someone says, "We've got this story, there was a killing, blah, blah, blah," and you say, "Well, it's not good enough"?

Sure. It's horrible. I'll probably burn in hell. (Laughs.) You make fun of it. It's like the "M*A*S*H*" syndrome. **You're basically looking at murder and mayhem every single day.** There are five, six, seven murders a day in New York City, and it's rare that we cover any of them now unless they have some real compelling interest, some mystery to them. Like, some young college girl is found with her head cut off in some nice suburban community where you'd never think it was going to happen. Well, then it's going to be a story, because it's unusual and people are like, "Wow, it's actually happening in a place that I think I'm safe." And that makes it a more compelling story for people.

What's your response to the accusation that you're not being responsible by not covering hard news?

I have this discussion with people all the time. My response is that we do what the market demands. **I would like to think that there is a responsibility in TV journalism, but there isn't. And I don't think there's ever going to be again.** There's too much pressure on news management to make sure that your news program rates. If it doesn't rate, you're off the air, bottom line.

How about the responsibility of how a story is covered. Do you have to consider that?

Yeah, I think about it all the time, on a daily basis. Journalism is not objective. You definitely have an influence on which way a story is going to go, and which way it's not going to go. For example, if someone doesn't like the mayor, you can go after him and make him look bad. That happens all the time. It's rare that it's so slanted that it's a problem. It's very subtle stuff. The editorial slant for all news organizations in the city is very similar. If you have a rich white person and something happens to them, it's going to get much more coverage than if it was a poor black person. No doubt about it. And that happens all across the country. When it gets down to it, it's more amazing for people when something bad happens to a white person. That's horrible, but that is the reality of the news business. But it's not just in the news business, that's society as a whole, and it's reflected in the news.

How about the stress factor of the job?

It's extremely high pressure. People do it for a little while, but they can't do it forever. I'm not going to be managing editor for more than a couple of years. **Producing a live show is one of the most hectic things there is to do in life. I have a stomach condition because of it. So many people I know in the business have ulcers or are alcoholics.**

Why?

Because it's a burn-out job. The job's a burn-out. I'm on call every weekend, one day a week. And being on call means basically working. I have a computer at home and I log in and I'm seeing what the stories are. I've got to read the newspapers. I'm on beeper all the time. I have a cell phone, so if I'm off somewhere I can call in. I'm in there at seven AM until six-thirty PM. I don't go out for lunch. I rarely leave my desk during the day because I have so much going on. You don't want to miss a breaking story, you have to be there.

I have to come home every night and watch the 10:00 PM news. And if I don't watch it then, I have to tape it and get up in the morning and watch it. And not only that, you have to be on top of the news all the time. You can't take a break. For me, the concept of leisurely sitting down and reading the Sunday *Times* is not leisurely anymore; it's part work. It's so consuming.

Sounds like a drag.

Another low is that you are in an environment where you have a lot of egos. It's a big-ego industry where people have ideas of what they want. The reporter has an idea of how he or she wants to do the story, and I have an idea. They're not just going to accept an order from me always; they're going to put up a fight. I get in fights with people sometimes on a daily basis. I've had shouting matches across the room with people. There's a lot of tension between people all the time.

So what's the payoff?

It's exciting. I'm a news junkie. There's a certain exhilaration being on top of the news as it happens. It's never the same thing. You walk in and you've got to figure out what your day is going to be like.

If you bust your butt, you really work a story, you get a good exclusive, it's good, and you beat all the other stations in town—it's a great feeling.

It sounds like it's real competitive with other stations.

It's very competitive. When you get a story that other people don't have, that you know is a good story, and they do it the *next* day because they saw it on your air and they missed it—and their news director says "Why don't you have that story?"—you laugh because you know they're getting kicked around because they don't have it. (Laughs.)

Brutal.

You do anything to get a story. You have to use tricks. You have to be nice, you have to be mean. You have to finagle people. You have to establish contacts so that people like you, and will talk to only you.

You can see why it's a young business. You see why people don't do it that long—because you can't. You can't live life like that. **I'm not going to live the rest of my life worrying about whether I missed a story or not.**

MICHAEL CATCHER

Casting Director, Liberman/Hirschfeld, Los Angeles

Twenty-seven years old

Background check—Some of the shows they cast are: "The Wonder Years," "Seinfeld," and "The Garry Shandling Show."

We decide it might be better to do the interview outside of the office during the weekend. Too many interruptions at work. So Michael picks me up where I'm staying in the canyons, and we drive around and settle on an empty, little, out-of-the-way restaurant. It's a quiet Sunday.

First off, you can tell this guy's *not* from L.A. He's just got that New York edge to him—goatee, sweatshirt, jeans—not affected in the least as you would expect an L.A. casting director to be.

Mid interview we're talking about how he can't go anywhere without running into someone he knows or has just auditioned. That's cool. I wouldn't mind running into a starlet. Hell, even meeting Fred Savage would be kinda cool.

After about a half an hour he says that he's surprised he hasn't run into anyone by now. I'm not. This restaurant is dead, deserted. Sure enough, literally two minutes after he says this, it's, "Hey Michael, what's up?" One of the kids from "The Wonder Years," cruises in. "See?" he says. "It's a small town."

Note: Michael went to Emerson College in Boston, where he graduated in 1987 with a B.F.A. in theatre.

What did you think you were going to do when you graduated?

Act. I had no idea that I was going to be in casting. It's funny. My friend who worked for Joy Todd (a New York casting director) wanted me to audition for a film called *Three O'Clock High*. I came in and tested for it and was joking with Joy about a casting job when I get out of college, and she said, "Sure." So I started interning there right after I graduated. And it got so busy that after about three weeks, she hired me full-time.

What about acting?

It got so busy there in the first three weeks, I didn't have time to even pursue what I wanted to do with acting. I knew that if I were casting, I really couldn't talk about acting at the time. I felt like it was a real conflict of interests.

What was extras casting like?

If you can communicate and you can talk on the phone, you can get a job done. It doesn't take much to learn how to cast extras. Besides, there's no one there to really teach you how to do anything. Casting extras is like being in an employment agency: you're not hiring someone for their talents, you're hiring them for their skills. If they can type, they're an extra. If they can walk, they're an extra. There would be a file of actors that were registered with Joy Todd. If you're looking for someone who has a taxicab, you look in the taxicab file, call them up at home, and say, "I have a day's work for you, are you available?"

And there's not a wardrobe person when you're doing extras. You're doing the whole thing. You're telling them what to wear, what time to show up. You show up at the set when they show up. You sign them in and then you can leave. You go back to work and work on the next day.

Long hours?

I was working really late hours, it was ridiculous. It just got to me. I started getting really bad stomach pains, so I went to get tested and they said I was developing an ulcer. **So at twenty-one I developed an ulcer.** That's one of the major reasons I left Joy Todd. Also, it got slower. It got boring.

So I sent my resume around and I got a phone call from a guy, Jeff Passero. At the time he was working with Deborah Aquilla, and they were casting *Last Exit to Brooklyn.* His sister went to Emerson College so he called me because he saw it on my resume. He needed help on this other show he was doing for HBO, *First and Ten.* Jeff was so busy with the film (*Last Exit*), he just called me and said, "Can you handle this?" And I said, "Sure I can handle it."

So that's how you met Deb Aquilla. How did you wind up working for her?

We were working at Three Of Us studios, which is one floor of all casting—different casting directors in every room. And Deb was working out of there. Deb saw how I worked with Jeff and asked me if I wanted to work for her. And I said, "Sure."

Why did she hire you?

I was working hard. **I was really good on the phone with people, you know, I had good phone sex.** I don't get angry unless someone fucks with me. Agents are pains in the asses. Managers are pains in the asses. I was very good at screening these calls so Deb didn't have to deal with them; I could always handle it. She didn't have to tell me what to do.

Sounds like she liked you.

She fired me the first week I started working for her. (Laughs.) I basically got blamed for something that wasn't my fault because I was the low guy there. And I was thinking, "This is fucking ridiculous." So I said, "Look Deb, this is what I want if I stay." I turned it around on her. I said, "You have to give me the freedom to think and be creative. You can't just expect me to sit there and get coffee and do this shit for you. I'm not going to do it. I'm there to make you a good casting director." And I was. **I was there to make them look good, which is what any good assistant should do.** So she took me back and I stayed there two years.

Damn. You were pretty straight with her.

I had rules with Deb and Don (her partner at the time). I wouldn't get coffee. I don't drink coffee. They could get their own coffee. It was a very funny thing because there would be producers there saying, "You know, can you get me coffee?" And I'd look at Deb and say, "He wants coffee."

They didn't get mad at you?

No, they actually understood. I walked out of the office once. I got so mad at both of them. It was a pretty busy day. The phones were going crazy. And every day I'd complain, "Look we've got to get somebody else in here man, 'cause the phones, I can't do all this fucking work." **I think by then I was already an associate. Which means, they gave me a title to make me happy, yet I'm still doing assistant work.**

So, I was really busy and in a pissed off mood because there was no help. So **I literally ripped the phone out and threw it against the wall and said, "Fuck it, I'm leaving," and walked home.** And I was thinking, OK, they're going to call me. They didn't call me. They didn't call me! So I was like, fuck, I'll go back to the office. So I went back and we had it out.

You mentioned being an associate, how did that happen?

I took the initiative without them having to tell me what to do. I was very eager, without being annoying. I've worked with people that are eager *and* annoying, and you don't want to work with the person. I grabbed responsibility and they gave it to me. They saw that I wanted it. They saw that I was very confident.

But not getting coffee. Isn't that a little...?

I showed respect for them, that's the thing—I wasn't fucking with them. When you're working for someone for $200 a week, making no money, they have to be aware that you're not going to do everything. I'm sure they thought I was cocky, but I was well liked by everyone who came into the office.

So what happened next?

We got this NBC contract to be casting consultants for all the East Coast. Every pilot that came out, we would work on. In casting, it's just a matter of knowing every actor's name so you can put them on lists. So we're making lists for each character for each pilot. Actors would come in and read for us. If we liked them we'd put them on tape and send it to NBC.

That's how I actually met my bosses now. They were casting different things for NBC from L.A. So when they got "The Wonder Years" for ABC, they called me in New York and asked if I would be interested in coming out there to cast "The Wonder Years" as a casting director. And I'm like, "Sure."

So you made an impression on them when you were an associate with Deb and Don.

They would talk to *me* and I would tell Deb and Don what the situation was. I was like a point man. Plus, I did my homework: I was making lists of actors that might be right for a role.

*Did you know that's how things worked, that that's how you
wind up getting jobs, from people that you talk to on the phone
in other situations?*

No, at first you don't realize it. And it's funny because **you *do*
burn bridges because you don't know who certain people are,
and you *do* give them some attitude.** Or, you don't do the job as
well as they want you to, and you have no idea who they are.

What did you think of L.A. when you moved out?

I hated it. I still don't like it here.

You don't really fit the "love ya baby" stereotype.

I get the same response from a lot of actors that come to my
office saying I'm like the mellowest, most down-to-earth casting
director they've ever met. And the thing is, I'm trying to help them
get a job. If they come to my office and I'm this fucking asshole casting director....(He shrugs, as if saying, "What's the point?")

A lot of times actors feel really comfortable with me and that's a
good thing because you're trying to get them the job. You *want* them
to look good, that's the whole point. You don't want them to be nervous. And you get a reputation where at the last second, when you
need to cast somebody, this actor will remember that I was nice to
them and they'll say, "That's cool, I'll go in on a day's notice. It's
Michael, that's fine."

Most actors I know hate casting directors.

Actors ask me, "How come when we call casting directors they're
always assholes?" And I say, "Look, you're calling someone who's got
a job, and they're getting flak from the producer who's telling him
they need this done. You have to respect the fact that when you call
up, they're not going to have the time for you, so you can't take it
personally." **Actors are dealing with rejection every fucking
day, but the thing is, casting directors are dealing with the
fact they have to reject them every day.**

I remember once an actor called me and I picked up the

phone—the call got through somehow—and they said, "Hello, is Michael Catcher there?" And I said, "Speaking," and there was silence. So I said, "What's the matter?" "Well, I've never gotten this far before." So I said—I was kidding with her—I said, "OK, I'll give you one question." She goes, "One question, one question...Can I call you back?" And I said, "Sure."

Do you ever feel bad for these kids who come out here with this dream, but you know the odds?

Sure, that they should become like a manicurist or something? Sure, I feel bad, but, it's my job. It's funny because Meg Liberman and I were talking, saying, "How come more casting directors aren't killed?" You know, actors coming in with shotguns and blowing our heads off? You're sitting there, you're rejecting these people and they're tired of it.

Everyone always asks, even producers, "Isn't it hard rejecting actors all day?" And I say "No, I'm nice to people." Our office, we're nice to people, so I don't feel that. I'm not lying to anybody. I'm not stringing someone along.

So, how does the casting process work? When do you guys get involved with a project?

I'm working on a new show now, a Castle Rock pilot for NBC. Right now it's just called "The John Mendoza Project." He's a comic who got his own pilot. NBC will call us and say, "Are you guys available for pilot season?" And we'll say yes. So we had a concept meeting yesterday with John Mendoza and his two producers about what they're looking for. And next week we're having a meeting with NBC, and they'll tell us what *they're* looking for.

We bring lists to meetings and show them the type and caliber of actors that we'll bring in. We'll give them the availability list of, you know, "This person's not available; this person has a deal somewhere else; this person won't do television." And names come up that you can't imagine with shows. You know, they'll ask, "Will Meryl Streep do it?" Something ridiculous like that. And you sit there and humor them and say, "I'll check." I'll usually say, "Give me a fucking break."

You know, "Hello, I know you think your show is number one but...."

After that, you put out a breakdown (agents get this "breakdown" list every day), which lists all the characters and the qualities each character has, and agents submit pictures and resumes of actors they feel are right for the roles.

Then from there we'll start having sessions. Whether we have pre-read sessions for us, or sessions for the producers. I read all the actors on all the projects because I'm a good reader and I like doing it. I'll usually do two or three scenes with each actor. I'll sit there and they'll either sit or stand, whatever they want to do. I put feeling into it, not like I'm doing this grand performance, but, you know.

Is it dreadful reading the same scene over and over and over?

Last week I read forty-six actors. Sure, by the thirty-fifth person you're exhausted and you've heard this a million times. And most of the time, the person walks in the room and you can tell if they can do it or not. As soon as they say hello to you, you can see what their personality is like. I mean, I work a lot on personality, because if someone has a really good personality and they're having a problem with the scene, I'll sit and work with them.

Why will you bother? There must be a lot of experienced actors out there.

I want the best people in the show. I'm not going to be lazy and just bring in the typical people you see in television. You see television shows that have typical people. You sit there and you know who they are. Whereas, you shouldn't always know who they are.

It sounds like fun. You get to act.

It's fun when there is some sort of electricity. It's fun when the person's really good. When they suck, it's really bad, *especially* when the producer's there. Because you're sitting there going, "This is terrible."

Don't you screen the actors—you know, see them before the producers in case they're not right?

A lot of times the actors won't pre-read with me before reading for the producers. The agent feels they've made a name for themselves so they shouldn't have to. And they'll come in, they're not given any notes, and they're wrong, they're absolutely wrong.

Why will agents send them in if they're wrong?

Because agents think they're right. They're telling me, "This person is perfect." And I'm saying, "No, I know this person, they're not right." "But they can do it," they'll say. That's not the point. I know the project. I have to approve every actor that the producer will see. And agents will tell me I'm wrong. And I say, "Fine, if I'm wrong, I'm wrong. I'm the one who's talking to the producer, they're telling me what they want. I'm the one who's reading the script and you're telling me what they want? How could *you* know what *they* want?"

I have friends that are those kinds of agents, that are so full of shit. But I can talk to them about it and tell them, "You're so full of shit." And they *are* so full of shit—but we're all buying it. That's the thing, we're buying it because they have this fucking attitude. Who are these people? **My joke is these are the people who have small penises; they know it and that's why they act this way.** I laugh at some of the people that call me.

A lot of attitude?

First of all, **speakerphone I hate. I won't deal with speakerphone. If you're going to call me get off the speakerphone.** The thing is, they're calling me to help them, and they're calling me on speakerphone?

And then the other thing is, they'll have their assistant call. I'll usually kid with them and say, "What are you having someone call for you for?" But if someone calls my assistant and says, "so-and-so for so-and-so," I'll say, "Put them on the phone and *then* get me." In this case I'm more important, they're trying to sell *me* something. "You tell *them* to get on the phone. We're going to play two ways now." I hate that. But fuck it. If they're going to do it to me, I'm just going to do it to them. But I'll usually make a joke of it rather than getting pissed off, because it's getting aggravated over nonsense.

Now that we're on the subject, what do you like least about your job?

Sometimes I wish I had more power. Not in the sense of a big head, but power over which actor I get to choose. I would love to just offer roles to people rather than having these actors that have done a million things come in for sessions with producers who don't know who the fuck they are. I wish they would just trust me. But I realize it's their show and they don't know this person. I can understand that.

I think the attitude more than anything. The fact that it is quote, Hollywood, I can't stand. It's stupid. The egos, I mean, I laugh it off. Because **the people who have the egos, when you meet them, you know why they have the egos—there's something wrong with them. They're real lonely.**

If you wanted to could you go from this to being an agent?

I was asked to be an agent somewhere. People always say I'd be a really good agent because I talk. But the problem is, I'm not an agent because I don't want to sell—I don't want to sell my mother. I think it's a sleazy business, this Hollywood business.

Such as the famous casting couch?

Everyone always talks about the casting couch and stuff. If it's there, I don't know anything about it, and I wouldn't tolerate it. **I see beautiful women every fucking day. But it's my job.** I've never picked up someone in a casting session. I have friends that call me and say, "Uh, I met this girl, I told her you were a casting director, can you meet her?" You know, so he can score with her. And I'll say "No, that's not fair."

But girls must take an interest in you because of what you do.

Sure, I've dated a lot of actresses. I married one. But my wife, I met at her birthday party. She read (auditioned) for me once, and I didn't know who she was. She had no idea who I was either.

Do you go out to spot talent or do you just take agent submissions?

A combination of both. Most of the time you don't have time to go out. It's good to go out once or twice a week to showcases. It gets real tough around pilot season 'cause I don't get home until around eight-thirty PM. But someone from our office will go out and cover it, and then we'll have a staff meeting to go over who saw who and who should meet so-and-so.

What about minority casting?

Color-blind casting? Yeah, we try to do as much as we can. It gets tough on shows like "The Wonder Years," which is very white-bread American. My joke is that it's the white supremacists' favorite show, because I've been casting it for four years and we've had maybe five black people on the show. But the problem is it can become tokenism. It gets tough when you work on a specific show that's dated. You all of a sudden have a black friend on "The Wonder Years," and it's an issue because it's an issue show, not a sitcom.

What should someone do to become a casting director?

I wouldn't go to New York to start in this business: it's so limited in New York. They should not think about making money when they start. You're not going to make any money. **You have to be willing to wipe people's asses.** I mean, seriously, you have to be willing to do shit work.

What else about working in Hollywood?

You mean Disneyland? Do I like it? It's work, there's work here. When I worked in New York it was a totally different business. New York it was a business. I don't find this a business—this is like life out here. You go home and your neighbor is in the business. Here you're dealing with it twenty-four hours a day.

Everybody knows each other.

Yeah, it's a really small town. Anything you say always gets back to the person. They'll always find out what you said. I've learned to just keep my mouth shut, just grin and bear it. It's just a job, you know what I'm saying?

WORDS FROM ON HIGH:
Advice From the Vice President of Human Resources at HBO on Breaking In

KIKO WASHINGTON

Vice President of Human Resources and Administration, HBO, New York City.

How do you go about hiring?

Since recruiting costs can be very high, we prefer alternative sources, the most successful one being the employee referral program. When you hire an unknown entity, you hope to do a good assessment. It's always better to get someone who is a known entity, and I believe employee referrals are the best way to achieve this.

When you talk about the entertainment industry, a lot of it has to do with contacts. If you know someone in an organization, you should let them know that you're looking, because there may be ways that your contact can get you in the company, or in the desired industry, because of his or her contacts. Relationships are one of the keys to life; there's nothing that can substitute for that.

Are internships important?

Yes! If you can, get an internship in a company even if it's unpaid and for credit, because it increases your contacts. People get to know who you are, so if there's an opening, they'll think about you. An internship separates you from the other resumes that cross someone's desk. A lot of people who have worked during the summer, fall, or spring semesters end up getting jobs in that company.

How else can someone land a job here?

We don't go to temporary agencies because we have an in-house temp program. Individuals in this pool work on a temporary basis for x dollars per hour. When an opening occurs, that person already knows people in the company so they're in a good position to get those jobs.

How many resumes do you get?

Five hundred a week maybe, depending on what's going on.

Not good odds.

It's the toughest for undergraduates because in many instances they don't have much work experience and you're comparing this individual to other people either with experience, or who were referred by employees, or past interns.

Are grades important at all?

I think if they're good, include them. I don't put a great deal of emphasis on grades. I balance grades against extracurricular activities. It's kind of like entrance scores: it can give you an indication of how someone might do, but it's not the only criteria. Did Einstein get good grades? I don't think so. He was probably bored.

Any creative accounts of someone going about getting a job with you?

We were starting the Comedy Channel a few years ago and this guy called a couple of times. I explained to him that we were still in start-up and I wasn't prepared to start seeing people. I said I would call him once we had a better idea what we were going to do organizationally. He understood. He was persistent—he'd leave messages saying, "Just checking in"—but he wasn't obnoxious about it.

Then one day—I get to work early, around seven AM—I walk in and this same guy is waiting in the lobby for me and he says, "I just wanted to know if you had a minute to chat. I know you told me already that you guys don't know where you stand, but I just wanted you to know who I am." I invited him up and he was a very nice guy.

Of course, if this had not been a fit, he wouldn't have gotten the job.

Another time, I received a cover letter where this person used a newspaper format. It was a *Wall Street Journal* article that he created with his picture and name and what he had accomplished for HBO, dated July 1st, 1995. I saw him too.

Did he get a job?

There was nothing available at that time. It's not what's available today, but knowing the people for the future. His goal was to establish the relationship.

So being creative can work for you?

You have to separate yourself from the pack. How do you do that? You can't be obnoxious and call a million times, because then you're separating yourself in a very negative way.

The company that you're trying to get into becomes the key. If it's a creative company, you have to be creative, you can't just send a letter that you would send to a bank. Certain personalities are attracted to certain industries. So you have to match your communication with your audience.

If you're writing something to the head of comedy, you want your letter to be funny so he or she thinks you are a match. Make reference to some of HBO's programming to let the person know that you know something about the company.

I can't tell you how many people just send a letter, "I will be graduating in May from the Darden School at the University of Virginia. I majored in marketing, my GPA is 3.78. I would appreciate a response or an interview." There are 8 million people writing that same letter. Why are you any different from anyone else? We would like to see everyone who's interested in working at HBO, but it is impossible.

Say who you are. Show your personality in your letter. Let the person know that you're a match for the company. First, you should be targeting companies that you're a match for.

So pick the company before the job title?

You should choose the industry and the company. It's OK to not know what you want to do. I don't care if somebody doesn't know what they want to do. If you say "I'm interested in marketing, but in order to get in I will do whatever it takes," you're providing the flexibility to get in. Then you create the focus.

How might people blow it in an interview?

Don't ask about money until you're pretty far along in the process. It gives the impression to the interviewer that money is the issue and not the job. You should have a rough idea of what jobs will pay, especially if you're coming out of school. You should do that research before you show up.

Communication skills are so important. It's hard to say, "Don't be nervous," but you want to have a conversation, not just an interview. If you can find out about the individual you will be interviewing with, where that person went to school, his or her background—all that stuff helps because it creates a dialogue beyond the nuts and bolts of the job. Chances are, if you're being seen, there's something about your background that fits the company. When you have the interview you have to show that you fit this company and its culture. I happen to like a sense of humor, it just helps, and also I think it's important in this company. First, you have to have the skills, you have to be qualified. Then it's about how you would interact with your co-workers.

You said to get into a conversation. Like maybe making reference to your trophy collection like I did when I walked in?

Someone walking in to my office should immediately notice two things that stick out; one, the trophies, and two, the cartoons.

I'll be honest, when I came in and commented on the trophies, I don't really care about sports too much, it was just a way of breaking the ice.

It's conversation, not an interview. Your reference to the trophies takes away the initial discomfort. And the sooner the discomfort goes, the sooner that person's just talking to you—just having a rap instead of an interview—the better off you are.

What else is it that attracts you to an applicant to make you want to hire them?

Direction. Drive. The desire to work. Emphasize that "I want to work here, and what I will bring is enthusiasm to the job. My resume says *x*, but don't think I'm not willing to do whatever it takes. Any department, entry level, I will be successful here." Know the company. If you come in and say "I want to work in entertainment/television," well, so do a million other people. What separates you from the next person? What do you know about HBO? Mention some of our programming. Read the trades of the industry you're trying to get in to—*Multi-Channel News, Cable World, Variety, Hollywood Reporter.* Know what's going on in the industry and let the person know you know what's going on.

Extracurricular activities, are they important?

Depends on the individual doing the hiring. I personally like people who are well-rounded. Sports, clubs, leadership positions.

How about advancement? How do you avoid getting stuck?

One, learn as much about the business as you can. Develop a global business perspective by learning how the company operates as a whole. Yes, you have to do a great job at what you're doing to be recognized, but don't see that as your only job. You have to know where the company is going and how it's getting there. Find out what we're doing from a programming perspective, what's going on with re-regulation, and how new technology will affect us. It's this knowledge that will impress others in various departments.

Two, meet people. Developing informal relationships are really the key and you can do this through participating in the extracurricular activities your company sponsors. With HBO, it's sports. We play softball and you can meet people from all over the company. You might wind up becoming friends with people from different departments. Talk to people, don't be intimidated by their titles.

Three, communicate with your boss. You want to be able to ask your supervisor, "How am I doing?" and have him or her be honest with you. You may have to force that dialogue from your direct supervisor and ask him or her what you should be doing differently. The corporate environment is really no different than one's personal life. It's difficult to tell someone negatives, but the negatives are more important than the positives because they help you grow.

For example, if you're not dressing properly, who can tell you this? The boss. But if you don't have a relationship with the boss, he or she is not going to tell you.

I had a guy who didn't bathe enough. He would work out and not shower because he was in a hurry, and it was affecting him. He was blowing it because of his hygiene. So I spoke to him. He changed his habits and he's very successful now.

So the type of person that succeeds here...?

A person who understands that they have to take responsibility for their own career. Some people get frustrated and they look to blame the company or something else as to why they're not successful. In the business environment it's very competitive and you cannot assume that people are focused on you or your career. People have their own priorities. You have to take responsibility for yourself.

6

Radio

"Radio is in an upheaval. There's a need for risk-taking and experimentation as never before."—Jeff Pollack, Pollack Media Group (*New York Times*, Feb. 3, 1993)

ECONOMICS

You can say that again. According to the National Association of Broadcasters, 59 percent of the 9,555 commercial radio stations operating in the U.S. lost money in 1991. Though the recession played its part, the sad fact is that more than 50 percent of all commercial radio stations have lost money in every year since the early 1980s. Why? Too many stations. In 1991 alone, 153 stations shut down operations. Despite this, there was still a 12 percent increase in the number of stations that same year. So while radio as a whole has maintained its share of the advertising dollar, that dollar is being spread thinner and thinner.

You'd be astute to ask why then have I bothered to include this limping industry in this book. It would be justified if radio, as a career, happened to be really lucrative; however, it's not. I will say that out of all of the communication mediums it is the most pervasive. There is a radio in 99 percent of American homes, one in almost every room. Plus, 95 percent of all cars have a working dial, in addition to the millions of Walkmans out there.

So, it seems to me there's lots of potential out there. Plus, the people I've run across who work in radio—from deejays to program directors—all seem to love it. Maybe that's enough justification. And considering radio play can make or break a band, well....

TOP GIGS

MUSIC DIRECTOR

This job involves a lot of contact with the record companies. The director gets the music together, keeps the music library going, updates computerized play lists, reviews what music is going to be included in the schedule (including what kind of new music will be exposed), and sets up on-air interviews with artists. This is also the contact person with the record companies.

PROMOTIONS DIRECTOR

Promotions is usually a well-funded area. This person will hype special features and events via on-air promos and serves as the media contact person aggressively marketing the station. He or she writes press releases, TV spots, print ads, bus boards, and subway signs.

SALES ACCOUNT EXECUTIVE

This job can be extremely lucrative. A sales exec gets no salary but a percentage of sales instead. Junior sales people develop their own client list. They'll do a lot of cold calling in the attempt to solicit new advertisers. There's a lot of rejection.

PRODUCER (SEE GARY DELL'ABATE INTERVIEW)

GARY DELL'ABATE

Producer, "The Howard Stern Show," on radio station 92.3 K-Rock, New York City

Thirty-two years old

Background check—Howard, the thorn in the side of the FCC, plays in fifteen cities across the country and is produced in New York City. If you don't know who Howard Stern is, you're not going to get the interview so I wouldn't bother reading it.

How come everybody knows who Bababooey is except for me? I'm on the phone with my ex-girlfriend. She asks, "What are you doing, you want to go for dinner tomorrow?" "Can't. I'm interviewing the producer of the 'Stern Show,'" I tell her. "Bababooey!!" she yells. "What?" "Bababooey. Bababooey. Oops, (phone call-waiting click) that's my other line. I'll talk to you later."

I leave the house to go have lunch on a bar stool where a friend works. "What's going on? You interviewing anyone interesting today?" "Tomorrow—the guy who produces 'The Howard Stern Show.'" "Bababooey!" the guy next to me yells softly. Dammit. Alright, tell me. "Bab*aboo*ey," he says, as if I'm a total idiot. "Gary Dell'Abate, Howard Stern's producer. You're interviewing Baba-booey?" "I guess so."

Next it's my roommate. That same evening, swear to god, we're watching the news. Howard Stern is in trouble with the FCC. They want to fine him like $600,000 or something for being indecent. "*That's* Bababooey," she points. "The guy kissing Howard's ass? The guy bending over to kiss Howard Stern's ass for the news cameras, that's who I'm interviewing for my book?" "Pretty sure that's him. Let me go with you. Pleeease!"

So I meet the guy, Bababooey, and I gotta tell ya, I'm a little underwelmed. He's this totally down-to-earth, mild-mannered, unassuming guy wearing jeans and a T-shirt with some goofy cartoon character on it. First things first. I ask him how he got his name. He told me the story. He collects animation art, and was telling Howard, on the air, about a painting he was going to buy of Bababooey, a cartoon character on "Quick Draw McGraw." Howard said, "It's not Bababooey, it's Baba *Loo*ey." And Howard, being Howard, won't let Gary forget this honest little mistake by calling him Bababooey, as does the rest of modern man.

What did you study in college?

I went to Adelphi University for communications. When I was in high school I was heavily into photography, so I thought I'd go there and take a couple of photo classes—that's what I thought I wanted to do. Adelphi didn't have a photography curriculum, so they said, "Go into communications; it's filmmaking, it's just like photography"— which of course it's nothing like. I took a radio class my first semester there and that was it, I never went back to photography.

What did you do when you graduated?

When I graduated I didn't find work for a really long time. I went to Europe for like six weeks, I came back, and I said, "Oh, should I look for a job this week or next." I just thought there would be a million jobs out there. I remember, I went out looking for a job on a Monday, and by nine-thirty AM I was sitting on the steps of the New York Public Library totally depressed. You'd answer all these ads in the paper and as soon as you walk into the agency they say, "How many words a minute do you type?" and the answer is I don't type any. I don't know how to type, so I ended up working odd jobs that are not communications related. I worked in a record store. I was a host at a restaurant.

So what did you do?

I had interned in the news department at WLIR, which is now WDRE, and my boss there was a really instrumental figure. He sort of took me under his wing. He would call me all the time and say, "I've got an interview for you." He sent me on a bunch of interviews. He was working at NBC at the time, and he told me that there was a job open as a desk assistant in the news department.

So I went to interview for the job and it turned out to be the assistant to the traffic reporter in the helicopter. That was technically my first job. I would sit in a little cubicle and there would be a map of Manhattan on the wall. I'd have a little police scanner and a telephone set up with a whole bunch of auto dials, and I had a little Shadow Traffic teletype machine that had a two-way radio. The woman in the helicopter would do a report and she'd come back after the break and say, "Gary, I just saw an accident in the right lane of the BQE just around the Lower East Side."

So I'd hit my auto dial and call the tow company and tell them there was a car there. It would be my job to keep calling the tow truck companies asking if it had been cleared yet. Once the tow truck company said they'd removed it, I would tell her, and that's when you hear on the radio, "That accident has been cleared from the right lane of the BQE."

Sounds easy enough.

It was, except the people at the tow truck companies had absolutely nothing to gain from it so they were fucking thoroughly hostile. I was bothering them in the middle of their busy day. I'd keep calling them. They would say, "Would you leave me alone," and they'd hang up on me.

It's got to be the lowest job on earth. Pulling cable has got to be better than that. I hated it because I had to get up at the crack of dawn, be in by six-fifteen in the morning. And I only worked three hours a day so my take home for that was $105 a week. So I'd work until nine-thirty in the morning and then I'd go work a regular job. I had this job in a kennel supply store so I could eat.

But hey, it was a start.

It was great, I got my foot in the door at NBC and I was going to make whatever I could out of it. **So I started going around and making friends with everybody and said "Listen, I'll do anything, just tell me what you want, I'll do anything."** I made friends with some people in the promotions department. They used to do a big promotion every summer. NBC was legendary for their bumper sticker contest. You would put this dorky bumper sticker on the back of your car and if you got spotted you would make money. So my next big gig was I got to drive the "N" car around. I would drive around and spot people with bumper stickers. It was great. I would call in live on the radio, you know, live to different shows and say, "Alright Mike, I'm following a white Chevy station wagon, New York license plate blank blank blank. Don't pull over, just wave to win." (He's saying this over the air, get it?) And then the deejay would say, "Is he waving,?" and I'd say, "Yup, he's waving," and he'd go, "Well, congratulations, you've just won sixty-six dollars."

A funny story is, I did that a lot of times during Howard's show; at the time he was on WNBC. And that was the first I'd ever heard of Howard. He was sort of this underground thing. I would drive during his shift and after four days in I was thoroughly hooked, I thought it was really great, really funny. One time—Howard's one of those guys that will take any contest or anything and just totally make it nuts and turn it around—I was following this woman (with a bumper sticker) and she didn't wave. So Howard kept me on the phone line and said to follow her until she pulls over. When she pulled over I asked her to come over to the car, and I put her on the phone and Howard proceeded to yell at her. He said, "Hey lady, do you know that you just blew six hundred and sixty-six dollars? What are you stupid, you put a bumper sticker on your car and you don't even know why?"

So that's how you got to know Howard?

Yeah a little bit, but he still didn't know who I was. In late August I heard that the guy who was producing his show was leaving. At the time they weren't even really calling it a producer—it was almost like a paid internship. Everybody wanted this job, even though it didn't really pay anything. They were getting a lot of outside resumes also. So one day I waited around for Howard. I got dressed in nice clothes and I waited around, and it just so happened that day that he was sick.

So Fred Norris and Al Rosenberg, who work on the show, they came in, and it was one of those days where they had nothing to do because Howard wasn't in. So they interviewed me for an hour, goofing on me and fucking with me. They were really giving me a hard time. They were going over every line on my resume and saying, "What's this, what's this?"—just fucking with me because they had nothing to do. They were bored. So I think during that, I think Fred took a liking to me. And I really wanted it, I made it clear that I wanted it.

So then they called me back and said, "Howard wants to talk to you." I went in and Howard spoke to me for ninety seconds. I found out he just wanted to look at me to make sure I wasn't an ax murderer.

When I first started they told me I was on a trial basis. I was so nutty to do good so that I could get the job. After two months I said, "So what's the deal?" And they said, "Oh, you got the job." I thought I was still on a trial basis.

What did you start off doing?

The job in the beginning was really three things: getting Howard's lunch, booking guests, and just keeping the office in some sort of organized state. The starting pay was $150 dollars a week before taxes. But it was great. The second I started doing it I said, "This is for me."

How did you live on $150 dollars a week?

I was working on weekends, and Friday nights I was deejaying at a club. But I didn't care.

You said you were trying to book guests. People weren't calling you to get their clients on the air?

No, no. At the time nobody called us. People weren't kicking our door down at all. In fact, we were lucky. We booked a lot of guests because when we would say "WNBC" that carried a lot of weight, they'd be like "Oh, NBC." But then they'd get in and it would be Howard and it would freak them out.

The first call I made was to Steve Martin. I tried to book Steve Martin on the show. And his publicist was incredibly hostile and she said to me, "You will never get a guest the caliber of Steve Martin on your show." And I thought, "Oh man, this is devastating."

What was a turning point in your responsibility or in moving up?

It's hard to say. **After I was there for a while Howard said "Why don't you call yourself the associate producer of the**

**show. Write that in your correspondence, it just looks better."
So then I became the associate producer.**

It's sort of weird, it wasn't like moving up the ladder because I've sort of had the same job for the last nine years. It's just the job has gotten bigger and bigger. I mean, I was the producer eight years ago and I'm the producer today. It's just the show is bigger and it entails more responsibility. But I haven't gone like from intern to program director to general manager to owner. It's just sort of naturally evolved.

Producers usually aren't on the air are they?

That's one of the things Howard took to a new level, putting a producer on the air. A lot of people didn't. **For the most part radio producers are kept in the background, seen and not heard, so to speak.** The second you start on this show you're immediately on the air, and that's a whole other role.

How long did you guys last at NBC? Didn't they kick you out?

I did one full year at NBC. Howard was there for three and a half years. We were doing great. The ratings started to go up. Howard was on the way up in a big way. But NBC was very much a family-oriented station. Howard was the true pioneer, innovator, wild man, and he was always at odds with management. They were always trying to get him to clean up his act. He wasn't doing anything bad, they just wanted a family image.

One day the program director came to me and said, "Listen, it's really important that Howard meet with John," the general manager. "John really wants to see Howard." He ended up meeting with the president of the radio division, came out, and said, "That's it, we're out of here." It was a complete shock. He had just had his highest ratings to date.

Howard took you with him?

So Howard got his gig at K-Rock. They had dished out a lot of money for Howard and Robin, and didn't think they really needed a producer and didn't want to pay for one. So I went out on a couple of interviews, which Howard has always teased me about on the air. He always said that I could never get a job because for one month I was out of work. Since I didn't get anything it proves that I need him to be employed. So after a couple of weeks he talked them into bringing me over too.

So what does a producer do?

Howard told me from day one, "Your job is to do everything in this office so that all I have to do is go on the air and perform. I don't want to have to handle the business. I don't want to handle the scheduling. You take care of all that and just let me go on and write and perform."

Our show is different, In reality, the producer of the show is Howard. The producer is somebody who decides what goes on and stuff. I'll give advice and suggestions, and he'll take those suggestions, but it's really his show. There are some shows that you can go to where the talent is a talking head and the producer is the real brain of the outfit, dictating what goes on. He'll say, "OK, what we're going to do here is we're going to play this record, and then you're going to talk for a while, then we're going to do the news and then we're going to do this." That's definitely not the case with Howard.

You guys don't even seem to have a format. Is that tough?

The hassle with the job is the same thing that is probably greatest about the job, and that is that there *is* no format. It's very undefined. So some days it can make you nuts because there's no rule of thumb. I mean, there's rule of thumb for certain things, but there are some days where it is completely helter-skelter, and whatever rules you have might be broken.

Like what?

We might book a guest and it might be that something bigger has come up. We might have something that we *said* we were going to do that day, and then decide that we're not going to do it that day. If there's something news-breaking, we drop everything and go for that now. And we'll say, "Wait a second, we have this this and this."

"Throw it out the window, *this* is important now. Tomorrow it won't be as important. Tomorrow everyone will be doing it, let's do it now." So that's what makes the show great. That's what the beauty of the show is.

This show is incredibly unstructured. Most radio stations have what they call a clock. You draw a clock on a piece of paper, and you write, "Zero to three, that's where we do news. And from three to eight, that's where we play a record. And then from eight minutes after to twelve minutes after, we play some commercials." Everyone else in the world has a clock that they abide by. You know, they do traffic at twenty after every morning and then do it again at fifty-five after the hour. Well, we have no clock. We never take breaks at the same time. We take breaks when he feels like it, when he gets to them.

How does your day begin?

I get in at like five-thirty in the morning. I get the show prepped for the day, which means I get the list together (of things they can do on air). I make sure the studio is set up correctly. If I know that we're having multiple guests in that day I make sure there's enough chairs in there, enough headphones. If I know that we're having a musical guest in I'll make sure we have a music set up, keyboards or guitars.

The guys will begin to brainstorm. They might say, "Dice (Andrew Dice Clay) is coming in today. Remember a couple of weeks ago Jay Leno was on and he said Dice was an asshole?" And Howard will go, "Yeah, that's great. Why don't you go pull that piece of tape and we'll play it for Dice." And then I'll go back to the computer, look it up, and find it.

Then when the show ends, we clean up the studio and then I start doing phone work. I can start making calls at around ten AM or eleven AM, because no one in the entertainment industry gets in their office before ten AM. And once you factor the West Coast time, I can't even start getting hold of those people until two PM.

What's that like, dealing with the talent?

Dealing with the guests is definitely one of the best aspects of the show, without a doubt. It can be the most fun, and it can be the most insane.

Why?

Sometimes people will come in and make demands, or the publicist will say to me, "You can't talk about this and you can't talk about that." And I'll go in to Howard and say, "Howard, you cannot talk about their first marriage." And Howard's great way around that is he'll say to the guest, "Well, I was going to ask you about your first marriage but your publicist told me I can't bring it up." And they always say, "Of course you can bring it up. Who told you that?"

It's tough man, it's very difficult. There are some publicists that are really great. You've got to understand something. My friends always ask me about this. They're like, "Oh, you talk to Chevy Chase, you talk to Cher?" No, I talk to *their people*. **Getting guests on the show, you don't convince Bob Hope to come on the show, you convince Bob Hope's *person*.** So now you're convincing a person once removed.

There's a lot of latitude in a publicist's job. There are some publicists who really take down the information and then they go to their person and say, "Listen, the 'Stern Show' called and they want you on." And then there are some people who make that decision in their heads themselves. They have decided that they don't want him or her on this show. And the celebrity may never find out about it.

Perfect example. Mark Knopfler from Dire Straits was coming to town and I called the publicist, a woman at Warner Brothers, and asked her to have him on. And she said, "OK, I'll check and I'll let you know." She called me back and said, "I asked him and he said no, but thank you very much." It turns out that later in the afternoon he was in the studio doing another show and I just happened to walk in for a completely different reason. I think I left something in the studio. And the jock that was on the air said to him, "Oh Mark, by the way, this is Gary Dell'Abate, he produces 'The Howard Stern Show.'" And Mark wheels around (in his chair) and he goes, "Wow man, Howard's a great guy. I really wanted to do the show, but the people from Warner Brothers said you guys didn't want me on," or something insane like that. And I thought, "Oh my God, I don't believe this." And I called the publicist back, and she finally did admit to me that she never told him about it. It's CYA, man, cover your ass. She just did not want to rock the boat.

The other difficult thing is that, listen, the show is very honest and it's very funny, but we don't do a fluff interview. **We don't do a hard interview, but I mean, you can go on Kathie and Regis and it'll be just one big party.** We ask funny questions and real questions. I mean, our show deals in reality. And there are some publicists who are so frightened. I think the worst quality that I deal with in publicists is they're frightened people. They're so scared to deviate off of anything that is potentially not perfect. The Howard Stern interview is a great thing to do if you're bored with the same stupid questions from everyone else.

I don't think I'd blame the publicists for being scared. It can be like a lion's den in there.

It can sometimes be a tough interview. We're certainly not *mean* to anybody. I think all the guests here leave feeling pretty good. And the response they see is incredible. Cab drivers and hot dog vendors and people all around the city will go, "Hey, heard you on Howard!"

We had Milli Vanilli on a couple of weeks. That was a big deal for them. Here they were, they were the laughingstock of the industry. The publicist called me on this one and he was very nervous. They always ask me, "Is Howard going to be nice?" The answer is always yes. Howard does a good interview and people leave very happy.

Did you want Milli Vanilli?

I wanted them right away. Absolutely. **My favorite thing is when somebody flips on the radio in the morning and goes, "Holy shit, what the fuck is that person doing on that show?"**

How did you get the President's brother, Roger?

Roger Clinton had called in on the show like three times, so it was time for him to come in live. So the publicist actually called me at home last night. I have two phone lines at home, one's a private line and one's a line that I give to almost anybody. And the one that I give to almost anybody, I usually don't answer, I screen. I give it out to a lot of publicists.

It doesn't drive you crazy getting calls at home?

I don't mind people calling me at home. So these people called me at home last night at like ten o'clock. And they said, "Roger's playing tomorrow night. Can we get another mention on this because it's a big event?" And I said sure. And they asked if he could call in tomorrow. And I said, "Well, he's in town, right?" This is where you have to sort of hassle and negotiate with them. I just had Roger Clinton on the phone last week. I didn't want to have him on the phone again, we wanted to meet him. I was like, "Listen, you've got to bring him in." They said, "Well, he doesn't like to get up early." And I said, "Listen, you want to put people in there tomorrow night (sell seats to a gig he was playing with his band), you get him in live and he's on for an hour. If you put him on the phone he's on for fifteen minutes. The longer he's in, the more we talk about the event." And they said, "Alright, hold on for a second," and they called him on the other line.

Does Howard ever piss off the guests?

Corey Feldman, the kid actor. I had to chase Corey to the elevator. Corey was literally in the elevator. He had one foot in the door and I had to physically grab him and go, "Please don't leave." He hadn't even been on the interview yet and Howard said something like, "Corey's been calling here and he wants to get on, he keeps bugging us." And Corey was really insulted by it. He was like, "Hey, fuck this. I've done an HBO show. I'm in *Ninja Turtles 3*, I don't need this bullshit." But he came back and it was his best interview ever.

What else do you do?

Part of my job is to screen calls while we're on the air. I've had a lot of celebrities call on my line, and I've had a lot of people who *pretend* they're celebrities to try to get on the air. I put a guy through who I thought was Joe Pesci, but he wasn't. It ended up being a really funny bit on the air. But I've had Cher call here. You have to ask people, "Well who's your manager. What label are you on?"

One of my jobs is a very convoluted pre-interview, if you will. I'll ask the publicist what's going on before they come in, but I don't really get to see the people before they come in that morning. So I'll go out there (in the waiting area) and I'll just start shooting the breeze with them and they'll tell me things. And then I can hand Howard a note, "Did you know that she's got a boyfriend in L.A.?" or whatever. And then Howard will ask her, "So how's your boyfriend in L.A.?" And she'll go, "How did you know I had a boyfriend in L.A.?"

So it's a pre-interview.

Yeah, but I don't say it is. I sort of chat with them—it's almost like spying to a degree. But I certainly wouldn't give away anything on the air that was hurtful or harmful.

When you hear Howard say stuff like, "Oh, she's got an amazing chest, she's not wearing a shirt and she's sitting on my lap"—does some of that stuff ever happen?

It's all real. When the girls come in and start to take off their clothes, they really take them off. When we do the Super Bowl party, we're all wrapped in towels getting massages from topless women. When we do Butt Bongo, that's the real deal, I mean people come in and play Butt Bongo.

And the women really take off their underwear?

A lot of times they do.

You can't do that on TV.

It's a much looser format, you can basically do a lot more. On TV when you're dealing with the visual, things have to be more precise and more thought out. And the thing about radio is that it's immediate gratification.

WORDS FROM ON HIGH:
Advice From the Personnel Director at WINS and WNEW on Breaking In

CECILIA QUINTERO

Personnel Director, 1010 WINS and WNEW FM Radio, New
    York City

Background check—WINS and WNEW are a couple of top
    New York City stations. WINS has an all-news format, and
    WNEW is AOR (album-oriented rock).

How many employees do you have here?

At WINS we have seventy-three. WINS has an all-news format,
so you need a tremendous staff to support that. We're really atypical
for a radio station. WNEW is AOR (album-oriented rock). They
have forty-five employees.

How many new hires did you have this past year?

Hiring levels have fallen. There was a time when I was always
recruiting for positions here at WINS. My hiring rate has fallen off
precipitously in the last three years.

Are people staying longer?

No. We have fewer positions than we once did. And as people
leave, sometimes there's a decision, "Well, do we need to replace this
position, or, can we reorganize that position somewhat so we can
eliminate it."

What do you look for when you're hiring someone?

I look for several things. I look for people who are really flexible—who are willing to take on more duties outside of a normal job
description if need be. I'm looking for people who have excellent
computer skills. People who can learn things quickly, and have a
knowledge, at least, of how we work. If an applicant comes in here

and says, "Well, how do you guys make money?" you know, that will raise a real flag for me. I want someone who's knowledgeable. Not necessarily experienced in our industry, but someone who has a sense of how we make our money and what our role in this market is.

How do you go about hiring?

Through *The New York Times* and other local papers. I always contact community organizations and industry organizations, as well as occasionally employment agencies.

What organizations specifically?

National Urban League. National Black Media Coalition. The National Association of Broadcasters. These have a pool of applicants: people who are either looking to move to a different market or people who are just unemployed who have skills and are looking for help in lining up work.

How many resumes do you get?

I probably get about twenty resumes per month. We get lots of unsolicited resumes. I'm sure it can be frustrating on the other side, because sometimes I can't respond to all of them. And for a determined job seeker, I'm sure it can be a little dismaying not to hear from a broadcaster that they've listened to. The people that stand out are the ones that call to follow up.

What do you look for on a resume?

At an entry-level job, obviously at that level they may not have a lot of industry experience. But I'll look for their activities while they were in school or if they volunteered at a station. I place more emphasis on the resume than the cover letter, that's my own personal style. If I see typos or misspellings, I'm pretty harsh on that. I look to see if they have technical experience, if they can edit tape. I look for computer experience.

I also look for the ability to handle pressure. I look for a past history where maybe unreasonable demands were placed on them. So if I see someone who was a waiter or a waitress at a busy restaurant, I like that. Especially if they were there for several summers, that tells me that they were very good at what they did. And many times young prospective candidates are embarrassed and don't even put that on. But that tells me that they can handle pressure and that they can juggle several things at one time.

For a younger person who doesn't have a lot of experience to offer, put a little personal section at the bottom with intriguing pieces of information as to what makes you different.

Are there common mistakes people make in interviews?

I've had candidates that have no notion whatsoever as to what an interview is all about. An interview is about selling yourself. You have to be responsive in answering my questions, but at the same time you have to be aware of what you're doing. You're there to market yourself.

People who are attractive to me in interviews are really focused. They seem to have goals in mind. They have a sense of what direction they want to go, what they want to pursue. That's very attractive. People who seem really wishy-washy or unclear, that really troubles me. Because my thought is, "OK, I'm going to place them in this job, but I'm not really sure they want it, so how long are they going to last here?"

How can you tell if they're wishy-washy?

They're not looking at me, they're looking out the window. If they're not looking at me, it indicates to me that perhaps they're not interested in the job. Or they're not focusing on what I'm saying, they're focusing more on their agenda.

You mentioned follow-up calls were important. Which is better, a letter or a call?

Letters. Follow-up calls are good; letters are better. Some of the hiring managers I work with really place a huge emphasis on that. It's like, "I can't believe that after I saw ten people, this one candidate who is really outstanding, who I really like, who is head and shoulders above the rest, didn't take the time to write me to thank me for my time and to tell me that 'Yeah, they'd love to come and work for WINS.'" What could have otherwise been an outstanding meeting is a little tarnished because they didn't take the time to do the follow-up letter.

How about grades? Do you look at them?

I'm not so concerned about grades.

An important thing—getting back to what mistakes to avoid when interviewing—if an employer tells you, "Please fill out the application," and you show up in your nice suit with your resume, and you think, "OK, I'll fill out the application kind of weakly. I'll just give them my name and address. I don't have to complete the work history, I've got my resume, I'm not going to take the time on that." Do not do that. I will want to see them complete the application, because that's a legal document. They're basically affirming on that application that "yes, these are things I have done." So don't have an attitude when they say, "Please give us your work history too."

Any creative accounts of people trying to get jobs here?

I've had people send me cookies and stuff. One person delivered balloons.

Did they get jobs?

It got them interviews, but I can't say it got them jobs here.

7

Publishing

BOOKS

Even though there are still more than 20,000 book publishers in the U.S. alone—an indicator that publishing is an extremely fragmented industry—fact is, it's basically a New York City industry, that is, if you want to join the big boys. And the big boys have become even bigger and more corporate. A flurry of mergers and acquisitions of the larger independent houses starting in the late eighties has put ultimate editorial control in the hands of publicly owned corporate giants. Hyperion Books is owned by Disney, Simon & Schuster by Paramount Communications, and HarperCollins by Rupert Murdoch's News Corp. Not that that means that all of a sudden editors are starting to dress like they actually have jobs (although my editor dresses fab), wearing skirts and ties. Not the case. There's still an air of creative casualness—a literate, academic look. A look perfected from years at prep schools, Ivy League schools, and summers in Nantucket.

Economics

Maybe it's a public reaction against becoming a Jetson family culture, nostalgia for simpler times of cooking and reading, I don't know, but book publishing has thrived in recent years despite a Blockbuster Video store on every block, the increasing number of cable channels, and "Roseanne" reruns five days a week. Spending on trade books (adult and juvenile fiction and nonfiction) increased around 13 percent annually from 1984 to 1989. The years 1990 and 1991 were tough years of little growth, but '92 sales jumped back up to a 13 percent annual growth rate.

Top Gigs

EDITOR

At the larger houses that exist almost solely in New York, you start off as an **editorial assistant**. The pay sucks, about $18,000 to start. Basic grunt work and lots of reading from the "slush pile"— those fabulous, unsolicited manuscripts. Next step is **assistant editor** which takes around two years to get to. You start to acquire your own books, but are still an assistant. After another two years you might make it to **associate editor** which means having a solid list of your own, doing most of your boss's work—editing their manuscripts and negotiating their contracts—and still photocopying and answering the phone. This is where you can get stuck for years, I am told, just waiting for an editor to die.

PUBLICIST

It's much easier to become a full-fledged publicist than it is to become an editor. Publicists stir up interest on a book six weeks before publication so that booksellers will buy it and the public will be eager for it. They try to get authors on TV shows. They schedule author tours and try to get books reviewed by major papers and publications.

PRODUCTION EDITOR

Every book has a production editor who oversees the production of the book from all stages until publication. They are responsible for making sure the book comes out in time, so they follow it through its line-editing, layout, and design stages.

And then, of course, there's the **designer,** who designs the inside and outside of the book, and the **sales rep**, who is on the road pushing books to all the bookstores out there. And from what I hear, if the sales reps don't believe in your book, good luck, sucker. The reps meet with authors when they're in their district, bringing them to signing and speaking gigs and maybe grabbing a beer. They're in their cars a lot listening to these tapes that all the editors put together describing the books that they're going to be selling.

MAGAZINES

The magazine biz, excluding those ever-popular publications such as *Girl Scout Leader, Elevator World*, and *Military Lifestyle* (yes, actual magazines), is really a New York thing, even more so than book publishing. Publicly owned companies such as News Corp, Reader's Digest, and Time Warner account for around 60 percent of magazine revenues, while Condé Nast and Hearst Corporation together share the vast majority of the remaining dollars.

Economics

Magazines haven't been nearly as successful as books in grabbing readers' disposable income. And when readership goes, advertising dollars follow, a reaction that killed off magazines in record numbers in the early nineties. Advertisers have become so fickle and unreliable with regard to magazine advertising that the magazines have taken to courting *readers* as fervently as they once did advertisers for their dollars. Magazines now depend on direct sales to readers more and more, and they therefore pay closer attention to what they really want. And so—as if just in time—publishers have turned to niche publications; very specific issues, like *Shape* magazine's "Guide to a Fit Pregnancy" and *YM*'s special, "Love." These one-time, special-interest magazines are selling like crazy.

Top Gigs

EDITOR

Magazines have a fondness for the word editor. If you deal with, in any way, the content—words or pictures—of a magazine, you're an editor. Fashion and photo editors generally do not write, so if you're afraid of the written word, there you go. All other editors are basically writers who do so for a paltry living and who wouldn't be able to attend the unending fabulous functions if it weren't for the fact that they got in free, and who wouldn't be able to pay their rent if they didn't write free-lance articles for other magazines.

RAY ROGERS

Editor, *Interview* magazine, New York City

Twenty-three years old

Ray Rogers, at first glance, is not what I thought he'd be. While he works for a magazine that furiously strives to showcase what will be the "latest," the next "thing," Ray himself is suspiciously conservative. Dark jeans, burgundy button-down shirt (Banana Republic?), conservative haircut, no earrings or jewelry. Good enough to bring home to mamma. But then you get to talking. Aha! This ultra-liberal, closet stage-diver spurts off clubs and bands that I guarantee the folks over at MTV have never heard of. But then again, that's his job.

He shows me around the halls of *Interview*. Again, I've been duped. Beautiful floor-to-ceiling wood-crafted shelves line the halls that lead to the library/conference room. *Esquire*? *The New Yorker*?—Yes. *Interview* magazine? I don't think so. Perception is *not* reality.

Let's start at the beginning. When did your interest in journalism begin?

The very beginning is I wrote and was editor of my high school newspaper. Then when I went to college I started right up with the newspaper there and the radio station too.

Where did you go to college? What did you major in?

I went to SUNY (State University of New York at) Albany and majored in sociology. Being a reporter or writing for magazines, having a background in sociology is pretty good. It's been very useful. People told me not to major in journalism, that it's a waste of time, that if you're a good writer you can pick up the skills. They said have a strong background in something else, like history or politics, but I chose sociology because I was interested in social issues.

When did you start writing for magazines? How did you start?

I studied in London my sophomore year and started writing for *Melody Maker*, a British music magazine. I just sort of called them up and said that I was a writer from New York. It wasn't a lie. (Laughs.) I went in with my jeans and a T-shirt and a little folder with ratty quotes, and they thought they were great, so they gave me some records right there to review. **The first thing I did was trash a Jackson Browne record which *Rolling Stone* gave like five stars to or something. Typical.** And then I started doing live reviews and little interviews for them.

I did an internship at *SPIN* magazine the summer after my junior year. That was a great experience. They're really good to their interns there. I wrote like eight stories that summer. Anything from short features to record reviews and little interviews with bands.

How come they let you write? They usually don't let interns write stories and do interviews, do they?

At *SPIN* I worked every day. There were like six interns there that summer but I was the only one that worked every day. I was really into it. I was really diligent. I would show up early and stay real late and come in on the weekends. But it really paid off because they gave me a lot of assignments and they trusted me. I felt like I was a part of the staff.

You had an opportunity and you went with it.

I totally went with it. I used it to every advantage. I did everything I could: fact-checked, wrote reviews, wrote interviews, came up with different ideas. I helped edit. I wound up cutting seventy-six lines out of the feature on Eddie Murphy interviewed by Spike Lee. That was pretty incredible that they let this intern do that. It's good at a small magazine because you can do everything from getting the publisher coffee to having a hand in editing their main feature.

What did you do when you graduated?

I moved to New York right after college without a job. I interviewed with Condé Nast and it seemed really promising. **They said that they had a job that I'd be perfect for, but I couldn't pass their typing test—a big faux pas.** So I took a typing class. (Laughs.) I figured, you know, whatever. Then I kept answering ads. I went to all these agencies and stuff, which really sucked. And then this came through here at *Interview*.

How did you hear about it?

I was in touch with Drew Hopkins (his old boss at *SPIN* magazine). We had become friends. I'd call him up every now and then and pester him for jobs or whatever. And he's the one that brought me on board here.

What was the job?

It was mostly a production job. The guy before me, that was the capacity he made it.

But you've made it something different. How did you do that— wind up writing reviews and stuff?

I was constantly giving them ideas of who we should write about. And for the first few months they kept passing up really great story ideas, or great bands that we should have been doing, that were in *The New York Times* or all over the press six months later.

What was the first thing you got to write?

The first month I was here I got a record review to do. It was a tiny band on a tiny label that none of these guys had ever heard of, but she's incredible.

How did you get to do that review—did they give it to you?

No, I was real persistent. They told me to be on the lookout for up-and-coming people and people who are cool and so forth. If I hadn't pushed for that they wouldn't have given me anything.

I saw an opportunity there and I grabbed it because I knew that I had to. **You know, they're not going to come to you with a little** silver platter and say, **"We would be honored if you would do a review of this new record."** Or, "We would be honored for you to write our next feature story on music. We'd love you to do that Ray." You know, they're not going to come to you and say that. So you've got to fight.

How did you go about it? What did you do?

As soon as I came in I started right away, boom, boom, boom, connecting with record companies. Calling them up left and right, finding out who is the hottest thing coming out. Who is the hippest, what is going to be great, what's going to sell, what's going to look great in *Interview* magazine? Who's got that right look and sound? What's going to be out there?

No one said, "Here, call these labels, see what's going on?"

No, I just took it on myself. I didn't want to be trapped in the production side or just answering phones. When I wasn't answering phones or typing, I'd be on the phone with publicists at record companies, you know: "What's going to be the best thing out in two months?"

And they'll talk to you because it's gonna help their band if they get in Interview *magazine.*

It works both ways. They can do something for you and you can do stuff for them. The thing is, you have to really be smart about it and keep your head on straight. And only do what you really feel is going to be great or is a really strong product, a really strong band. **Don't sell your soul for a free dinner. That's my motto. Not everybody has that motto. Not everybody at all.** I mean, lots of people really get off on wining and dining with their new best friends at record companies or publicists. Being taken out to dinners at fancy restaurants, feeling like they're part of this hip thing.

And they'll pay because they know that you can make someone's career.

It can definitely help out bands, or anyone, such as directors, that we spotlight. It can definitely help their careers. It's sort of like,

"Well, *Interview* says that it's good, there must be something there."
We just put the Lemonheads on the cover and it's going to make
their career. I mean, that sounds really haughty, but it will. It made
Marky Mark's career. He was on the cover, naked from the chest up.
He was huge after that. That issue sold out all over.

So is that how it all works—schmoozing with the record com-
panies?

A lot of times it does work like that, but you don't have to. Not to
blow my own horn, but I feel like I've really gotten where I am without doing that. And **I think people really do respect you a lot**
more when they know that they can't buy you.

A publicist at Geffen Records invited me to a Nirvana concert
before they were huge, and I popped up on stage and dove out. I
stage-dived. And two days after that I get a letter from another person from Geffen that I had met that night: "Dear Ray, the last time I
saw you, you were diving off the stage at the Nirvana show." So that
was a big plus for me 'cause they saw that I'm not one of these tired
old rock critics that sit in the back, barely clapping, looking smug.
I'm just like the rest of the kids in there, that's what I'm into. They
respect that. If they think that something's really cool and explosive
and happening, they know that I'm top of it, that they can go to me.
I'm not that boring "Oh, ho-hum, it's OK. Doesn't this remind you of
'78?" "No, it reminds me of '93."

Exactly. Fuck Woodstock. It's kind of funny seeing music writ-
ers use highfalutin words to describe rap or something. I mean,
who are these guys?

That can be annoying about music writing. Music writing can
really get self-indulgent. That's something that you always have to be
conscious of and not fall in to. Just because a lot of other writers
write like that, it doesn't make for good copy. Listening to music is a
really personal thing, so you just do it honestly. How it affects you or
how you think it might affect other people. What might be something universal that people can get out of listening to this band, or
why might people want to listen to this band.

You mentioned that they told you to be on the lookout for what's cool, what's next. How do you do that?

I go out and hear music at least four nights a week. Check out what's at CBGBs, or at Maxwell's in Hoboken, or Brownies on Avenue A. (These are the cool underground clubs that have launched many an alternative music career.) Reading a lot of music magazines and being in touch with people. Having a good network of friends.

I love music. I'm an addict for it. I don't have needle holes in my arm, but I have scars in my earcanals from my Walkman headphones that I have on ten hours a day, even while I'm here. It's sort of a joke in the office. I'm always wandering around with this loud music. But that's my job, so they allow it—to know that there's a huge scene in Chapel Hill and we have to cover it before everyone else does. That keeps the magazine hip—them letting me blast my Walkman.

Watching MTV?

I don't have MTV. Isn't that weird? I have to get it. But the thing is, musically, I'm like three years ahead of MTV, just because I have to be. Being totally ahead of things, and discovering new, exciting people. Going to search out these people. Going to CBGBs and not just going there to see the Breeders, but going there to see the two opening acts *before* the Breeders. Checking them out.

Say you find a band or someone you really like, how do you get them in the magazine?

You write a proposal and bring it to the magazine and just try to be persuasive about them. Maybe I've gone out to CBGBs or Under Acme, or wherever, and saw a great band and called up their manager or their record company. And it turns out they just got signed and they're going to have a record out in three months or something like that. So I just write a little paragraph of what they sound like, why I think they're going to be big, or why I think they're great, and hopefully it will work. When you've got three people at a magazine where music is their thing, it can be competitive towards getting those few slots, getting your bands covered.

You've got to fight.

After you get to a certain level those things become part of your duties and you don't have to push for whatever every month. Now, basically, in our editorial meetings we sit around a table, and Ingrid (the editor in chief) says, **"OK, Ray, baby. What have you got for me? Who's the coolest, what's the hippest act coming out?"** And I'll say (whatever), and she'll say, "Do you really feel strongly about this?" And you say, "Yes, this is going to rock your world," and she'll say "Do 'em!"

If you're consistently on the mark, they trust you. Now they trust me here because they see the stories I'm doing are popping up all over the place after we've done them already. And that's great for them.

Do you like interviewing people?

Yeah, I love it when people are fascinating. Not everybody's fascinating. That's the thing, and sometimes your editors don't understand that. **Sometimes people make fascinating music, or create fascinating art, but are not fascinating to speak to and don't have a ton of things to say.**
The point of the journalist is to get people, or when it's stars, to get them when they're not scripted—to get to the real person. Like when I met Bono from U2 backstage after a Zoo TV concert, and I asked him, "Do you ever feel lost up there among that huge setup?" And he looks at me and instantly says, "No, I feel lost right now talking to you." And I was saying to myself, "You're full of shit." So I said, "Really, why?" And he said, "It's just that when I'm up there I'm in my element." And I'm like, that is so scripted, why couldn't he give me an honest answer. Everything's a script.

Or else they don't say anything.

Yeah, that's really frustrating. Especially if it's a Q and A. You need sound bites and all you get is "yes," "no," "oh yeah." And you're like, "Oh, my god." I interviewed Kim Gordon (Sonic Youth) for this magazine that's not even around anymore, and she was awful. She wouldn't answer any questions. She was like, "yes," "no," even to questions that weren't yes or no. That was really frustrating because I'm a really big Sonic Youth fan, and I've seen her be really articulate and really fascinating and her songwriting is really passionate.

That can be really frustrating if you can't get people to talk. 'Cause you go to the editor and they're like, "Well that's your job, to get people to talk." It can be a reflection on you. Maybe you didn't do your job. Maybe you didn't really push. Maybe you got intimidated. You can't let yourself get intimidated. To get good copy and to get good quotes from people can be stressful. If you're doing an interview and you're not hearing anything really exciting or interesting, that can put a real strain on you.

Are they often uncooperative?

Most times they're cool. Most times they know that it's part of their job to talk to magazines. We wanted to do a page on this one nasty little band from the Seattle area called Beat Happening. Well, they didn't want to be in our magazine. It was really this old elitist, indie-rock, punk-rock ethic thing of, "Oh, fuck you." But I did a review anyways.

You trash them?

No. I gave them a good review. (Laughs.) It's still a great record and people should still know about it. A lot of writers might decide to trash someone for that. They might be like, "Oh, fuck them, I'll show them."

What's the working environment like?

It's crazy, like most magazines. There's always last-minute changes, and you always have to be up-to-date to the minute. You do everything three months ahead of time, so it comes down to the wire on what you're going to cover. Can you get this music that's going to come out in April—can you get it three months earlier? Can you get *enough* of the music that's coming out so you know what's really good, the *best* thing that's coming out. It's a lot of long hours. But the staff is really great here. Really cool people.

When's it most stressful?

When we're on deadline. Every three weeks we have a two-week period where it's crazy. Twelve-hour days. It's really exhausting. But you also get a rush too, because you've got to get it out and you've got to make it really great. It's a lot of pressure. I guess that's part of the charm of *Interview* is that it does take extra time to come up with great product, but it takes a toll on you too. There's not much time to do other stuff. You don't have an outside life for those two weeks. No time to even go swimming at the Y which closes at nine-thirty PM.

The hours can be a real problem if you can't handle it. Sometimes you don't have time to even do your job—going out to see music and to be on top of things—if you're here until all hours. You're exhausted, but you have to come in the next day and do it all over again. And the next day, and the next day, and the next day. People get burned out.

Where is the magazine printed?

I forgot. I think Kentucky. Yeah, it's Kentucky, 'cause sometimes they'll say, "Uh-uh, we're not going for this penis shot."

They keep you in line?

For a magazine we're pretty far out there compared to just about anything in terms of what we will run or won't run. You know, like a Bruce Weber spread of naked guys kissing, or Drew Barrymore naked on the cover with her boyfriend and dog. That caused so much controversy. We got so many calls, and so many news stations came and taped. But I think it's great that we did that.

How about office politics?

What's frustrating at some magazines is when you see that so-and-so's friend got assigned a story because it's their friend or their boyfriend or something. It's frustrating and kind of gross. If you have a real sense of integrity it can be frustrating to see that go on.

You don't play the game?

I don't really think about it so much—making alliances. I try to do a great job while I'm here. And just by learning to be a good editor, a good writer, and a good commentator on things out there, that to me is what will take me further. I didn't start out knowing somebody. I didn't have an uncle in publishing. I wasn't connected in any way. You can get by on being a good writer and by being an agreeable person to work with. You can definitely do that. **Some people happen to be beautiful and get by on their looks or something. That's a way for all you pretty people out there.** But people see through that eventually.

How is the pay?

Lousy. Small. You don't go into publishing if you want to be rich. Don't go into publishing if you want to even live a comfortable life for the first few years. But my entertainment's free. Whenever I want to see a band I just call up and they put me on the list.

Anything surprise you about the corporate magazine world?

I guess what surprised me is how gay it is, which is great. Just how open it is about everything. I guess just coming from a small town where it's sort of conservative, and then coming here and half the staff is gay. It's so cool. And nobody thinks twice about that. **You going to be able to make an interview out of this? I feel that I didn't give you good copy. If I were in your position I would be like, "Oh no, I don't have any good quotes."**

Don't worry about it.

JENNA HULL

Editor, HarperCollins Publishers, New York City

Thirty years old

Background check—Owned by Rupert Murdoch's News Corp., HarperCollins is, as any person who reads books will tell

you, huge. This book, the book you're reading, is a Harper-
Collins book. They do real books too. Offices are in New
York City.

I first learned who Jenna Hull was while I was in the hospital
with strep throat. My agent called with good news about my book,
"HarperCollins is very interested." "Who? What editor?" I asked.
Craig Nelson's associate, I was told. Cool. So I called my friend who
had just left HarperCollins and asked her about this person. "Jenna
Hull. Sure I know who she is. She's really aggressive, she's good. I'm
sure she's going to be made a full editor really soon," my friend said.
She told me I should be psyched because Jenna had been very successful at getting money out of HarperCollins to buy the books she
liked.

As it turns out, it wasn't Jenna who loved my book proposal, it
was my first wonderful editor, Lauren, who has since moved on.
Jenna had already been promoted to a higher position, just as my
friend thought she would be. What else did she say about Jenna?
"She's very serious. Nice, but serious. Not much into small talk.
Doesn't hang around the water cooler too much." So when Jenna
agreed to this interview, I was pleasantly surprised. Serious? Eh, I
guess. I don't know though, because my memory of the interview is
of us laughing with our feet up on her desk, chain-smoking.

Where did you go to college?

I went to Hampshire College in Amherst. I majored in women's
studies and political science.

What did you think you were going to do when you graduated?

I didn't have the faintest idea. I was really in a huge panic over
what I was going to do. I moved to D.C. and waited tables that summer for money. I used to go into a bookstore all the time on Dupont
Circle called Kramerbooks. I walked in one day and a guy I'd gotten
to know there was frantic. I asked what was wrong and he goes, "We
need someone to work here. Everyone just quit." And I said, "I'll
work here." And he said, "When can you start—now?" So I started

working that afternoon. I really liked that because I'd always liked books. I wound up managing the store pretty quickly, and I was on this profit-share, so it was very lucrative. I wound up leaving there after three years, which made my family happy. It was the family horror that I was working retail, they were so appalled. But that turned out to be my entree into this world.

How?

I was dating someone who lived up here in New York, and moved here for all the wrong reasons. I moved up here with no plans, no nothing. I knew a sales rep from Random House and he told me, "You know, you can't work at a bookstore in New York and support yourself." Then he said, "A friend of mine at Random House needs an assistant. Do you want a job?" I'm like, "Sure!" He said, "Do you want to know what it is?" And I said, "I don't care." He said, "It's in marketing." And I said, "What's marketing?" "It's similar to what you do in the bookstore." And I said, "Great! I want to work at Random House."

So I got hired there because I had the bookstore stuff. I liked the people that I worked with a great deal, but I hated every moment of the job itself.

What did you do?

I did things like tracking sales of books in independent book-stores, and wrote a lot of catalogue copy. I tried to think of innovative things to do with books, whether it's a display or a contest. **The first books I worked on were Trump's book and Roxanne Pulitzer's, and I was like, "I can't stand this, I'm going to kill myself."** It was horrible, especially when I realized that what I really wanted to do was get into editorial. It seemed that all the fun stuff was happening there.

You couldn't get a job in editorial there, at Random House?

I interviewed with a couple of people there. Random House, like most places, has to post in-house all the jobs that are open. We do the same thing here, down the hallway. At that house, like a lot of other houses, it's really hard to move from these other departments into the editorial department.

Why?

There's just a stigma about it. There, anyway, there was a real snobbery among the editorial department that anything else is lower level, and you don't want someone who's been doing one of these lower level things. It doesn't work the other way. You can go from editorial into anything else very easily. So I knew I would have to go out of house.

What did you do?

I just sent letters everywhere. I went through LMP (Literary Market Place) and I picked the people with the most interesting names at the publishing houses where I wanted to work. I sent a letter to Hugh Van Dusen at HarperCollins, whose name I liked. He knew that someone was looking for an assistant because his assistant had just quit with no notice, as had some other people. And Hugh, who had a special fondness for people who worked in bookstores, 'cause he had worked in a bookstore in college, gave my resume to him and he called me that day.

So what did you start out doing here?

I started out as an editorial assistant. It was very exciting but a big pay cut. **I took a pay cut to go from book selling to doing marketing, and then another one to do editorial.** They're the hardest jobs to get, and they're the lowest paying.

Because everyone wants to do it because of the glamour?

There's some of that. There's also a tradition of it being a money profession, where people coming into it had family money.

So what did you start doing?

My boss said, "Here's the deal: I'm way too busy. In six weeks I want you to be able to do everything that I can do." That was the big appeal of it, because a lot of people start, and you're doing photocopying and you're answering the phone and you're making travel reservations and you're typing. And he's like, "Look, I type eighty-five words a minute, I can answer my own telephone, that's not what I want."

He hated to negotiate contracts, so I learned our contract really quickly. I started doing all the negotiating with agents. It's really the way that you learn. You make all of your contacts this way. You're talking to the agents who are calling for your boss. Nine times out of ten, they're not going to get your boss on the phone, they're getting you. "Can this author have another free book?" "He doesn't like his author photo." "Can we change chapter six?" "Where's the money?"...It's all with the assistant.

I had developed a nice rapport. When I got promoted, several agents took me out for lunch, which is totally opposite. Because the way things are set up, *we* pay for food. **Agents will call and say, "Let me show you some books," and they get a fifty-dollar lunch.** So it was very sweet that people were like, "I'm going to take *you* out for lunch." And that was because while I had been somebody's assistant, I had a really nice working relationship with these people.

I was also doing a lot of line editing of manuscripts, because my boss was acquiring a lot of books. You know, if you're going to publish fifteen books in the fall, they're all going to come in within four weeks of each other, and they all have to be line edited. And that's very time-consuming. It's a lot of night and weekend work.

What exactly is line editing?

Line editing is basically fixing it, seeing if the author is doing what he or she wants to do. Cutting, asking for more things, stepping in when they're getting confused, when they're getting lost; it really varies from manuscript to manuscript. Some need very little and some things you end up completely tearing apart, rearranging the order, everything. Throwing out chapters here, asking for more chapters there. Once we're done with our line edit, we have copyeditors who go over grammar, spelling, syntax, continuity, all that stuff.

Does every editorial assistant become an assistant editor, or is that a hard move?

If you have a brain at all it's not a hard move. It can be very time-consuming though. Here, the average is about two years. It's just how long can you stand to do this job with very little pay. It can be very tedious.

When you move up to assistant editor you start being rotated into editorial meetings. **People generally begin taking the time to learn your name, which they won't have done before.** The big thing is that you're acquiring things (buying books to publish). Then you can start calling yourself an editor as opposed to being somebody's secretary, their assistant. It just feels that you're finally not in college anymore.

How did you start acquiring books?

I would screen all the manuscripts that came in for my boss, and there would be things that he wouldn't want—things that weren't necessarily right for him. Or an agent might make a pitch to him: "I have a book on oral history of women in the fifties." And he'd say, "God, that's not for me at all, but Jenna might really like this." So he was steering some stuff towards me too. We had very, very different interests. So when serious nonfiction was coming in, it was going to come to me.

So you'd get a book in that you liked. How would you go about acquiring it?

If you find something that you like, if you're crazy about it—which is about one out of every hundred things that you see—you go to the editorial meeting and you bring it up. And if the group doesn't *pounce* on you, and your editor in chief basically says OK, then you take it into the acquisitions group. In the acquisitions meetings are finance people, vice presidents, and sales people, and a lot of people that don't want to spend money. You run numbers and figure out if it's going to make money, at what level, how much you can pay, how much it will sell, how much the art is going to cost, how much the printing is going to cost—you have to do an overall accounting thing. And then you drink a lot of coffee and write the best little pitch letter you can write.

Then you get called into this frightening meeting where they all want to say no to you, and you pitch your brains out. If you're lucky they'll say, "OK, go bid on it." And then you go bid. And usually there's other people bidding, and so you do a lot of running back and forth, begging your finance director for more money. And then, if all goes well, the agent will accept your offer and then you'll go from there.

So your success of being an editor or an assistant editor is your ability to be a salesman with the acquisitions committee?

Especially with the first few things. **The first couple of books you acquire, people are totally taking on faith that you have the faintest idea what you're talking about.** It takes a mix of confidence and arrogance, especially the first couple of times.

There's a lot of pitching all the way along. I talk to people and they're like, "Oh, I love books. I love to read. I should go into publishing." And in some ways it's not suited to people who like to be quiet and read a lot, because there's a lot of other garbage that you do.

Do you have to write at all?

It's a funny sort of weird promotional writing; it's not English-thesis, school writing. It's very short, very concise. It's the flap copy basically; the inside of the hardcover and the back of the paperback. You're trying to get somebody's attention in the thirty seconds when they pick up a book and look at it. Some people are good at it, and some people like me just struggle. It's really hard. The one part of my job that I really dread.

I always had the perception that editors were either frustrated writers or at least very good writers.

I think it is a perception that you have to be a great writer to be an editor, and it's really not true. I think it's the wrong job for somebody who wants to be a writer. You have to read some pretty bad stuff. If you're trying to write, and you're reading a lot of bad work... I think a frustrated writer is the worst editor in the entire world. On some level you're competing with your authors, because you really want to be doing what they're doing, which is hard. There are exceptions, because there are editors who publish and who are successful.

How did you go from being an editorial assistant to associate editor? How long did it take?

I was an editorial assistant for a year and a half. Then I was an assistant editor for about that long again, about a year and a half. And then I became an associate editor. Basically my boss just yelled and screamed and we begged and pleaded. He's like, "Look, she's doing all this work, she's acquiring her own books, and she's doing my books." I was pretty pushy: "It's time to promote me. I need more money, I need more money." **If I'd been like, *this* much pushier I would have driven everyone insane and been fired.**

How did you make it to full editor?

When I was associate editor I felt trapped. We have a big company, and we have editors and senior editors who are in their mid to late thirties, so nobody is leaving in the next twenty years. So you hit a ceiling. When you get to be a full editor you're really talking about expanding the size of the company. It's like, "Does the company need another full editor?"

It's also hard to move somewhere else when you're not a full editor, because there are enough other unemployed editors in town looking for jobs.

So, I was still Xeroxing for my old boss while I was acquiring my own books as an associate editor. **I thought if I had to Xerox one more thing that didn't belong to me, or answer one more screaming author on the phone for a book that wasn't mine, I was just going to jump out the window.** I was really miserable for a while. And so I approached the paperback publisher about creating this position.

What kind of position?

We publish hardcovers and paperbacks, and everybody used to do both. So I just lobbied for a full-time position doing the paperback line. They had been sort of thinking along the same lines. So they officially created the position and a bunch of people applied for it. I bit my nails for three weeks and then found out that I got it.

Why do you think you got it?

Half of it was being aggressive and half of it was just luck and timing. In my case a position was created that I pushed a lot to create for myself. And since I'd been thinking about it for six or eight months, I knew exactly what I would do.

As an editor, do you have to be in touch with what's going on?

The nice thing I realized when I got the job is that all of the stupid stuff you do when you're younger that you think has no applicability all of a sudden makes sense. You're in an editorial meeting and somebody brings in a book on Zanzibar, and you're like, "Oh, yes, I know about Zanzibar." It's like people who do crossword puzzles and play "Jeopardy!"—ridiculous and small amounts of knowledge come in handy.

What's a normal day like for you?

Right now I'm hounding people who are supposed to deliver manuscripts by the end of the year. I've got a lot of writers who are supposed to deliver by December 31. This is the time you start calling and saying, "Well, is it going to come, or not?"

It really varies from day to day. You're always reading proposals and submissions, but there's always more to do. Today I was fixing flap copy on a book because we changed the title. And then I was working with a designer because I didn't like the design she was using on the inside of one of my books. I was on the phone with a journalist I'd like to do a book for us. I'm on the phone all day—authors, agents, potential authors....

What do you do with a book when the author hands it in?

You read the manuscript, you edit it, you see how it looks—if it makes sense. Sometimes it's in great shape and it's ready to go. **Sometimes it's just a living nightmare. The author's had a nervous breakdown, they've lost their way, their research isn't good, they've discovered they can't write.** They get overwhelmed because they're just living with this book and doing nothing else day after day after day.

If the editing is heavy, it goes back to the author for rewrites or clarification. If it's light, and if it's in good shape, it goes to our copy editing department and to our production department. And basically, the copy editors go through and look for things like, "Jane had a red bow in her hair on page 7, but on page 284 it was a green bow"— you know, that kind of stuff. It also goes to the designers who design the inside. And then you start rolling.

Any stress?

There's stress in a couple of ways. One is just the number of acquisitions. You are supposed to buy a fair number of books every year. About ten to fifteen books a year at my level. So yeah, there's the stress of, "Am I getting enough books in and am I getting good books?"

If there's a really good project, you're hoping that you're the person in the house that gets it, as opposed to another editor. Agents are dealing with people at every single publishing house in town and you want to make sure that you're getting the best projects from an agent.

There's the stress of trying to convince people here who deal with the money to give you enough money to buy your books. And then there's a huge stress after you've done it, you've bought it, now is it going to work? I mean, you pay $100,000 for a book—is it going to sell? Are we going to make money on this or are we going to lose a lot? Are you going to see these royalty statements twice a year that say, "We paid $100,000 and we've made $5,000?"

What surprised you most about this job?

When I started I thought I'd get to read and edit manuscripts. I'll read and edit, read and edit—my two favorite things. And that's about 2 percent of the job. It was surprising just how much paper pushing there is to do and how many other things go on. It's surprising how little reading and editing it is.

How about working with writers?

Since I'd worked in a bookstore I had a sense that authors weren't these wonderful magical people that you want to run off to an island with. Writers would come in and want to know why we didn't have fifty copies of their book. You have authors who are just your best friends for the rest of your life, but you also have people who are really difficult. They're word people, word-on-a-page people. They don't work, they don't have jobs, you know? They stay home. They stay home way too long.

What's the best part about your job? Where is the satisfaction?

On a not terribly glamourous level, the best thing about it is that you do everything. This book comes in and it's your baby, and you're doing everything. If you're not doing it directly, you're overseeing it. You're conceptualizing the jacket in your head and working with the art people. I'm doing photo research because I want to get a better jacket for a book. You're doing the marketing. We have a marketing department and we have a publicity department, but if you *really* want your books to work it takes all the creative stuff you can think of. You're working with the copy editor, the legal department, this and that. You have to love all the day-to-day stuff. There are glamourous aspects, but the flashy stuff is only about 2 percent of the job. You're the liaison between the author and the rest of the company, and any problems that arise with the book are your responsibility. You're the book's representative and you want to publish it as well as you can while keeping the author and the company happy. Sometimes everyone will have different ideas and it can be a real tug-of-war—you have to be diplomatic.

How much of what you do are you passionate about as opposed to doing it solely because it is commercial?

I feel that I'm finally at the level where about 80 percent of what I'm doing is stuff I feel really, really strongly about. If you don't care about something, you can't do a good job with it, I don't think. Because you really have to be able to trust your instincts. But if you're bored your instincts suck. About 20 percent of the time you do things that you think make sense for the house, that will make us some money, but that I could care less about.

What's the most frustrating thing about this work?

When you're starting out, that's the hardest part, because you feel like you're a really smart person, you've been in college, and you're Xeroxing and answering the phone all day. It can feel really demeaning the first couple of years. And the pay is so bad. When I started, it was $16,500. It's so hard to live in New York on that amount of money. The first year it's not so bad, but then it's not fun anymore.

You begin to think that checking out things at K Mart would be more glamourous than working here. Law school starts looking better and better. Meanwhile, everyone you know thinks it's just so cool. Your parents think it's great—"She's an editor at a New York publishing company"—and your friends think it's terribly glamourous.

There are good perks though. You're on all the movie-screening lists. You want any *Home Alone II* paraphernalia? I've got a whole box of it. You get to meet exciting famous people. I've got a great Rolodex. **When I wasn't making enough money to pay my rent, I was hanging out in the Green Room at "Letterman" with my boss and Roseanne Barr, and Sandra Bernhard took me to the gym with her because I didn't have enough money for membership.** You get a ton of free books. There's this whole wonderful underground black market where you'll never pay for another book in your life.

Do you recommend being an English major?

Traditionally we're full of English majors, but I think more and more it doesn't matter. I think your basic liberal arts degree makes the most sense. Somebody who's well-read and smart. It's more important that you're well-read than that you be an English major.

Do you read for pleasure anymore?

Less for pleasure. **If I've been editing a manuscript for six hours, the last thing I want to do is sit down with a good book.** And then you get into a thing where if something is not really well written it drives you crazy. You go into editor mode, "Ahh, look, that should have been a semicolon. Look, that doesn't make any sense." You start editing what you're reading, which is really annoying. Unless I'm on vacation, it's not much of a recreation anymore. It's not an escape.

Everybody in the world is writing a book. And then once you start working here, everyone you know is also writing a book. The person you sat next to in high school English class, your mother's best friend, all these people that you have to be nice to. This is in addition to the huge amount of stuff that we're getting in from agents.

But you like being an editor.

I can't imagine doing anything else. Despite all the headaches, it's a pretty terrific job. You're looking at ideas and writing that fascinates you and you actually have the power to get this stuff into a book. It's also the most entrepreneurial job you can possibly have and still work for a corporation. There's a tremendous amount of freedom and discretion in deciding just what I do every day. There's a lot of pressure, but it's also like, "What am I interested in?" I'll read a magazine article and say, "Wow, this should be a book." Also, you can call anyone you want in the entire world and say, "Hi, I'm an editor and I'd like to talk to you about a book project." **It's amazing who will have lunch with you when they find you're an editor at a big publishing house.** And you also have the old-fashioned satisfaction of seeing an actual, physical finished project for all your efforts. At the end of the day, the author's worked hard, you've worked hard, and you have this beautiful finished book in your hands.

A lot of editors compare our work to midwifery, and that's not a bad analogy. There's a lot of struggle and yelling and screaming sometimes—but in the end you have a terrific book, and somehow it's all worth it.

WORDS FROM ON HIGH:
Advice From the Director of Personnel at Condé Nast on Breaking In

FREDDY GAMBLE

Director of Personnel, Condé Nast, New York City

Background check—Condé Nast is owned by S. I. Newhouse, Jr., who also owns Random House, *The New Yorker*, and thirty newspapers. Condé Nast magazines include: *Vogue, Architectural Digest, Glamour, Mademoiselle, Brides, Self, GQ, Vanity Fair, Gourmet, Bon Appetit, Condé Nast Traveler, Details, Allure, Street & Smith's Sports Books*. All magazines are published in New York City.

How do you go about hiring? Are connections important?

Connections are useful anywhere. What a connection will do is get you an attentive hearing. A lot of employees will refer people. That's a big source for us. Occasionally we advertise. Occasionally we work with employment agencies. But that would be more for the nonpublishing jobs, like for accounting for example.

Do you recruit at colleges?

We do a little bit of college recruiting. We tend to concentrate on East Coast schools where people would be likely to come to New York after school.

Do you pay close attention to the Ivy League Schools?

Yes, that would usually be our concentration. There is a greater likelihood that a greater percentage of people coming out of those schools are going to have the sophistication and outlook and the ability with the language that would be important for us. The reality is that we're dealing with magazines that are geared to a relatively sophisticated audience. So if someone is out trying to sell a page of advertising in *Vogue* magazine, or prepare a piece on fashion, what we would tend to look for is someone with a relatively sophisticated outlook.

Say someone were interested in getting in marketing at one of your magazines. Would you look for a marketing major?

We're usually not especially focused on one particular major over another. It would be exceedingly unusual for us to say "A degree in marketing required," as many companies would do. The head set and the apparent capacity to carry out a job would be much more important to us than a particular degree.

How many new hires for '92?

Including temps—for example, people that worked for a summer—there was probably slightly over 300.

How did most of them get the jobs, do you think?

Employer referrals are always an important source for us. In many cases, someone who is in a job, and doing well at it, might tend to have friends that would have the same kind of spirit and interest and talent.

How many resumes do you get a week?

When last we tried to estimate this, it was about 10,000 a year.

What do you look for?

I look for something that's going to stand out of the crowd. If someone is looking for a graphics position—well, how does their resume look? How is it laid out? Is there an interesting typeface used? If someone is looking for a job as a copywriter, well, the cover letter is probably going to be as important as the resume.

I remember one case where someone wrote in, someone right out of school. The letter started off, "Words, words, words." And it talked about how he enjoyed words and what they could do on a page. The letter was simple. We called the person in. It ended up getting him free-lance work and it led to a staff position. And that was sent to "Dear Personnel Department."

The objective is to make your application stand out of a crowd. And I think with a large organization of this sort, I would probably suggest stopping by, leaving a resume and a letter, who knows, with a velvet ribbon wrapped around it. I'm not saying that that's the approach for everyone, but something to make it personal. Something that says, "I really want to work here and it will be worth your time to talk to me because I'm a little different in a good way. And I care about your company."

It is shocking, shocking, how many resumes and letters we get with typos in them. And that is not a plus in a publishing company. Are they stupid, careless, or both? If you can't spell, pay a friend. And you might want to say that *liaison,* I've come to believe, is the most frequently misspelled word which almost always appears on a resume. You could do your readers a big service if you remind them how to spell that word.

How do you go through the resumes?

You develop an eye. Things sort of pop up at you. Some things are really basic, such as, are things spelled right? Or where does someone live? Alabama? If they come from out of town, they should put some explanation of how they're planning to live here.

One encouragement I have for young people regarding cover letters is, write them in English, not in Personnel-ese or job-letter-speak. That's going to make someone stand out. A letter that starts off, "Help, I really want to get a job and I'd love to work at your company, dot dot dot." That's going to capture my attention much more than, "Attached hereto is the blah blah blah...."

The *way* it is expressed is much more important to me than *what* it is that is expressed. Is it expressed with literacy, a certain style, with a sense of humor? We are a very unstructured company. Face it, you're looking for people who are going to fit into our world. And most of our world is inhabited by people who are smart, ambitious, push the edge a little, colorful, a little irreverent, arrogant.

How about interviews. Any advice?

The things that make me take positive note is someone who appears to have done a little homework about the company. We don't have an annual report—we're a privately held company—but my goodness, someone can read a couple of magazines before they come in. Subtleties. Somewhere in the interview, in some way or another, discuss a recent piece you've read.

So if they're interviewing with Mademoiselle, they should show that they've at least read the magazine.

Someone at *Mademoiselle* doesn't want to hear about someone saying they want to work at Condé Nast. They're waiting for that person to jump over the desk, grab a magazine issue out of their hands, and say they want to be on *their* magazine. A relatively strong personal presentation is going to be an important criterion for most of the jobs on the magazines.

When reviewing certain applicants, I've so often heard department heads say, "Well, *this* person really wants the job." It's absolutely important to share that in person, and in a follow-up note. The follow-up note should be one more demonstration of interest in the job.

So thank-you or follow-up letters are important?

I've seen thank-you letters that have cinched the job, and I've seen thank-you letters that have killed the job. A thank-you letter can have a typo in it too. (She laughs.) Stupid or lazy?

Is typing important?

Typing is important for almost all jobs. There are very few jobs I can think of where it isn't an issue. Pretty much all the entry-level jobs are going to involve some administrative stuff, which is going to include some typing. And the sooner you can get through it, the more time you have to learn other things. The hope is to get someone who can do the scud work real fast, and then have a little time for the more fun things. (It depends, but somewhere between forty and fifty wpm.)

Do you look at someone's GPA?

Yes. I pay some attention to it. I don't obsess about it. I weigh it in with everything else. We want people who are going to be achievers. We want people who are going to work hard and contribute. You try to talk to somebody about their college experience and get a sense of who they were and what they were and what they did during those four years. And you might get a sense that someone had a 2.6 average, but opened up a boutique. You're not going to get a very rigid set of requirements for any kind of job from me.

Any last advice?

My encouragement for someone who's going out for a job early on in life is that they, if they're really interested in the company, walk around the building the day before. Walk through the lobby. Who do you see coming in and out? What do they look like? You're probably going to see a different kind of person in our lobby going in and out than you would in an insurance company or even at Time-Life. Because, what do you want to do in the course of an interview? You want to give the impression that you belong there. I'm looking for someone who's going to fit in.

8

The Art World

The art world was, by far, the hardest industry to research for this book. First off, just trying to get the interviews was such a major pain in the ass. Nobody wanted to talk on record. Nobody wanted to be quoted. You'd think they were inventing the cure for cancer behind their doors.

The New York gallery world is so small, so closed, and so private. The players don't talk to each other and they certainly don't talk to the press. And unlike all the other industries in this book, there's no publication that covers the industry: who's buying what, who's doing well, who's not, who just sold what? This is precisely why rumors run rampant. What artist is leaving what gallery? Who is shutting their doors? What collector was seen lunching with what gallery director?

Since the pulse of the American art industry is geographically concentrated in New York City in the downtown Soho area (in addition to a handful of top galleries uptown), it naturally demands one to constantly be looking over their shoulder. It's called paranoia, babe. Quite understandable, considering that just like every other industry, it all comes down to money. And in the art world, it's not as if there's tons of people dishing out $500,000 dollars for something to put on their wall.

Therefore, one's reputation and the perception of one's success are the gallery owners' intangible keys to prosperity. Not even prosperity, but survival. So, a gallery owner's fear that their underling might say anything even remotely controversial, wrong or indemnifying basically scares the shit out of them. Enough so that every time I asked someone to participate in this book I'd get, "I'm sorry, my boss said they'd rather me not." Or, "Policy dictates that we simply do not speak with the press." (Note the eloquence of their rejections.)

I think maybe they were afraid of being exposed—of coming off as not knowing what they were talking about. Listen, I can't blame them. When you're talking about art, a painting, it's all pretty subjective. It wasn't my intention to, but I could well imagine that they were scared to death that I could expose that they don't have the slightest idea of what they're talking about. Imagine their fear.

> Me: "So why did that painting sell for that amount of money as opposed to the other one?"
> Them: "Ah, ah, ah, ah."

I did luck out though, and actually wound up getting two very influential, young, and confident art players to talk about what they do.

The Commercial Art World

THE PRIMARY MARKET

These are the galleries, the **art dealers**. A gallery represents a roster of artists, shows their work on their walls, and sells to private collectors, museums, foundations, or whoever is buying. They exist to make a profit. A fifty/fifty split is the most common arrangement between the gallery and the artist for a work sold.

THE SECONDARY MARKET

This term refers to **secondary dealers**, which don't represent any specific artist but which sell that person's art. Say you bought a painting from a gallery and now you want to sell it for whatever reason. This is what the secondary market lends itself to. This is referred to as resale—it was once sold and now it's being resold.

THE AUCTION MARKET

When a collector or museum needs the dough, or they simply don't want a piece any longer, maybe they want the money to acquire something else (with museums they call this "deaccession"), they'll put it up for auction at one of the auction houses such as Sotheby's or Christie's.

Museums

Museums, as opposed to galleries, exist to preserve and keep, not to trade and sell. They are concerned with acquiring for their collection. They are supported by governments and corporate and private donations. Many museums, however, have taken to selling works presently in their collection in order to acquire different pieces. It's called deaccession and it definitely has its opponents. "This field fancies itself as noncommercial, and yet here are all these guys having a great time playing the market. It's such a closed, clubby little group, and nobody will talk about the problem. It just surprises me that people are not worried about it. It's very worrisome, and it's starting to erode what museums are all about" (Tom Freudenheim, former director of the Baltimore Museum of Art, as quoted in *ArtNews,* May 1990)

ECONOMICS

The contemporary art world is a baby industry. Galleries first appeared in New York in the sixties, so we're not dealing with a long history. Most galleries are mom-and-pop shops and they play it very close to the hip. With successes and disappointments, dealers simply do not talk. And unfortunately, no one will talk for them. There's not an organization or publication that does any kind of statistical research on the gallery world.

And how could someone compile prices or sales when dealers don't "sell" the first place? You see, they don't call it "selling." They call it "placing." Say I'm an artist. A dealer would never say, "I sold Mr. X a fabulous Drozdyk." Uh-uh. What they'd say is, "I **placed** a fabulous Drozdyk with Mr. X." This phrasology shows the art world's—I'm searching for a big word here—weirdness. I think it also suggests a denial that they're actually taking part in a monetary transaction and that they are part of the world of commerce. In other words, that they're in it to make a buck. But I won't get too psychological about it.

Yes, the art scene did explode in the eighties and brought to it a lot of attention. Million-dollar sales for young, unknown artists became almost expected, and prices for the masterpieces went to outer space.

The recession in the early nineties brought prices back to earth. Auction prices at Christie's and Sotheby's dipped, and many pieces being brought to auction aren't finding buyers. Meanwhile, certain galleries insist that they were actually booming during the recession. But with eighties prices? They'll never tell. Doesn't matter, really. Galleries are still out there doing their thing just like the auction houses; the jobs are there if you want them.

The one area of the art world where the recession had the most profound effect was in the noncommercial, nonprofit museum world. Museums, large and small, and artists who depend on government grants, witnessed them, in many cases, disappear. Right-wing, conservative zealots blew the whistle on what they perceived as government-supported "pornography" and slashed the National Endowment for the Arts (NEA) budget, forcing many smaller museums and art spaces to close down. Their argument: Why should the American people pay artists to make pornography, or art for that matter? And to do so in a recession? Forget it.

TOP GIGS

In Galleries

DEALER (SEE LANCE FUNG INTERVIEW)
ART PREPARATOR

The art preparator, who is usually an artist, is in charge of gallery maintenance, installation of the shows, and the transportation of art to and from the gallery. He or she also deals with wrapping and packing artwork, insurance, getting pieces through customs, delivering to collectors, and installing pieces in buyers' homes.
REGISTRAR

The registrar works hand in hand with the preparator. This person does the paperwork for all of the movement of the art that the preparator is doing and keeps track of what comes in for a show. This is an important function, for if you don't inventory every piece when it comes in, it can then go into storage somewhere and you'll never know where it is. The registar also does sales commission reports and is in charge of the library, which contains archives for every show listing every piece that was made.

Museums and Related Industries

CURATOR (SEE THELMA GOLDEN INTERVIEW)

MUSEUM DIRECTOR

You're the boss. But consider this advice from John Lane of the San Francisco Museum of Modern Art (as quoted in *ArtNews*, May 1989): "Anyone going into the field at this point must realistically face the fact that ninety percent of your time will be spent on management and administration and ten percent or less on artistic program. If you don't like these odds, then maybe you should be a curator, not a director."

CORPORATE COLLECTIONS CURATOR

In the art world there are corporate collections, some of which employ directors or curators. There are also private foundations, founded by private families or corporations and they sometimes have curators. They distribute money to artists and give grants as well as doing exhibitions.

ART EDITOR

There's a whole publishing aspect of the art world. You might want to be an editor of art books or an editor of an art magazine where you determine the stories and what shows are reviewed.

LANCE FUNG

Director, Holly Solomon Gallery, New York City

Thirty years old

Background check—A highly respected gallery whose artists' works are in museums and great private collections around the world. You probably wouldn't recognize the artists they show by name, except for maybe William Wegman, who is known for his crazy Weimaraner portraits.

Van Gogh died a poor man. Probably not the fate for the artists Lance represents. Not to say artists and dealers are only in it for the money: those folks disappeared with the super-inflated and hyped art market of the eighties. Nevertheless, Lance's artists are not starving by any means.

Besides his work at the gallery, the second biggest thing in Lance's life—and I'm not sure you can separate it—are the frequent dinner parties he throws. Artists, museum curators, competing dealers, critics, collectors, and would-be collectors assemble around his custom-made-for-the-occasion dining room table at least twice a week in his Soho loft.

There are a few reasons why Lance throws these so often. One, is his intent to develop the next generation of collectors via acculturation and assimilation into the art world. Another is simply the desire for good conversation and a good time. Yet another reason for these soirees is to expand the *diners'* network of friends and acquaintances. "Whenever a friend is out of work and needs a job," Lance says, "I'll throw a dinner party and they won't need a job anymore." Lance at work.

Lance insisted I attend one of these dinners so I could see what it is he does. Intimidated by the type of people I knew would be there, and uninterested due to the type of people I *thought* would be there, I said "We'll see." My plan—do the interview and blow off the dinner. Lance's plan, make Charlie attend a dinner party and *then* give him an interview. Ah, well. I'll be attending my third Lance Fung dinner this Sunday. A little culture never hurt anyone.

I turn on the tape recorder as Lance and I are in the middle of discussing a particular artist I've been following. And when I ask him, "Didn't he recently change galleries?" Lance responds:

"That kind of art gossip is profuse and frightening because it terrorizes the city. (Laughs.) Outside of my gallery, I listen to the gossip, which can be interesting and fun, but nothing is factual, so I never dare repeat anything unless I know it's fact. And in this case, I don't. I knew the answer as fact probably four months ago, but I don't know if it is a fact any longer. Things happen so quickly in the art world."

Fine. Next subject. Where did you go to school?

I went to school at the University of California at Davis and studied pre-med/biology as well as art studio. Then I came out here and went to the School of Visual Arts (SVA) to get my master of fine arts.

How did you wind up in the gallery world?

While I was at graduate school, I went into galleries every day and thought it would be interesting to see what real artists—professional artists—did. I thought it might be interesting to get a job behind the scenes. As an artist I felt it might be helpful or useful to know some dealers or other professionals who could look at my work. Not to kiss ass to get into a gallery, but more to get top-quality input on my work so it would take me to the next level with my art. So I got an internship at a powerful midtown gallery.

What gallery?

I'd rather not say. (Laughs.)

Ok, what did you do?

They were having an opening, and the mailing list wasn't complete, so I stuck on labels for the invitations announcing the show. And just that was absolutely fascinating. And I thought, Gee this is *worth* my four hours—looking at names I'd never heard of, and a lot of names I did recognize, friends of my folks, it was almost shocking.

For the opening they had me bartend and paid me $8 an hour. I thought, wow, I'm really chic now, I'm in the art world! All of my friends from art school said, "Oh, look at him pouring wine." I was tucked away almost in a closet pouring white wine to some arrogant and nasty people, while others were extremely nice, even asking me who I was and what I did. **It was great, the whole process of being**

ignored and stepped on, and the converse of also being noticed.

The next day the gallery offered me a part-time job. I became the assistant to the registrar. And through a series of events of people getting fired and replaced and blah blah blah, I kind of moved up the food chain to assisting the owner of the gallery. This was over the course of one year.

Why do you think you got to move up the food chain?

As an intern I worked hard. I put those labels on real fast. I was probably the fastest label stickerer. When I first became the assistant to the registrar I worked long hours. I didn't know a thing about the computer when I started. I didn't know how to turn one on. By the end of that first week I knew every system backwards and forwards. I had that computer system down pat. I came in early, I stayed late. They knew I was a hard worker. I came in every day with a happy face and I left every day with a happy face, and I made people enjoy their jobs. It was fun for me. When I first started I took home every catalogue and every press package on each artist, every article, everything I could find on every one of our artists and I read it all.

You had a shot and you went for it.

Actually, I had no idea I would end up being a dealer.

What did you get out of working there? Did you make a lot of contacts, what?

In a very superficial and subtle way. In this particular gallery, and the way in which most galleries function, is, there is an owner who makes absolutely every decision. Every decision, from where to put the name on the mailing envelope to, of course, who's showing, how to exhibit the work, and how to install the show. Every decision is usually made by the owner and only the owner. The director then fills in the minor decisions, and there the primary key is to sell. Then **you have a support staff that does not ask questions and does what they're told. The grunt work.** You hear the nasty stories of picking up the owner's laundry and doing their personal errands, well it is sometimes true. However, the art world is a glamourous field. You're dealing with creative and intelligent people, and it's worth doing the shit work. And that's what I did in those two and a half years. But I never thought of it as shit work.

So two and a half years of that, then what happened?

Luck would have it that a peer of mine at the School of Visual Arts was an early collector of the Holly Solomon Gallery. Over the course of graduate school he kept saying, "Oh, my friend Holly Solomon, you should meet her, you should really work with her." Because I was so satisfied at my current job—I loved what I was doing, my salary was just fine, all my friends worked there (at the other gallery), and this was not my career—I never entertained the thought of leaving.

Until I met Holly. She was so gracious and friendly it shocked me. **You don't get into the inner sanctum of the art world, and if you do, it's generally not so friendly.**

Holly invited me to lunch across the street from the gallery that I was employed at. We sat at the window table and I could not eat a bit of my lunch, thinking that my boss would see me. Then Holly told me she was looking for a director. Of course, I did not tell her how I was not qualified, and that I did not know too many collectors. Basically, I was unqualified. But I thought, OK, this would be interesting, let's entertain this thought. It's a nice ego stroke, right?

So I went in. I met everyone; I liked them and everyone liked me. She apparently led the staff to believe that I was being hired to fill an entry-level position. This was a way for her to get honest feedback about me from them, because if she told them that I might be the director of the gallery they would automatically resent me.

And soon they did. In the art world there are few galleries, even fewer good galleries, and even fewer directorships. Everyone takes an entry-level job and wants to move up the chain, and that rarely happens within one gallery. So Holly's staff had been there between three and five years, some people there seven years. That's a loyal staff. They were loyal to Holly, her gallery, and the artists. Then **you hire a little snotty twenty-seven-year-old kid over them? It doesn't go over well.**

So why did she hire you and not someone that had been at her place for many years?

Good question. (Laughs.) I, of course, asked her that. Of course, I didn't get an answer then. And, of course, little did I realize, I was on nothing more than a six-week trial period.

So a month before I graduated from SVA I started working for the gallery. The first day at work we had a staff meeting where Holly introduced me as the director. That did not fly well. Of course, no one was nice to me. And then came the grilling, "Who do you know; what do you know?"

I remember, that day a gorgeous 1969 Neil Jenny painting came in, a magnificent landscape piece. We represent Neil. Holly priced it around a half a million dollars and said to the two women there that had called themselves the assistant directors, "Alright, who can we offer this to?" I interrupted and said that I thought I knew someone (a collector) that would be interested in the painting. Of course, they all looked at me. It was a fifty/fifty gamble. If I didn't make it (the sale), they'd laugh at me more than if I'd said nothing. This all happened on my first real day. I placed the call, and the collector came in that afternoon. The next day she told me she would buy it, and the following week she dropped off a check. And that sealed things.

Then over the course of three months, one woman left and then the other. And within three months Holly said something fairly close to this, "Lance, here's a corporate American Express Card—I've never given one to a staff member before—here's a key to the gallery, here's a key to my house, and here's the key to my heart, dear. Go for it. Do whatever you want, and let's see what we can do." And since then she hasn't questioned me.

So what does a director of a gallery do?

There's managing of the gallery, which means basically running the gallery—making sure that everything functions smoothly and properly. You also work with the artists—from encouraging them, doing studio visits to learn what's current, to getting them shows with other galleries or museums or alternative spaces, to hopefully having them receive commissions for public sculpture or from private collectors. And there's selling the work, of course.

How many artists do you represent?

We have a huge stable actually, probably one of the largest. I think the last count was around eighteen artists. Several months ago I added a new artist to our gallery. He's a twenty-eight-year-old Italian artist. I gave him his first one-person show, which was a phenomenal risk that Holly let me take. And we sold the show out within three days of the opening. And to major collectors.

How did you find this artist?

I was traveling in Italy with my family for summer holiday. We were in Rome. And, of course, in every city that I went to in Italy I had about five million appointments—visiting galleries and having lunch and dinners. **There's no such thing as a vacation and there's no such thing as a day off. You eat, sleep, and live work seven days a week, twenty-four hours a day.** For Holly and me our work is thoroughly enjoyable, so yes, every day and every minute is work, but every day and every minute is play. I could be in Venice taking a water taxi down the Grand Canal, and then I'm off to a gallery to see art? How can you call that work? You can't call that work. To answer your question, I first saw Tristano's work in a catalogue at a friend's gallery in Rome.

Several months later I was in Paris for an international art fair in which all of the major galleries take a space in the Grand Palais and install group shows. My friend Valentina was there representing her family's gallery, and once again there was a piece by the artist Tristano di Robilant. And I said, "This is absolutely fantastic. How much is it? I want to buy it." And then I thought, Give me a break. If I want to buy a piece, I should *show* the work.

I was so moved by the piece, I really wanted it, so I said, "I want to do a show. Let me find out when I can do a show." I bought the piece with the promise to do a show if Holly would allow me. Ultimately, she's the owner. So I asked Holly when I returned from Paris, and she said, "Whatever you want to do, I trust you."

Tristano had a group of work ready. He flew out here, he did the show, and it was packed to the gills with crème de la crème people....

How come they came for an unknown Italian artist?

I called continually. I called numbers from my Rolodex maybe four times. The gallery sends out press releases for a show to press people and museum curators a month in advance to let them know what's up. Then we send invitations to our collectors, friends, etc. And we also place ads in the art magazines. But, of course, they could hear in my voice that I was enthusiastic. I told them the story that I just told you, "This young artist I saw in Italy...," which is really a wonderful story. The work struck a chord immediately and intuitively in me. It wasn't about, "Gee, I can make a million bucks selling a whatever." It wasn't about that at all. It wasn't about networking. It was just, I loved the art. And it certainly wasn't about money. They could tell in my voice that I was sincerely psyched.

What's your relationship like with the artists?

Our artists are all great. Not only are they talented and focused, but they're down-to-earth, sincere. They're not affected. It's not about being hyped and being on the cover of every magazine. They really just want to do their top-quality work, and they want a dealer who will represent them with some kind of dignity, and not misrepresent them. All of these artists are a complete joy to work with. I speak with all of our artists at least weekly on the phone.

Really, what do you talk about?

Well, there are many inquiries about our artists. For instance, with one of our artists, somebody wants to reproduce an image in a grade-school book, so I'll check to see if that's something she wants to do. Producers want them for talk shows, such as William Wegman. And when people want to buy their work there are all sorts of business questions I may need to consult the artists on. Sometimes it's just to touch base and to find out if everything's going OK, or if we should get together for dinner or what have you.

I also think I'm fortunate, and I think in a way they are too. The fact that I studied art studio in addition to art history is a plus. I'm not a business major, so it's not only about business and making money. With most of the artists, we have conversations on all levels: the content of the work, the process of the work, how to represent the work, and how to sell the work. Most artists really leave all the PR and sales to the dealer because that's what we do. And most dealers leave the art-making to the artist. But I'm privileged when they say, "Well, what do you think of this painting?" And they really *want* to know what I think and not for me to just say, "Oh, that's really great. Let's have it in the gallery and I'll sell it."

There are a few of the artists who don't need my input, because they are focused and they know exactly what they're doing. I might say, "This is what I think about the work. This is what I see into it. Is this what you want perceived from the piece?" And then they'll say, "Exactly," or, "Oh no, no, where did you get that from?"

But when you go visit their studios, you pick what you think is going to sell. There's a bottom line to consider.

Right. But it's not really a bottom line, because you're dealing with artistic people, people that have put their complete passion and life into a work of art. **I would never pull rank on an artist and say "Look, I just don't think this piece is completed. I don't want to show it."** They've invested their life into that painting or sculpture. And that work is just as valuable to them as one that I think is salable.

But what's salable is not always necessarily good. Isn't there a lot of schlock and hyped up things that pass for art?

The art world is a subjective business. You may walk into a gallery and you personally may not respond to the art either emotionally or intellectually, but obviously, the dealer responds to it in some way. So there needs to be a place for everyone.

So it's subjective. Nothing's good; nothing's bad. It's personal.

Certainly there are guidelines of what good art is. And again, all of those rules are fairly subjective, and it's for you to digest and personalize so you can decide what's good for you. That's what a collector should be doing. There are collectors who buy art to speculate to make big profits, but they can also lose. In these cases, I think, instead of looking at art, they're listening, and that's where hype will fall into play.

As a dealer, I only show what I believe in, not what I think I can sell. If I believe in it, then I think I can sell it. Because people feel it in my energy. There are dealers, I'm sure, who think that they're great sales people, so all they need is *something* with the right look, the right history, the right person, and the right price. I'm not that type of a dealer and I think most quality dealers are not that way either, because dealing comes from a passion. The great dealers are smart, educated, astute, talented, and skilled. If they wanted to make big money, they could easily go to Wall Street, become bankers, and make lots of money probably easier and faster.

But you can make a lot of money selling art. There are collectors out there who spend a lot of money on art. Why?

I think if you've been around art, and you love looking at art, the next logical step is to live with art, because you're able to look and live with it every day. It's a wonderful experience. It's a privileged experience. Some people can live with posters and that can be just as fulfilling for them.

Now we don't want to overlook the obvious. People in the eighties *did* collect art for speculation. It was a validated business. Big business, big money. A lot of people jumped into the art world, both as artists and professionals. Now we have hit the nineties, and we have a levelling recession on our hands. **I think the people who entered the art world for the wrong reasons, that being primarily money, will leave or have left. The diehards are still around.** Speculative collectors have obviously slowed down. The diehard collectors still collect.

Challenges?

A big challenge was growing into my own shoes. **Being a twenty-seven-year-old dealer was a big challenge. The first**

year I wore suits. I thought that was a way to look older. That was an insecurity that I had, though I think it was valid. You don't spend a million dollars with someone who's younger than your son or daughter, except if they say something that a sixty-year-old would say, right? But now I don't give a shit. People have come to respect me even more because they understand that I don't give a shit, and that I am telling them exactly what I believe in, take it or leave it.

It's a challenge not to be jaded the way a lot of people have become, saying, "Oh, nothing's interesting. It's all derivative. Nothing can sell." You know, not losing hope is not easy. Not thinking that the art world is just about money and a bunch of nasty, nasty people. I mean, that's a challenge, not buying into that belief.

There we go. Money and nasty people—this is the stuff I want to hear.

Galleries are very competitive as we know—even though everyone's known each other for a million years and they're friends, and their kids have gone to school together, and blah blah blah. However, it's competitive and nasty at the same time.

And elitist?

I wouldn't say it's my **opinion that the art world is elitist. I would say, however, that it's probably the general opinion that it's elitist.** Seeing that I'm in it, and I am a so-called player, a dealer, I don't think I'm elitist. I certainly am accessible. I'm proud of being accessible. And I'm proud that the owner of the gallery is as accessible as I am.

But it is snobby, come on?

Within the art world, from what I hear, it is...(searches for proper word) it can be difficult. We all know it's competitive because it's so over-saturated with artists, with dealers, and with people that want to be dealers. How many top positions are there? Very few. And the people in these key positions stay there until they die. **So within the employment portion of the art world, it's ruthless, it's brutal, it's backbiting, it's backstabbing, and I don't think it's neces-**

sarily the most pleasant environment. However, I really think if you're true, you're smart, you're aware, and people can see that you're sincere, then you can break in. I really do.

Let's talk about the selling aspect. How does that work?

A collector may come in and may want to look at work. I'll bring in work and we'll talk about it, the artist, and the history, etc. I'll talk with them and show them slides of other related artists; we'll go through a carousel of slides. Maybe they'll say, "Gee, we like, Africano, MacConnel, and Majore," and from there we'll pull out works by all of those people.

Someone may come in and be only interested in conceptual art, so I'll show them Matta-Clark, Barry, Huebler, Hutchinson, etc. I'll show one or two examples of each artist to see what they like and what they respond to. And we'll just talk about the work, just have a nice conversation.

I also work with consultants and private dealers who then have *their* clients. They may say, "I have a space *this* big," and that their clients want figurative work. Or, "Gee, I want a museum-quality Nam June Paik piece." These consultants can be extremely different. Some are educated, some nice, and some have no clue about art but are expert sales people.

The other thing that I do is have people up for dinner at least two to three times a week at my loft. The number of guests range between six and twelve. Entertainment is not new to this business. **Collectors, museum people, press people, and all sorts of people *love* to be wined and dined,** including artists and who knows who, right? What I enjoy doing is to have them up to my home rather than taking them out for dinner at Chanterelle's and Harry Cipriani's, which dealers enjoy doing—and Holly does have a permanent table at Harry's. (Laughs.) I spend a lot of time deciding who to invite to my dinner parties, at what time, where to seat them, what to serve. It is amazing how much time I focus on my dinners. And it's only because I love it so much that I want it to be successful. I don't want a bomb.

And maybe they'll take to one of your artists on your walls?

What I wanted to do with my home and my art collection is to show people how you can live with art. I live with it and it intermixes with my lifestyle. For me that's what collecting is about. For someone else it might be something different, and that's alright too.

Don't you have anything bad to say about the art world?

I think I'm very lucky. I'm in a bubble right now that is most likely an isolated situation. It is so great, and it is always rewarding and glamourous, yet stressful too. I assume most other gallery positions are not equivalent to mine. **My friends that work in galleries at all different levels do nothing but complain. It's abusive, hard work, monotonous, demeaning, they don't travel, they don't entertain.** I don't know. I hope that if I'm ever interviewed in the future, let's say ten years from now, I'm just as excited and passionate as I am now, and that I will never become jaded. I don't actually think I will become jaded—I'm having too much fun. But, certainly, it is hard, hard work.

THELMA GOLDEN

Associate Curator, Whitney Museum of American Art; Director, Whitney Museum of American Art at Philip Morris.

Twenty-eight years old

Background check—Founded in 1931 by Gertrude Vanderbilt Whitney, the museum is highly regarded for its extensive permanent collection of American art (more than 10,000 works), and is probably best known for its Biennial: a large group show of important American artists' work that takes place every other year.

Scene: Whitney Museum. The Biennial.
What a drag. A beautiful day outside and I've got to go to a museum. To that crusty, old, nasty word that sends waves of fatigue through my legs just thinking about it. So I get out of the cab and

walk past this life-size, plastic Tonka-toy fire truck that's parked out front. Huh? A *life*-size, mammoth, red and white, completely non-functional, completely plastic (right down to the tires) fire truck. A disturbingly friendly sight, this children's dream. (But don't try to climb on it kids! or you'll have to contend with one of the twenty-four-hour guards that's hired to protect it.)

I make a mental note to interview the Tonka-toy guard on the way out, and then walk through the front door into the museum. I take out my wallet and pay the admission price to a twenty-year-old kid in a T-shirt who's sporting a nose ring and at least seven earrings in his left ear. Way to make a first impression, Whitney—nose rings and giant plastic fire trucks. Can't be too uptight. Maybe this isn't going to completely suck after all.

So I walk around for a while. I'm not even going to attempt to explain it, you just can't. I will say, though, that by accident (I swear I didn't see it), I did step on a piece of art that was exhibited on the ground. It was a plastic vomit sculpture (?) installation (?). Anyway, it didn't have its own guard like the fire truck, so I was cool.

I had seen Thelma's picture with a small feature about her in *New York* magazine. There she was. A five-foot tall, young black woman who is easily one of the most influential and sought-after under-thirty art-world power players. After getting blown off by many, many people who just refused to be interviewed—were they afraid of saying the wrong thing, or did they just have nothing to say?—I called her immediately. "Sure, it sounds great," she said. Finally, someone who had something to say.

Thelma went to Smith College where she majored in art history and Afro-American studies. She graduated in 1987.

Where did the idea of being a curator come from?

When I went to college it was weird. I didn't necessarily get to college and meet many people who wanted to be a curator. It wasn't something that there was a path for. In terms of being a doctor there's a path. You're pre-med and you take all the courses you have to take. If you want to be a lawyer, you might not major in anything specifically, but you know there are things you have to do to get in to law school. Whereas being a curator, it wasn't that clear on a certain level.

Was that scary being that there is no path?

Yeah, it was scary. I didn't always know if it would actually happen. There are people who purport a path though. People say, "Oh, you'll never get a job in New York." They say you should go to a smaller museum outside of some of the major art centers, New York, L.A. Get some experience, go back and get a master's in art history. **There are a lot of things people told me I should do in order to do this, but I didn't really do any of them.** I was more willing and more interested in just coming to New York and sinking or swimming. I was either going to do it here or not do it. And if I didn't do it I would just get a real job like everybody else.

What was your first art job when you graduated?

My first art job was at the Studio Museum Of Harlem as a curatorial intern, which was a ten-month position. It was funded by the state council and the NEA to allow the museum to hire people, because museums don't have a lot of money. I worked for the curator and I did everything that revolved around the exhibition program. I did research, I did all the clerical work, answered the telephone, typed, filed, etc. I was just the all-around, help-everybody person; I just did whatever needed to be done.

The Studio Museum did exhibitions on a three- or four-month basis. So every four months you had a new show. So I learned the pace there; get a show up, get another one down, get it up again. I learned a lot of technical things. We worked with a fabulous exhibition designer there who was able, with not tons of money, to get a show up and make it look beautiful. So I learned about how to put up a show and how you make the art look great—without building new walls.

After that—my internship was over in June—I knew that Richard Armstrong, the curator at the Whitney, was looking for an assistant. So I applied for the job and got it.

*So you wouldn't have even heard about the job if you hadn't
been in the inside.*

**You can't even find art jobs when you're in college. You
have to be here and do the whole—go talk to people a million
times to see whose assistant might be leaving in six months—
to get a job.**

What did you do at the Whitney?

I did a lot of purely secretarial work. I made all of Richard's
travel arrangements. Richard had a dog, so I'd call the kennels. I did
everything, but it was very balanced. That job gave me my first real,
hard-core, in-depth entree into the art world, in that I was answering
the phone and majorly famous artists would call, and major dealers
would call constantly.

All curators at the Whitney get tons of slides from artists who
want their work to be looked at, so I organized that. I'd open them
up, get them in the carousel, Richard would look at them, I'd take
them out and send them back to people. That was ongoing. Hundreds of them, always.

And you liked the job, or no?

I loved the job, it was great, but I wanted more. A good friend of
mine was the visual arts director out at an alternative space in
Queens called the Jamaica Arts Center, which was started in the
early seventies as a community arts center. And it had distinguished
itself as an extremely high quality, extremely diverse and interesting
exhibition program. They were often of a subject matter that museums in the city just didn't do: artists of color or artists from other
places—South America, Africa, Eastern Europe. I was hired to be
the assistant visual arts director there.

How did you hear about that job?

Working at the Whitney gave me a lot of access in a sense that in
the curatorial department we got every art magazine known to man.
We got announcements from every gallery. I saw tons of shows just

because I knew everything that was going on. So the person out there (at the Jamaica Arts Center) and I had remained friends. I went to see most of her shows and I actually helped her with the research, because the Whitney has a library and I had access to a lot of information. And she knew I wanted more. She approached me and asked if I would like to come work for her. So I asked Richard what he thought and he said, "You should do it—it's a lot more."

So you took the job. How did that go?

Jamaica Arts Center was funded primarily by the City of New York, the State of New York, and the NEA. There was the funding crises in 1990 and 1991 that slashed my funds significantly, so I was laid off. **It was a real turning point in my career in a sense that I didn't have one anymore.** (Laughs.) All of a sudden I was on unemployment. And they ask you there (at the unemployment office) what you do and I said, "Curator." And they're like, "What's it closest to?" And I'm like, "Nothing."

But by that time I had made lots of contacts in the field. Right before I had gotten laid off, the directorship of the Philip Morris branch (of the Whitney) had opened up and I applied for it. I really didn't think I was going to get it. It was going from running a small alternative space program to...this. My budget at Jamaica was like $80,000. My budget here is like five times that. Well, I got the job and started in April 1991 as the director of the Philip Morris branch.

Why did they trust you coming from a small alternative arts center in Queens?

David Ross (the new director of the Whitney) is a very interesting guy. He's a musuem director, but he's only like forty-three years old. He's very young to be running a major museum. He had his first museum job as a curator at like twenty-one, so he's not really fazed in certain ways by age or even on-paper experience. I feel like I did some great projects at Jamaica Arts Center on very little money where it was just a question of working with artists to do really exciting things, and I think David really liked that.

So what do curators do?

Curators organize exhibitions. That's their primary responsibility in a museum like the Whitney. Secondary to that you're involved with finding and looking at work that is appropriate to acquire for the collection. These are the two main areas.

What does organizing an exhibition entail?

You get an idea that you want to do a show of Georgia O'Keeffe. You sit down and decide of all the Georgia O'Keeffes out there, what work best exemplifies your idea about Georgia O'Keeffe. So it means travelling: you have to go look at them all and figure out which ones you want. Then, laying out the show that creates a narrative, that is, which paintings go first, which go second, what are the relationships between them. Then, writing an essay for the catalogue, the book that promotes this idea of what it is you're saying about Georgia O'Keeffe.

What do museums get out of showing works that they don't own?

A temporary exhibition allows us to, in a more focused way, show a commitment to the artist who we find important. They're important because they bring together work in a way that the public could never see, because work is spread out. The Matisse show is a great example.

Those Matisses were all over the world. As much as people might love Matisse, and they might go to all of the different museums to see a Matisse, there's no experience like seeing them all together. It's a major achievement to get them all together for the public to get to see them, and that's what museums are supposed to be about—doing that, bringing it together. And it's the role of the curator to have the intellect and the enthusiasm to do that.

How do museums support themselves? Where do they get the money to do this?

Museums are nonprofit institutions. We don't sell work; we don't make money. We get funding to do exhibitions from public sources

like the NEA and from private foundations, from individuals, and in
many cases from corporations like Philip Morris. We generally get
the money for the museum in a project-basis way. That is, if you
have an exhibition that you want to do, you fund-raise for it.

*You mentioned that the second main function of the curator was
acquiring work for the museum's collection. Why do you
acquire works?*

Because museums seek to be the places that document, in a his-
toric way, the achievements of any given period, or any given group
of artists. In the Whitney's case, it's American art of the twentieth
and then into the twenty-first century. So we buy work so that our
permanent collection can stand as a document of American work. So
that fifty years from now, what we bought in 1992 might give an idea
of what was going on.

How do you keep on top of what's going on out there?

I spend a lot of time looking at work, so I spend a lot of time out
on the street: downtown, Soho, Williamsburg (in Brooklyn), South
Bronx. I go to Soho to the big galleries. I go to alternative spaces on
the Lower East Side, Hoboken, and Jersey City.

Then there are artists who I'm interested in who I go see in their
studio to see what they're doing. Sometimes it's with the intention of
a show; other times maybe I've done a show already and I just want
to see what else they're doing.

What's the difference between museums and galleries?

Galleries are commercial. Galleries show art for sale. Galleries
are the people who represent artists and are their agent, quote,
unquote. Commercial galleries are set up with the premise of having
a group of artists who they represent and showing their work so people can come see it. They're the people who sort of help curators. If
I'm interested in an artist I call their dealer, and then that person
will give me their slides, or send me a resume, or tell me what other
work is available.

How is that relationship?

There are a lot of dealers I have a very good relationship with, in that I can be honest with them and they're honest with me. They'll show me something and I'll either say if I'm interested or not. Then there are others, of course, who are much more pushy. Every dealer thinks that their artist is the best artist, and I can't blame them: that's how they should be.

Are you creating, then, what is contemporary art by what you pick and then show, or are you following it, or finding it? What's going on?

I really resist the notion that I'm creating a scene, and every time I hear it, it sickens me a bit. I'm often one to shun what people consider this power that I have. I *do* know when I show somebody (at the Whitney) that it is seen in a different way than, say, when I showed them at Jamaica Arts Center. I showed an artist this year, David Chung, who I showed at Jamaica Arts Center, and we laugh about it. Because when I showed him then, nobody cared. But I showed him here and then David Chung becomes an important artist. That's because this is the Whitney Museum. And I think that's great, because I feel that some of the people I'm showing never have this access.

Are you accessible?

I try to remain accessible. But again, it's hard because of this power. Access brings a whole lot of weirdness with it too. You know, I love going out to alternative spaces and going to people's openings, but it's becoming increasingly weirder, because as much as I just look at myself as Thelma, the curator, some people make it into more than perhaps it should be. So it becomes a little harder.

For so long I remained anonymous in the art world that I miss it a little bit. I miss being able to go in galleries and nobody knowing who I am.

Do you ever wonder who your friends are?

No. I know who my friends are, who are not, and who's trying to schmooze me, and I really kind of ignore that. That's not problematic. I guess what is problematic is just that there are so many artists out here trying to make a career, and I truly feel for them. And the options are pretty limited, especially in this weird financial climate. There aren't tons of places to show. There aren't lots of collectors buying work. It's not the eighties anymore. So I understand people's persistence. It takes a lot to commit your life to making art, and then it takes a lot more to make other people realize that commitment. So I don't necessarily mind what I see as artists just trying to make their careers happen.

Do you conceptualize ever as far as what the artist will produce?

No. Never. Usually I have ideas. The last installation here at the branch was Suzanne McClelland, a painter, and I had an idea that I wanted a painter to work in the gallery on the walls. I wanted a painter to work off the canvas, and that's all I said to Suzanne. I didn't say how, I didn't say how much, where, whatever. It was up to her what to do.

Gary Simmons wanted to make a piece that would be a huge fifteen-foot azalea garden in the shape of the KKK's cross. Do we plant azalea plants and grow them? How do we get them in, how do we water them? So in that, yes, we conceptualized together. It was like, "Alright, this is what you want to do, this is how we're going to do it."

I have an artist who's doing a piece that has lots of labels that have to be typeset. I'm overseeing that. There's one artist whose work, part of the piece is in Germany, and now the big challenge is getting it here because it's kind of spread out. I just work with them, and depending on what they're doing, it depends what I actually do.

I have a painter and I just have to kind of make sure that we are done on time. I have to keep calling and just say, you know, "How are you? Good. What's up?"

When you see something, what hits you? Is it visual, emotional, technique or what?

It depends. It's just, I see things and they interest me, and I remember them, and then I perhaps pursue it. Sometimes I see things that interest me that I don't pursue, and I don't know why. But maybe I'll see it again a year later and then I'll do it. That's the part that's hard to explain, and I think all curators work differently and I don't really know how I work in that realm.

I don't have a *thing*. Sometimes you hear people, they're a photography curator or a painting curator; I'm just not like that. I just know that this is what I do now. And it's hard too, because people always want to pin you down. And I say that quite often, I say, "Look I'm doing this now. Three years from now it might be something completely different."

Do people ever say, "Boy, she missed the boat on this show or this artist—what was she thinking?"

It happens all the time. **I think there's this fallacy about the "expert." I just don't believe anyone is an expert.** I don't really believe that anything is objective; it's all arbitrary and it's all subjective. Now, I'm not saying that as a cop-out. I truly believe when I look at things and I think they're good, that they are. But I also leave it open that people are not going to.

Are there any issues that concern you in the art world?

What worries me the most is this issue of inclusion. The fact that *I* exist in this institution, but there are very few people like me in other institutions across the country. I wonder what that means. It worries me that I still get invitations for shows that read something like, "Contemporary Hispanic Art Now." I wonder what that means. Why is it that people still can't just show artists because they're good and not put them in these packages?

People often try to pinhole me into the multicultural debates, and I'm not interested in them. **I don't believe that multiculturalism can exist in this kind of packaged way, the way in which it's been sold.** I don't believe that multiculturalism can exist in this kind of packaged way, the way in which it's been sold. People call me up to do things for Black History Month—I'm not interested. And it's not because I don't believe BHM is great, but I have to question what they do for the rest of the year. If an institution is committed, then why can't they be committed on another day besides February.

That's probably the worst part of it. The fact that I feel that I'm chipping away at a huge mountain sometimes, because I would like what I do not to seem so unique. I would like it not to seem weird to show a white woman who's in her early thirties and who is a single mother back to back with a black man who is thirty-five and gay. People make that out to be some big, huge political statement and so unique and so different. That's life. You know what I'm saying? What's weird about that?

What helps someone to be a good curator?

I think you have to be interdisciplinary. I don't believe that art happens in a vacuum. I feel like you have to know what's going on in other realms. I think it would be very hard for me to deal with artists, especially some of these young artists, if I didn't know about music. **You can't talk to one of my artists without talking about Sonic Youth.** And it's not just because he loves it, but there's a real link there. There's this whole thing going with Sonic Youth and all these grunge bands with this notion of objection; artists who are dealing with this notion of antimastery—not wanting to aspire to the masterwork but going on the underlevel of things.

There are artists who are inspired by slasher movies and *Mad* magazine: seventies culture being regurgitated out of these artists in the nineties. For example, Mike Kelley is an artist who is at the forefront of this. Weirdly enough, he and Sonic Youth are friends. He's done two of their album covers. Kim Gordon is one of the people who has written most about his work. His work is about the weird sexual awakening of children—all these things that are not nice things to talk about, which I think a lot of music is about. It's also a nihilistic approach. Like Nirvana and all that new metal, it totally relates. The "end of the world right now" mentality. Fragmentation, disillusionment—it's all there.

Someone else who I've shown, Gary Simmons, is totally into hip-hop. His work is all about urban angst, black male anger, the whole thing. You can't talk about his work without hiphop. So I feel like you have to be into contemporary culture to be a contemporary art curator. Maybe there also is a way in which you could just focus on art and let the art just deal on its own, but I find it almost impossible. I need the whole thing.

It seems that artists are pushing the envelope of acceptability to bring attention to their work, like with the NEA.

I don't know if that's the case. I don't think people are making this work just to get into a scandal. I think at any moment in history, always, artists have always made things that oftentimes, in the beginning, have seemed objectionable. We look at paintings of Manet now and they seem quite traditional and quite beautiful, but when Manet started painting those pictures they were seen as being completely objectionable to France of that era. I think artists make things that interest them or that sometimes haunt them. **I think a lot of work that's happening now about the body and about sexuality is coming out of a very distinct era, and that is the age of AIDS.** The sex-death correlation, as well as the sexuality-death correlation is really forming a lot of people's psyche.

I find it quite interesting that during that whole NEA controversy about Mapplethorpe, whenever you walk past any of those porno bookstores on Forty-second Street, it's filled with nothing but upper middle class businessmen. But yet Mapplethorpe does this and it's like, "Oh, it's pornography." Well, let's talk about people who consume this, but privately.

Do people ever say, "Oh, you work in a museum—how nice"?

People think curators are these old white men with half-reading glasses with British accents. Artists often say, "God, it's kind of weird that you're a curator," because people have this impression of curators being bookish.

I think there's a fallacy of what museums are about. I think people have a vision of museums as being these dusty old places with a lot of dusty old things like mummies and dinosaurs. And I think once people understand what's there, more often than not, they'll come see it.

The museum world in general is a field that needs people, in a sense that museums are changing, and different people have to work in them. And I don't just mean that racially. It's a cultural thing. Because we are living in a real diverse culture, we need all kinds of voices.

WORDS FROM ON HIGH:
Advice From the Personnel Manager at the Guggenheim Museum on Breaking In

NAOMI GOLDMAN

Personnel Manager, Solomon R. Guggenheim Museum, New York City

Background check—The building that houses the world-famous museum of modern and contemporary art is itself considered a masterpiece. Designed by Frank Lloyd Wright and completed in 1959, it is the youngest building in history to be designated a New York City landmark. An extension of the museum—the Guggenheim Museum Soho, an exhibition space—opened in 1992 in downtown Manhattan.

Who is likely to get a job here?

We tend to hire people who have been in our internship programs because they have a track record with us. I make that the pay-off for working for nothing. Internships and summer jobs are vital experiences for anyone in this environment.

You look for that experience?

If they don't have that, forget about it, because the educational process of acculturation is going to be that much more difficult. There's so many different things that they need to learn in their first year of work here that it's just too much.

How about typing and computer experience?

If somebody hasn't used a personal computer, they're basically unemployable. The idea that they're not going to type is completely unrealistic. They're going to type. I type. We all type.

Any things to avoid putting on a resume?

"Extensive experience." Recent college grads, they don't have a hell of a lot of experience; they've had a *taste* of certain things. They're just not old enough to have extensive experience. There are certain words that I don't like. These are personal: "creative," "growth," "career path." These are impressionistic statements that a person who's interviewing you for a half hour can't possibly understand what you mean. So what it says about you is that you are unclear.

Language skills are very important here. So if you have good Italian, German, French, and Japanese, probably, that plays very well here.

What about sending a resume blindly to you. Do people get hired that way?

Yes, people actually get jobs like that. The problem is, is that I don't always have time to look at them. I'm really busy right now, so resumes from three or four months ago are sitting in my office because I just haven't looked at them.

How many resumes do you get generally?

A lot. It depends if I'm running ads. Hundreds a month. When I was interviewing for the reopening, I got 1,500 resumes a month.

Is it important to major in art history?

No, I don't think so. But I think there should be a demonstrated interest in wanting to be at a cultural institution.

Does the college you go to make a difference? Isn't the art world sort of a privileged world?

I think there's an economic thing that goes on in the art world. You're earning nothing working in a cultural organization. So you have to think about who can afford not to earn too much money, and who is going to get supplemented from their family. So there is a built in gradient there, which is unfortunate, but it's true.

What do you look for during an interview that will help someone get a job?

The people I hire are the people who tell me, "I'll do anything." The person that says "I'll do windows, doors, floors, I'll do anything, I just really want to work here." In an interview I'm really looking for that excitement. You know, "I want this job above anything else. This is what I want." It's their passion I want, because it's the passion that's going to keep them here, certainly not money. I want people who are *dying* to work here.

In an interview you have to be yourself. But don't be negative, always be upbeat, and don't say anything critical about former employers. That's really important.

Is this a demanding work environment?

A high level of performance is demanded here. A high level of commitment; these are not nine-thirty to five-thirty jobs. The expectation that you will work nine-thirty to five-thirty is totally unrealistic.

Is it important to send a thank-you note after an interview?

I expect a thank-you note. That's really common fashion for me.

How about follow-up calls?

If it's a place that you really want to work at—again, I want people whose passion it is to work here—touching base with me every couple of weeks or months is a good idea. I think that that's a totally admirable quality, without being a complete nudge.

Are connections important?

I'll definitely see people who were referred from people internally, that is important. But it doesn't get you a job—it just gets you in the door.

Is someone's GPA important?

I don't care to hear what your GPA is. I don't want it on the resume. The fact that your GPA was high does not mean that you're a functional working person. And the expectation that it's going to wow me.... You know, it takes hard work, tenacity, enthusiasm, it takes a good attitude. It takes a flexible personality to function in the workplace. The fact that you were an exceptional college student doesn't really hold that much weight. In a law firm it probably does.

Any last advice on getting a job?

You never know where your next opportunity is going to come from. Everything is an interview. An exploratory interview is not necessarily an interview for that job, but you should still always be on your best behavior. Everything is laying the path for something else. I used to have this expression, "You don't know underneath what rock your next job is going to be."

9

Music

"In the early '80s it didn't even enter your mind to deal with corporate labels, because they weren't dealing with underground music," says Thurston Moore from Sonic Youth, *Interview* magazine, August 1992. And then there was Nirvana (Geffen Records) in '92 and alternative hell (officially) broke loose in the corporate rock world.

"Alternative" no longer meant a limited audience base and low sales; thus, the bigger, corporate labels started tripping over each other in the attempt to sign them up. And the alternative bands that signed with the big corporate labels did so out of necessity; it wasn't and isn't a sell-out, as I've heard people say. These acts were being limited by the inability of the independent labels to print CDs and tapes fast enough and to distribute them on a massive scale. The Big Six (listed below) have cornered that market, so any small label or band that wants to break through to a large audience is forced to play ball with them. That's why you've got underground, independent labels merging with, or at least taking distribution deals with, one of the Big Six, which account for 90 percent of U.S. recorded music sales.

THE BIG SIX LABELS AND DISTRIBUTORS

Los Angeles, and to a lesser extent, New York City, share the billing of "music mecca" and are, therefore, the homes for the Big Six.

1) Bertelsman Music Group (BMG): Is a German company that owns and distributes RCA, Arista, Jive, etc. Also owns Bantam, Doubleday, and Dell Books.

2) EMI Music: Is owned by Thorn, an English company (and is sometimes referred to as Thorn/EMI). CEMA is the distribution company for labels owned, partly owned, or in a distribution agreement with EMI Music, which include: Capital, Liberty, EMI, SBK, Virgin, IRS, and Sparrow.

3) Polygram: Is owned by Phillips N.V. of the Netherlands, which also owns Propaganda Films, Interscope, and Egg Pictures (Jodie Foster's company). Polygram labels include Mercury, PLG, Island, and A&M. PGD is the distribution company.

4) Sony: Columbia and Epic are the major labels owned by this entertainment giant. Chaos and Def Jam are a couple of off-shoot labels.

5) MCA: Bought Geffen records and was itself bought by Matsushita, owner of Universal Studios. UNI is the name of the distribution company owned by the parent company.

6) WEA: Is the name of the distribution company owned by Time Warner. WEA is comprised of the labels, and stands for, Warner, Elektra, and Atlantic Records.

ECONOMICS

The music industry isn't afraid of anyone. Even though Joe Schmoe can turn to MTV and even network TV to get his music fix, it hasn't slowed his tracks to Tower Records; in fact, it seems to have quickened it. In the 1986-1991 period, spending on recorded music hip-hopped to 11 percent annually. CDs can take the bow for causing this growth. In 1986, CDs represented just 8.6 percent of all recordings sold, while in 1996 it is projected they will account for 50.5 percent, 9 percent higher than what they did in 1991.

TOP GIGS

Record Company Gigs

A great way to break into the music biz at a label is through a college rep program. Sony Music, for example, has around forty-five
college students around the country who get a small salary for working their asses off pushing new releases to college radio stations and
to small retailers. They get involved in arranging for the concerts in
the local towns. They go into stores and put up posters. They push to
try and get announcements and articles about the label's bands in
local newspapers. Placement into a full-time job at the label after
graduation for these people can be as high as 75 percent.

A&R (ARTISTS AND REPERTOIRE)

A&R is probably the most coveted of all the record company
gigs. Usually when somebody says they want to go into the record
biz, this is what they're talking about. These are the folks that discover and sign new bands. Yeah, their faces are younger and their
hair is longer, but A&R dudes are landing their jobs by means other
than the proverbial mailroom. Instead of developing talented ears
from within—work your ass off and pray—the major labels wind up
filling A&R positions from the outside. Managers of obscure,
unknown bands that break through, as well as founders of small,
independent labels are often plugged into these jobs. It's a way for
the labels to acquire proven and successful ears, as well as to gain
instant street credibility. What's more, established musicians—as is
the case with Thurston Moore (Sonic Youth) and Geffen Records—
are being tapped to discover and shepherd new bands to the labels.

PRODUCT MANAGER

The product manager works closely with A&R folks on all aspects
of the release of a CD. He or she creates development concepts and
materials for merchandising, helps arrange tours, sets budgets for
music videos and basically serves as an in-house manager. The
smaller and medium-sized labels sometimes don't have product
managers, so then it falls within the responsibilities of the A&R person who signed the band to do this stuff also.

ARTIST DEVELOPMENT

This person deals with making an act's presentation better, such as giving them a certain look if that's what they need. Making their hair different. Getting the image together. Looking at the repertoire—maybe adding and diversifying the music a little. He or she works very closely with A&R.

SALES REP

The entry-level sales job is account service rep. You develop and implement in-store displays, product positioning, and develop unique in-store promotions, as well as take care of inventory counts.

Non–Record Company Gigs

MANAGER (SEE JANET BILLIG INTERVIEW)

AGENT

Agents live their lives on the phone calling up promoters and venues telling them what band is coming to town that they represent and asking, "What venue can you give me?" Big agencies like ICM and William Morris represent most of the huge acts as well as the struggling alternative bands.

PROMOTER

The promoter will buy the show from the agent. They'll guarantee the band a certain amount of money, which means the promoter might take a bath or make a nice chunk of dough if the show sells out. They buy all the advertising, i.e., radio spots and newspaper ads. They put up billboards and posters. They decide what venue they're going to rent for the show based on how many people they think they can draw. They hire the sound system, lights, the crew, production and catering.

A good entry-level job towards being a promoter is that of **venue assistant**. The promoter pays you to meet the band when they pull into town, show them where everything is, help them with whatever they need. Filling the beer trays with ice and making sure the towels are dry. This can lead to coordinating the whole show, making sure the sound and lights get in there and stuff, and then to a promoter's position.

JANET BILLIG

Manager, Gold Mountain Entertainment, New York City

Twenty-five years old

Background check—Some of the bands Gold Mountain man-
    ages are: Sonic Youth, Beastie Boys, Hole, Breeders,
    Dinosaur Jr, and my favorite band, the Lemonheads.
    Offices in New York and L.A.

7:00 PM. The offices of Gold Mountain Entertainment. Janet
talks on the phone behind a frightfully messy desk. To her right, on a
shelf and on the floor, stacks of demo tapes that need to be listened
to, or not. On her left, a large TV tuned permanently to MTV. No
volume.

Janet talks with Courtney Love, lead of the band Hole and wife
of the late Kurt Cobain from Nirvana. Janet to Courtney, "If you say
yes to *Melody Maker* (a British music magazine), everybody else will
be pissed. When we say no to press, we mean no."

7:15 PM. I walk out of Janet's office and hang with the assistants.
They seem happy here, like they're not kicked around. I go back into
Janet's office. A new phone call. "Unless I *fix* him, he's not going to
be *able* to tour." She's telling someone why they've got to fork up
some money for her client's physical therapy. A bad arm I'm told.

7:20 PM. Janet looks up at me, holds up one finger, and mouths,
"One minute."

7:45 PM. Two phone calls later. Janet talking with somebody
about the Breeders and why they need a truck with four seats in it,
and where can they get it.

8:00 PM. I think Janet feels bad for making me wait. I go chill
with the assistants. They're still around.

8:05 PM. Janet's associate, Dana Millman, comes in for a conference call. "We don't need to make a $200,000 record. We want to
make a record for $125,000." Pause. "No. The musicians' salaries are
non-negotiable." They're being hard-asses, but they're really cool
about it. I'm impressed.

An assistant walks in and interrupts with, "Courtney's on the phone." Janet takes the call from her couch phone, keeping an ear on the conference-call conversation. Janet to Courtney: "They want two hundred fucking thousand dollars to produce the Lemonheads' next record."

Courtney sings a song for Janet on the phone and she lets me listen in, but only for like half a second.

8:15 PM. Janet gets a call from Japan where the Lemonheads are on tour. She pleads with the person to keep Evan away from the Japanese girls for fear of their fathers' killing him. "He likes girls," Janet tells me after the call.

8:30 PM. I reschedule with Janet for Saturday afternoon when things might be a little quieter.

Saturday.

So how did you get your start in the rock business?

I started working really young. I had my first job when I was like fifteen. I've been doing this for ten years. Not managing rock bands, but in the rock-and-roll biz.

Starting out doing what?

I was working at a club downtown. I started out doing coatcheck. Bands used to come in all the time and I ended up working with merchandisers a lot, because that's where they used to sell merchandising, right next to the coatcheck. So I used to meet all these merchandisers and learned about it. You'd see the same people working in this whole merchandise thing. The same people come through month after month. **I lied about my age and got a job doing merchandising.**

What did you do?

I'd go out on the road. I didn't sell shirts. Sometimes you'd go out and sell if it was a smaller tour, but I did mostly bigger tours. You do logistics and stuff of getting enough merch (slang for merchandise) to each venue. You know, when you're dealing with stadium tours and arena tours, you're talking about a mass quantity of merchandise. You're also organizing sellers.

What about college?

I would go to college back and forth in between working and making money. I went to school in D.C. for a while and graduated from NYU. When I graduated I wanted to stay in New York, so I got this part-time, shitty job at this new independent label called Caroline Records just doing anything I could. And that just grew into a real job as it grew into a real label. And I was there for four years.

The merchandising was worthwhile experience?

Doing the merchandising you learn about the rock-and-roll business 'cause you're out there. You're out there seeing how promoters work, seeing how bands work on the road. **You learn all sorts of that weird shit. Just that general interaction of rock-and-roll people, who are the weirdest of the weird.** On the road, especially, living in close quarters with a crew of forty or fifty people for six months. I was this sixteen-year-old girl very much in this male world. It was fun. My parents were super supportive. I was the youngest, so by the time they got around to me it was kind of like, "Whatever you want to do." I come from a very liberal, New York, intellectual Jewish family.

How did you hear about the job at Caroline Records?

I started part-time while I was at school. It was just mutual acquaintances. I spent a lot of time at CBGBs and got to know the local people, the people who hang out there. So I'd met someone who knew the woman who started Caroline, and she said, "Yeah, you can start here." It was really just part-time shit work, just whatever needed to be done.

How did you get over doing just the shit work? Were you aggressive?

I think there's a certain balance. You have to be assertive but not too aggressive, because you don't want to create these horrible power struggles. Just working really hard and being really aware of things. Taking responsibility for things that you wouldn't necessarily, things that aren't in your job description.

With rock and roll and the rock-and-roll business, you're dealing with so many flakes and so many people who don't want to take responsibility for things, so you have to double up and take on more responsibility than you usually world. And I think it has a lot to do with not being afraid of that—being responsible for other people's lives.

How did you get the job here at Gold Mountain?

It was really strange. Courtney Love, basically (from the band Hole). I had signed Courtney to Caroline. And, I had known Nirvana for a really long time from their first record label, Sub Pop, which we distributed. So I'd known Nirvana (whom Gold Mountain formerly managed). They'd slept on my floor when they toured and stuff. So John Silva (from Gold Mountain) suggested, "Why don't we bring in Janet to manage Courtney, and she'll get other bands too." And the next week I picked up three more bands and had a roster. (Laughs.)

So what do managers do?

You do everything. You just do everything. It's so...God, what do you do? (She's almost too flustered and tired to even explain it.) OK, you start with finding a band. You find a band that you want to work with. I'd never work with a band that I don't like. I'd never work with people I don't like. You work so hard, there's so much to do, and you have to deal with these people ten times a day, every day. I deal with their careers and have a vision for them. Maybe that's the most important thing, is someone you know you have a vision for.

Why is that?

You have to sell your artists to so many different facets, it's not just a record company, it's a booking agent, it's a publisher. **You have**

to sell all the time, so you've really gotta fucking believe it.

You send out tapes to every A&R person you know. (A&R people are the folks at the record labels that sign bands. See Todd Sullivan interview.) You invite everyone to come see the band. And you hope someone thinks they're as great as you think they are, they give them a load of money, and then we take a commission. (Laughs.)

So after you get your band a record deal, do you still have to deal with the label?

Eighty percent of my job is motivating a record company. You know, a company like Warner Brothers puts out three-hundred-some-odd records a year. How do you get people to pay attention to yours? The Lemonheads: this is a band who had sold 12,000 records on their last release. Really, no one gave a shit. And no matter how good a record is, if a record company doesn't embrace it and feel enthusiastic about it, they're going to talk about Mick Jagger on the phone to the press or to radio stations. You know, they're not going to talk about the Lemonheads. Who are the Lemonheads to them?

Half your job is motivating a record company to pay attention to your act, and also not to whore your band—to keep the band's ethic alive. You don't want to become some sort of Karaoke band, you know what I mean? When the record company goes, "oh, we don't like your singer, so we're going to get you a new singer." It's a manager's job to represent the band the way the band should be represented at the label. That's really a giant part of the job—dealing with record company people.

What are they like?

There's some really, really great ones, and there's some really, really awful ones, and you've got to work with both of them. You call them on the phone, you go out, you go to the record company, you have meetings. Like with Dinosaur Jr, who has a record coming out, I went to Los Angeles three times before the record came out. **You just get in people's faces, "What are you going to do for me? What are you going to do for my band?"**

When you go and have meetings with the radio promotions

department, you talk about what tracks they're going to push to radio; what should be the first single; what should be the second single. How many radio stations are we targeting for this song and how big do you think it can be? And then when they come back with an answer, you go, "Well, I think it should be bigger."

Why should they listen to you?

They want to have a success story also. They also look to a manager for things. I mean, a record company's job doesn't end with just having a record: they need the band to promote the record; they need the band to be out on tour. They need the band to do schmoozy radio shows. So they need me also to help promote the band. **The labels want to have successes. It's my job to make them think that my band is the one that can be a major breakthrough.** My band's the one that can be Nirvana or Pearl Jam or David Bowie or Phil Collins.

Do all bands have managers?

No. It makes it more professional. It gives them someone to call and say, "We need this." Look at my desk. It's filled with faxes from record companies.

What do they want from you?

They call me and go, "When can Evan (from the Lemonheads) do interviews?" So I go to Evan and say, "Your record's coming out. You're going to do phone interviews Monday to Friday every morning, ten AM to noon. And then I'm going to bring you to New York and we're going to do in-person interviews from the eleventh of the month to the fifteenth of the month. And then we're going to go to Los Angeles and we're going to do them from the twentieth to the twenty-third. Then we're going to go to London, Paris, and Hamburg and we're going to do interviews there." That's just organizing the setup of a record. This is just promotions, not part of a tour.

Will you travel with them?

Sometimes. With someone like J from Dinosaur Jr, people think he's really strange. The record company thinks he's really weird. I give the record company someone to talk to so they don't have to talk to him. He doesn't want to talk to the record company either. They won't send him anywhere unless I go. They gladly pay for me to go. He doesn't talk a lot. He alienates people. A writer will ask him ten questions and he'll just sit there and won't say anything. And he'll make the journalist feel like an asshole and they'll leave. So we had to figure out a way to make the interviews different so he'd do them.

That's also a manager's job, to come up with ways to make things a little different, and to make a record company work a little bit differently than they're used to, so they kind of get a little more excited. That's a big part of the job—to get people to think more creatively about your artists.

Might that mean getting creative with them—you know, helping them with an image?

To maintain an image or to change an image if it's bad, that's part of it. I'm not so much like the mad scientist, you know....

Like, "Wear cowboy hats?"

Yeah, exactly. How about some flannel—get that grunge thing going. No. I represent artists and I want to represent who they are, which is why I choose to work with them. And they choose to work with me because I don't say, "I think you should wear glitter pants and platform shoes."

What else regarding record companies?

You ask them for money all the time: money to make more expensive videos, money for tour support if you can't break even on the tour. Or if you want to have a huge light show, you ask them for money for that. You ask them to spend more money on artwork, for everything. They ask you to do something, you ask them for money.

Do they hate you?

It's kind of this weird adversarial relationship you're supposed to have. They expect you to ask them for money. And it's their job to say no, and they'll try to get it down.

What about touring? What do you do?

The first thing you do is you make a schedule. I sit and I make a year-long plan. You go, "I want to do the U.S. in April. And then we'll go to Europe in May. And then we'll go to Japan and Australia in June and July. And they'll we'll come back to the States and tour again in August."

Although I have an understanding of it, every tour is kind of like this giant *thing* you have to put together into a nice little box and send it off, which is really hard because every tour's different. Every band wants to tour differently. Do they go in a van, do they fly everywhere, do they go on a bus, do they go on two buses?

Is managing a tour tough?

Everything can go wrong on a tour. This whole job is crisis management. Dinosaur Jr was doing four shows at East Coast colleges. I talked to them when they got to the venue after they went to sound check, and everything seemed fine. So I'm walking out of the office at nine PM and the phone rings. It's the tour manager saying, "They won't let us play, we're too loud, they want us to turn it down." So I have to call the promoter. **I tell the promoter, "This is really fucking crazy. You brought us the sound system that makes it be this loud. You don't want us to play, fine, give us the check, we'll walk."** And the guy says, "No, we're not going to give you the check. If you're not going to play, we're not going to pay you."

So what do you do? It's ten-thirty PM and I'm talking to their lawyer. Meanwhile, the band was *supposed* to go on at ten PM. So I'm fighting with this school's lawyer, screaming at each other back and forth, back and forth. He's telling me that their decibel level is so loud that they're endangering people, and that they want me to indemnify the school. They want me to send a fax indemnifying the school, that we're responsible for these kids' ears. "*You* booked the show," I told him. "There's absolutely nothing in the contract limiting the decibel level."

So they called me back and said, "OK, we've decided to pull the show," and I'm like, "Fine, whatever. I have to go. I have dinner."

What happened?

The minute they decided to pull the show, the band went on and played. They're like, "Fuck these people." No one told the band they pulled the show. And it was fine.

It would have been a riot.

Well, that was my other sell to them: "You want to pull the show, *you* go out, you make a fucking announcement and tell 800 kids that just paid ten bucks that you think the band's too loud." There's just tons of crises. There's one every day.

Like Evan and the Japanese girls? I overheard that phone call the last time I was here.

Evan, you know, has a thing with girls. And my one concern in Japan is that they'll castrate him. It's a really serious concern. And Evan is someone that's not going to think about that. So I have to trust my road manager to really watch out for him.

You've really got to look out for them.

Being a woman in this guy world, you know, I personally tend to be a lot more of a caretaker by nature. You know, you think, am I their manager or am I their best friend? They *pay* me. Where's the balance, is there no balance? There *is* no balance. I'm here to sort out their business affairs. I'm here to make sure they make enough money and get paid properly. But I'm also here to be the person that they call and cry to.

It's so important that when someone does become a huge star, that you have a relationship with them, that they trust you and know that you're not in it only to exploit them for their money. Like with Nirvana. They need to know that I've been there since day one. I'll always be there. I care about them as people, not because they make millions of dollars, which is a real concern of famous people.

Is it a pain though when they become huge? You know, the egos?

It's a very strange industry. You know, all you're dealing with is huge egos; not only the egos of artists, but the egos of record company people. Everybody wants to be the person behind something, you know, "I did that."

I start with, bottom line, everybody I work with has a huge ego, but that's only natural. Whether they're selling 50 records, 50,000, 500,000 or many millions. It can be a pain in the ass, 'cause what if you call with bad news? How do you say "Your record's failing," or "no one wants to play your song on the radio?" Or, "You got a really fucking horrible review."

Do they ever blame you for it?

Oh yeah, sure. "Why aren't you making this happen, why aren't you making this happen? It's your job to make this happen. I pay you to make this happen." Sure. But that's why you have to have a solid enough relationship with your artist where they can say that to you without you shrivelling up, or without them firing you. My career solely rests on them keeping me in employ, you know? I mean, I have nothing without my clients.

You get blamed for everything. Things that are out of your control, you get blamed for.

Like that show the other night. It's not my fucking fault that the goddamn school didn't want them to play loud. The school bought the show. I assumed they knew they were buying a loud band. I don't think I'd get fired over a show, but if there were a whole tour like that, and every show they showed up at there was a fuck-up, and things didn't happen right, and they weren't happy, they weren't comfortable, they hated the hotels, they weren't getting the right kind of attention, and the advertising wasn't right—there weren't posters at every show—and the shows didn't sell out, and there's this whole horrible series of events—you'll get fired for that, sure.

What are the highs?

I like hearing new stuff and getting excited all over again—that's the thing I really dig. I just heard this tape last week that was unbelievable. This band from Ohio that no one I know has ever heard of. Really fucking great.

You going to sign them?

I don't know, I can't really find them. I don't know who they are really. I called the record stores in Ohio three or four times and people are like, "I don't know, I *kind* of heard of them." But I can't take on another band right now, I'm really too busy. I have two bands in the studio, three bands, no, four bands in the studio, two bands on tour....

Who were you arguing with on the phone last time I was here? Something about studio costs for the next Lemonheads album?

A producer's manager. He manages the producer that we want to use to make the next Lemonheads record. Everybody's got a fucking manager. (Laughs) So we were arguing about how much money to spend on a record. The label guaranteed a certain amount of money, and this guy wants us to go and ask for more. And we don't think it's necessary. Because the money you spend to make a record is a loan from the record company, basically—you pay that back. The record company just doesn't *give* you money, ever. Everything you take from the record company you pay back.

Do some bands not understand that?

Yeah, it's hard to understand why you're $400,000 in debt to a record company. That's normal. You spend a couple hundred thousand dollars on an album, you spend $50,000 on a video, you take $80,000 in tour support.

What's your involvement when they're in the studio?

Make sure they have money, make sure they have a place to live. Whatever. If they want a kazoo player, if they want a string section, find them a string section. Anything they need, you know? If they want their girlfriend to come out, you buy their girlfriend a plane ticket.

What about music videos?

On the videos I deal with directors, producers, putting them together, getting budgets approved. You usually work with a video person at the record company in putting it together. Finding the right director to go with the band—someone they're happy with. If the band and the record company have different ideas, you have to talk the record company into the band's idea.

That's a common one. The record company wants you to use such and such a director because they owe him a favor, or for whatever reason. And the band's like, "No, we want to use so-and-so, our friend, or this guy who made this video." And you have to be the mediator and tell the record company that it's the band's creative vision, and that's what we're selling here. And bring them back to, "No, it's not your aesthetic, it's our aesthetic."

Do they often come with—

Ridiculous, crazy ideas? Yeah. It's amazing. For the Dinosaur Jr video, I told the people at Warner to get treatments. (A treatment is a written concept from a video director for a video describing what type of video they would make.) So I get these faxes, these treatments, while me and J were in Germany and Paris doing a press tour. They got these two current, big-name directors. And they were both, like, "there are live dancing dinosaurs coming out of a volcano." It was so horrible, I didn't even show them to J. So I called up the record company flipping out, like, "How could you possibly think this is anything...." They just didn't get it. "I can't believe you sent this." I was like, "Don't worry, I'll find the video director."

What about MTV? Do you have involvement with them?

We try to. MTV's this giant evil monster. (Laughs.) You just try to get them to play your videos. "I know you're playing the Lemonheads a lot. Put them in more." Yeah, MTV's tough. It can basically make your band.

I felt like this week Warner Brothers didn't push Dinosaur Jr hard enough to MTV, because I was up there and I just felt like they weren't pushing the band enough, so I wrote a bitchy letter. It's both of our jobs to pitch to MTV. I mean whatever makes it happen, whatever makes it work.

How do some people get on MTV more?

If there was a formula, man, I'd be using it. There's none. Mondays and Tuesdays...(She shakes her head.) These are when they have the two meetings at MTV when they decide what they're going to put in rotation. So you usually know on Tuesday about six PM if you get in, or if you get moved up. Like if you're in overnight rotation and you get moved up to afternoon rotation, from two plays a day to six plays a day. There's this big giant meeting and you don't know what they do in there, I don't know. **You love MTV because they make you a shit load of money, and you hate MTV, they're evil. (Laughs.)**

What are some other things you have to deal with?

I'll show you the latest fax. I think I threw it out I was so mad. The first Dinosaur Jr show of this huge tour was tonight. I get this fax from the UK company that says, "We gave away on this radio show flights to Glasgow, two tickets, and backstage passes to the show. We need to know what time the two winners can meet the band." (Long pause. She's still pissed and still can't believe it.) People don't go *meet* Dinosaur Jr. J's just not that kind of guy. His *fans* are scared of him. They don't want to go near him. He's weird.

So I called them screaming, "You gave away J!" That was my whole thing. I was like, "How can you give away the band?" and I went on this whole tirade. This is not a band you give away. It's not like backstage is anything exciting. You'll see J getting his arm massaged, being grumpy.

So I called J and I said, "Listen, they gave you away. I didn't know anything about it." That's another thing. "They did this contest and I didn't know about it—sorry." It's my job to know what they're doing to promote the record. So I have to call my client and say, "My job wasn't being done. Nobody told me they were doing this. They gave you away. These two kids are coming to the show. They're supposed to meet you as a prize, which is like no fucking prize to anybody because you're evil. So these kids are going to be there. If you see them don't kick them—they won."

WOODY NUSS

Rock-and-Roll Tour Manager

Thirty-two years old

You can't visit Woody at his office to do the interview. Doesn't have one. Doesn't even own a car. Just rents when he's in town, in L.A., which isn't often. You hop in his rental. What's this? Who is this guy? You thought he'd have long hair, or at least a leather jacket or something. Doc Marten shoes, at least. He wouldn't be wearing a sweater, jeans, and sneakers. God. How boring. How uncool. I point this contradiction out to him and he comes back with something like, "This town's already got enough of that." Good point.

Hollywood. He's right. The whole town has a rocker fantasy going, you realize, as he weaves the rental tin box in and out cars on Melrose Avenue. (Obviously he's had many years of practice on the road.) Here he is, a professional rocker, a guy with a job most of these misdirected punks would die for, the real thing...and *he's* out of place. I guess when you're actually doing it, you don't need to *look* like you do it.

But this down-to-earth, regular-guy image he's got makes you feel a little silly with your writer-goatee thing going. Ah, what the hell. I'll drink a few cups of coffee, smoke some cigarettes, and never see him again. Unless, of course, I have to hit him up for tickets to a Lemonheads gig (recently on the cover of *Interview* magazine), my band of choice this month, which he just happens to tour manage.

When did you start working behind the scenes?

In high school. My high school tried to be like the *Fame* school of performing arts but it was in Atlanta. There was a real theatre there and a three-person tech squad, which was a bit more appealing than the guys that ran the projectors. It wasn't quite the nerd squad. It was a good way for me to cut class. So I learned lighting and sound there. I mean, sound there was like, "Plug in the mike, plug the box into the speakers, and go." At least I knew which end to plug the mike in and stuff.

I had a friend who was in a band, and I figured out a way of putting together a sound system for him. And that was it. **I started doing sound for a bunch of fifteen-year-olds with shitty equipment, playing backyard parties. It was a way to have fun, hit on women, and party with the guys in the band.**

What about college?

My freshman year I went to Georgia State University, which had a promotional music school. It was a music-business institute kind of school. That was ridiculous because I already knew more than the guys there.

So then I went up to Athens where my friends were and went to school there. We'd do open-mike nights and stuff. And eventually what happened is, the house sound-guy at this one bar was a baseball fan and a gambler, so if he had money riding on a game, he'd call and I'd come in and mix for him that night. So that's how I got my break, because he'd bet on the Braves, which at the time was a really stupid bet. A few times the band turned out to be R.E.M. So I did the earliest R.E.M. shows there and some shows out of town with them.

Why didn't you stick with R.E.M.?

On one out-of-town show everybody had gotten really drunk and fucked up and nobody could drive the car back. So R.E.M. made me drive the car home with the trailer attached to it. I had never towed anything before. So we're going down some road in Augusta getting ready to get on the highway, and we pass the entrance ramp. So I put it in reverse and started to back up, and Peter looks up at me and goes, "Be sure not to jackknife." And as he says the word, of course, we jackknifed. Did some damage. So, partly due to that and partly due to the fact that my sound system was really shitty anyway, they switched and started using a different guy's sound system. So that was the end of my R.E.M. career.

Were you making any money doing those gigs?

The standard of living was really low in Athens. If you made thirty-five bucks a night you were doing fine. So, yeah, I was doing alright.

But then it got to be kind of a rut. You know, I was doing the clubs in Athens, but nothing was really going anywhere. And I was seeing what these bands were doing on the road. R.E.M. had really blossomed; they had two vans now and were going all around the country. I could see that I was stagnating. The next band that was really doing anything was a band called Love Tractor. So I approached them and said, "Next time you guys go out (on the road to tour) you should take someone to do sound for you so you won't be at the mercy of these clubs." So they were like, "Yeah, sure, great, let's go."

What about college?

I was at journalism school at University of Georgia. It was ridiculous. Nobody there knew what they were doing. **It was a real collegiate look at the TV and movie industry by people who'd never been in TV. It just didn't make any sense to finish school.** I think it was winter quarter of my junior year and I just was like, "Nah, I'm going to go out on the road with the Tractor." And I never went back.

What was that tour like?

It was complete poverty. We got stranded a couple of times with no money because we didn't have a real record label, we had a small independent label that had no money. It was six guys in a van with all the gear. Sleeping on top of the gear. You know, you'd build a little shelf where you could lay down over the gear. Or you go to a hotel and tell them there's one or two of you, and the rest sneak in a back door. You throw the mattresses on the floor, and two guys sleep on the box springs and two guys sleep on the mattresses. You bullshit the maids into giving you enough towels so everybody can shower.

You get stranded in Arizona sleeping at a girl's place that the guitarist used to go out with but doesn't anymore, sleeping on her floor.

Fun and organized, huh?

Yeah. Pulling into Baton Rouge and finding out we're playing in a gay disco and *Cruise* magazine is there to interview you. And you're looking at each other going, "Well, I guess there aren't going to be any chicks tonight."

We played this show in Saskatoon, Canada. We found our contact guy, and he's like, "Well, we can't get the venue. It's too expensive to get the club we were going to use, so we're going to find someplace else to have our show." So we ended up doing the show in this guy's house. We moved all the furniture out in the front lawn and like two hundred people paid to get in. And during the middle of the show the guy comes running in and is like, "Wait, wait, stop, stop." I thought the police came, we were too loud or something. And he's like, "No, the northern lights!" So we all ran out of the house and sat in the furniture on the front lawn and watched the northern lights for like twenty minutes, and then went back in and played some more psychedelic instrumental music. It's different than what I'm doing now, which is tour bus and first-class hotels and all that crap, but there's better stories from then.

You needed to do that, though—pay your dues?

A bit. There's plenty of people who haven't done that, who have jumped right in and gone on bus tours. But it did make a lot of difference. Just the fact that there aren't very many surprises that I come across now because I did so much touring in those days.

How did you wind up going out on tour with bigger acts?

I went out with the Tractor for like three years. And due to that I got to meet a lot of other bands and their agents in New York. I became friends with the woman who was the bookkeeper for Love Tractor's agent, and I'd tell her that I was looking for something else. I was interested in Robin Hitchcock because I'd seen his videos and stuff, and I knew that this agent also represented him. So I called this woman and said, "I'm a huge Robin Hitchcock fan, do you know anything about them, are they going to play down here, can I come see him?" And she countered with, "Well, as a matter of fact, they may need someone."

So I convinced this agent to take a chance on me. I just jumped in the deep end with a band that was much bigger than a band I'd done before. They had a record deal, a bus, they were older guys. I started doing all the advancing, doing the pre-tour work of the tour manager.

What's "advancing"?

Advancing is calling all the venues, calling all the promoters and making sure they have what you need. Making sure that they're hiring the right sound system and lighting system, and that they're advertising the show. Just making sure that they're going to have everything there when you get there so there are no surprises. That they're going to have the bagels and cream cheese set up for you when you walk in and all that crap.

Then you put it all together. You call the travel agent. You book all the hotels. You get directions to the venues. You plot out the distances and figure out how you're going to arrange the driving. You rent the gear and rent a truck to haul the gear. You gather up the musicians. You get them to the hotel and check them in and out. Then you get the guys to the venue. You've got to get them to all their interviews and find time for them to get their laundry done.

Total control.

You've got to be a control freak and you've got to be organized. You wake them up in the morning and make sure they eat and have clean clothes and all that stuff. **Try to give them enough time to party, which there's never enough time, because you've always got to be somewhere else.**

Sounds like you've got to be a hard-ass.

Yeah. But you also don't want to be a fuck-face about it either. I mean, I know a lot of guys who are really professional and who can't keep a job because the musicians hate them. And there are plenty of tours I've done where the musicians hate me by the end of the tour. Because you're the one that's saying, "Get your ass out of bed," and "No, you don't have time to have a long breakfast, you're just going to have to grab something quick." And you know, **"I'm sick of your bullshit, just wash your clothes in the sink and get moving."**

If I said to you, "OK, this is what we're going to do today. We're going to drive four hundred miles, we're going to stop, get something to eat, drive another hundred miles, go to some place, set up, do a sound check, go to the motel, have a drink, maybe get a bite, ·come back, play a show, pack up all the gear, maybe have a drink, get back in the van and drive a hundred miles." You'd think I was fucking insane. I mean, most people in the world, if they're going to drive four hundred miles, they spend a month planning it. Think about your parents taking a four-hundred-mile drive to the beach. They fucking spend a week deciding you know, which blankets they're going to take and this and that. No, every day you get up and you drive four or five hundred miles, you're in a different city or a different country. **It's hard to maintain your sanity. You just want the musicians to be comfortable. You don't want them freaking out all the time.**

You get in a lot of fights?

There's a certain amount of babysitting and hand-holding and ego smoothing that happens when guys start fighting or whatever. In any kind of group dynamic there are going to be arguments. You take five anythings and put them together, that's going to happen. It can drive you crazy too, because you can't make a decision as a group. You know, "so where are we going to eat?" **When five people have to agree on where you're going to eat, you know, you're fucked.**

To them you're the guy that's making them do this stuff. But you're just keeping them moving; it's the record company or manager that's making you do it. But you're in their face every morning saying, "No, get up, you can't sleep another hour. I'm sorry you got drunk last night. It's not my problem."

You ever leave someone before?

Yeah, what are you going to do though, you could do it all the time. I've actually done that. But when you do that you've got to arrange their contingencies. It just happened in San Francisco. One of the guys in Gallon Drunk is a compulsive shopper. And I was like, "OK, meet here at 2:30," and it was 2:45 and he was nowhere to be found. And I was like, "That's it, fine." So I wrote a note that said, "Mike, you're late, fuck you. Take a taxi to Greyhound, take Greyhound to San Jose, take a taxi from the Greyhound station in San Jose to this address. You pay. You fucked up. Love, Woody." And I left the note on the door. And the guys in the band were like, "He'll never do it. You can't do that 'cause he won't figure it out." I'm like, "He figured out how to get on a bus and go shopping wherever the fuck he is, he can take a Greyhound bus. He's not that inept."

You usually end up waiting and you just try to discipline them somehow. But that's really stupid too because you're like, **"OK, I'm going to fine you because you're late." Well money doesn't mean shit to these guys.** What I did to one guy once was, he's kind of a really girlish man and he had this robe that he wore every morning, this satin bathrobe thing. So I took it from him. You know, I was like, "I could fine you, but it doesn't mean anything 'cause you've got plenty of money. And I could beat you up, but it would be like beating up your sister, that doesn't do anything. I'm gonna take your fucking bathrobe. I'm gonna take something that's precious of yours and hide it from you as penalty."

Were you joking?

No, this was it, this was my retribution. You have to exact some kind of punishment. It's like being an elementary school teacher. So I took away his robe, and the guy who was sharing his room said, "You should have seen him last night. He was like, (in an English accent) "Where's my gown? What have you done with my gown?" And he was like, "Woody took it to piss you off for making us wait."

It's another lifestyle. Sounds like family.

Yeah, it's very strange. That's another aspect of it, it is very much of a family. You get to feel like you really care about these guys, and they're your brothers and you look out for them. So sometimes you just kind of cradle him in, you take care of him. You want to find guys that are nice and that you care about, that you get that family feeling for.

When I was out with Red Cross, I didn't really care for their music or for them as individuals, and it sort of reflected in my attitude. They would say, "Why isn't there a crowd here? What's going wrong?" And under your breath you'd say, "You guys suck. Your last record is shit. What am I supposed to do for you?" You can't really say that, but it comes out. If you're thinking it, it comes out in other ways.

What else does a tour manager do?

You've got to find time for them to go sit in a laundromat. Get them across borders, you know, arrange all the immigration paperwork. Check and make sure there's no roaches in their pockets. Keep them from buying drugs, if that's their situation.

Sometimes you have to deal with merchandise. You know, if you don't have somebody out on the road selling your T-shirts, which is what happens quite a lot, you have to find somebody in every city to sell your shirts for you. You have to find some guy or some friend or some waitress or someone that will sit there and sell T-shirts. And you've got to count them in and count them out, and do that money also.

So whose job is it to pick out the girls for the guys to sleep with?

None of the bands I've worked with are getting laid all the time 'cause I'm doing all that alternative-rock stuff. **Sex is the last thing on these types of girls' minds; they just want to drink cappuccino with Michael Stipe.** The sexploitation on heavy-metal tours is enormous though.

Do you ever feel left out of it as the manager?

Yeah, there are times. **You're just the other guy, the other guy that nobody really introduces.** And that happens a bit. Like with the Lemonheads, there were plenty of times where they'd all go to someplace cool, and I'd be like, well, fuck, I've got to go park the van at the hotel and put this piece of gear in safe storage, and I'm not going to get to go to this party and hang out with the guys.

Explain the money thing to me. You're like a road accountant, right?

You have to keep all the books. You have to keep all the receipts for every nickel you spend. It's nickel and dime. Everything that comes in and goes out you have to account for back to management, or, in larger bands, a tour accountancy firm. When you take an advance from a record company to cover your tour support, they want to see that you didn't take this $12,000 and blow it on yourselves. They want to see all your hotel receipts and this and that. So you do all the bookkeeping—you know, I spent this much on hotels, we spent this much in a music store, we got this much from the venue, we got this much from T-shirt revenue. You've got to keep an eye on how much money you have in your budget. You also pay out per-diems—expense money to the bands and the crew.

So there's a lot of accounting?

Yeah, but it's not complicated accounting. **If you can balance a checkbook you can keep a tour going.** And that's what's surprising to me—the accounting is the easiest part of the gig. But I get a lot of calls from people who are happy with their tour manager except for his books. He can't fucking turn in books. It's so easy. You stick all your receipts in one pocket and at the end of the night you write down what all the receipts are for. It's no big deal.

Do you collect from the venue?

Yeah. You go to the promotor or the bar manager, whoever's going to pay you. You've got to keep an eye on what's going on, for things that look suspicious. There are different ways promoters can rip you off. You'll watch how the booth goes to see if they're doing anything strange, like if they're letting a lot of people in for free, or if they're not tearing tickets in half. Because you look out at the room and you see a thousand people and the guy says, "Well, only seven hundred people came in. Here's the three hundred tickets that were never sold." And you're like "No, these are people that you took their ticket and you never ripped it."

Does that happen often, promoters trying to rip you off?

It happens every now and then. Sometimes you just call the agent and tell them and they shut the guy down. They spread it around that the guy's ripping bands off, then he won't get good agents' clients. Sometimes you've just gotta make a deal on the spot; settle out-of-court, as it were. **Sometimes you decide you want to trash the guy's club and take it out physically on him or something.** There was a time in Louisville where I chucked a pool ball through a plate-glass window of a guy's club. You know, I'll just take it out one way or another.

The Lemonheads did this show, a college gig. And the college advisor came, the neck-tie guy who wrote the check for the university. And he was like, "You know, your contract says a sixty-minute set and you guys played about forty-eight minutes. I think we should prorate your check. I just don't think the university got $3,500 worth of entertainment." And I was like, "No. Bring the crowd back in and we'll play another fifteen minutes. It's not going to happen."

What about your role with your bosses—the record company and the band's manager?

Managers and record companies will put bands in impossible situations all the fucking time. Because they never go on the road, they have no idea what the stress is like. Typical example on a recent tour. We had to do a photo shoot for a cover of a single this band is putting out. We were in Austin, Texas, and at seven PM I called the manager and she said, "Tomorrow you have a photo shoot in Dallas at noon." And I'm like, "No, we don't." And she said, "Yeah, we just scheduled it. You have to be in Dallas at noon, so just get up early and go to Dallas." And I'm like, "Fuck you, it's a four-hour drive.

We're not going to get up at nine o'clock in the morning to drive to Dallas to do a photo shoot when they'll be so fucking hungover they won't be able to do a photo shoot anyway. Send the photographer to Austin."

What's the best part about your job?

I like being in different places all the time. I mean, I'm a tourist at heart. I like being in different cities and checking out the cool places to go, you know, finding the funky place to get pork barbecue in South Carolina.

How's the money?

Starting out you work for whatever you can get. I've seen guys go out for $350 a week. At my level it's in the neighborhood of $1,000 a week. Morrissey's tour manager probably made $3,000 a week on the last tour. You can make a lot of money.

People must think you're pretty cool. Seriously.

But it's related to the interest they have in that band. **If I went up to somebody and said, "I'm Michael Bolton's tour manager," they'd go, "Well you must be a total dick."** When actually, being Michael Bolton's tour manager is a tremendous amount more responsibility than being the Lemonheads' tour manager.

What else is cool about being a tour manager?

I've been to Japan, all over Europe. It's pretty easy touring in Europe because the promoters there always give you a guy, he's your driver, etc. There's somebody there to take care of you. The challenging part of that is doing the money conversions and doing different kinds of press. And when you go to Japan, you don't do anything as a tour manager. They give you a promoter, they give you a translator, they give you a driver. They do everything. The minute you get there it's white-glove treatment. You point to your bag and some guy goes and puts a baggage tag on it, and the next time you see it it's in your hotel room, and you're lucky if your socks aren't folded. They're so efficient.

Sounds pretty cool.

I've never had a straight job. I've never had a job where I have to shave every day and wear a tie and tuck my shirt in. And that's a lifestyle choice I made. I live a really casual kind of lifestyle on the road. **I don't want to work for a record company and be an ass-kisser and go to meetings and that kind of stuff.** And that's part of why people perceive it as arrested development. No, I'm not wearing an Armani suit and going to work every day, and I'm not on this path of corporate success or whatever—it doesn't matter. I make plenty of money, and I work the kind of job that I enjoy doing.

TODD SULLIVAN

A&R Executive, Geffen Records, Los Angeles

Twenty-six years old

Background check—Bands on the Geffen label include: Nirvana, Guns N' Roses, Peter Gabriel, and Aerosmith.

You're hanging out waiting for your interview victim in this recording studio in Hollywood, and you can't get a handle on any of it. Is that your interview down there? The guy with the goatee, flannel shirt, and nice, heavy, wide corduroy coat, or some rocker I should recognize, but don't?

And where the hell are you anyway? They've got this fake log-cabin wood panelling and shag-rug thing going that's got the Partridge family written all over it (not literally). Depressing mauve everywhere, pre–"Charlie's Angels". Early seventies, the golden age of rock. Makes you think of Foghat and beanbag chairs. Pretty cheesy. The seventies. Bigger and bolder and more in your face and between your toes—the shag rug—than you care to remember.

How much did it cost to do this place in retro, or have they just not redecorated in twenty years? You have a feeling it's the latter, and so you're wondering why the label that made a killing off of bands like Nirvana and Guns N' Roses couldn't afford to record at a studio that was a little nicer maybe. Huh?

But then Todd—yeah, it was him—leads you into one of the studios. Alright, you're impressed. Definitely the latest. A mixing board twice the size of the Brady family's dining room table, and all these other fancy and expensive-looking things. The guy sitting down plays something for Todd to hear. What does he think? "It's still a little slow. Can you make it just a bit faster," he says, as we cruise into the room that's on the other side of the glass. You know, the room where you always see the singer recording their thing, and always with their hands cupped around their headphones—like in the "We Are the World" video? (Hey, an eighties reference.) *That* room.

When I talked to you on the phone, you mentioned you started out playing in bands. Did you want to be, like, a huge superstar?

I think there was that thought, but there was always reservations. I didn't think as a musician I had the discipline to do it. I was always frustrated because I couldn't write a song. I think that song writing is so much a natural ability, and I couldn't write a song.

So you went behind the scenes. Where did you start?

I started to volunteer at this college radio station. I didn't know what I was going to do. I thought maybe I'd just file records or something like that. But they said, "Well, do you want to be a deejay?" and I was like, "Yeah, of course I want to." I was there for about six months and then I became the music director.

What did that entail?

Records would come in from the record companies and I'd decide what was going to get played. I would listen to everything that came in, so that's where I started to really figure out what was good and what wasn't good. Then you have to organize your on-air staff. You're responsible for these volunteers that are coming in to do shows, so you get people calling you at three in the morning saying, "I can't make it," so you gotta wake up and drive down to the station and do their show.

How beat.

It was just nonstop. I was also going to junior college and managing a record store for money (the college radio station didn't pay) and also being in a band. But it was great. I had such an energy to do it.

Then a friend of mine who had an internship at Geffen Records said, "There's a guy who does regional promotion for Los Angeles who is looking for an intern." So I decided to quit school. I just felt like this was an opportunity to get into a record company that I'd never seen before.

What did you do?

I went in three days a week and helped him on all the piddly stuff: doing mailings, calling radio stations to find out what they played and what they added to the rotations, running errands. We worked out of his house. **It was nice 'cause we would set up the phone in the backyard, catch a tan, and do work.**

This was for no pay?

Yeah, but he was great and really up front with me. He said, "Unfortunately I can't pay you, but this is the experience you'll get, and you'll also meet some people." A lot of it was tedious, but at the same time, I could just see what was going on. We'd go into the main office and I'd just observe and absorb everything.

He would regularly talk to people at the label about jobs for me, and after a year, Geffen offered me a job in the mailroom. **Here I am working for a year for no money and then they get me in the mailroom. And I said, "Well, I'm still willing to do it."** You know, David Geffen got his start in a mailroom, so I didn't think they would try to keep me in there.

How did you get out?

After I worked a year in the mailroom, Tom Zutaut (the A&R guy that signed Guns N' Roses to Geffen) got some sense of my musical knowledge. He would have to go through the mailroom to get to his office every day, and I'd just be working and listening to what I was listening to, and every once in a while we would talk. He'd say, "What are you listening to?" And I'd say "Oh, I'm listening to this and this." And he'd say, "Cool, that sounds cool." And he asked if I wanted to listen to tapes for him.

Was this an intentional strategy of yours to get his attention?

I was never forceful, saying, "God, I really want to get into A&R. I want to work for you." He just had some kind of understanding— he spotted something in me. All the demo tapes that came to him were piling up so he said, "Start listening to these tapes on your own. Keep working in the mailroom and we'll see what happens."

So I started taking tapes home. There was like six hundred tapes that I went through in just over a month, writing comments on each. I picked out about five things and he liked them. So then I was hired as a full-time tape listener.

He just asked you?

One day I get to work and the office manager calls me into her office and says "You're working for Tom Zutaut full-time now." And I'm like, "What?" It was a shock. I was floored. That was my first real step.

So they came to you, you didn't go to them and ask for it?

I was always turned off by people who did that whole schmooze thing. I always wanted to just let my actions or personality speak for itself. **It was frustrating a lot when I was working in the mail-room. I thought, Fuck, it's not going to happen, I've got to do it some other way.** But I never changed that philosophy that I wasn't going to attack these people and say, "Gimme a job." I think Tom saw that I just worked hard and didn't have a problem with sticking around and doing work late. He saw that and said, "This guy's willing to work."

So you were listening to tapes. You didn't have to do any secre-tarial work at all?

No. Nothing like that. It always drove me crazy just being a tape listener because I always thought, This is ridiculous. How can I be getting paid for this? I'd do this anyway. The company is going to have a bad stretch and I'm gonna be out of there. They're gonna get rid of me. That was my big fear. I thought if any part of the company is easily expendable, it's that part. So I always felt real unsure of the job. I just wanted more and more music coming to me—that way I could stay busier. I'd read something about some band in a magazine and call them up and say, "Get me this tape."

I was also out in the clubs six nights a week when I started, seeing bands. Tom said, "Right now you're just going to be my eyes and ears. You're going to be going out and seeing bands, and I want you to keep a low profile, because if people know that you work for me, people are going to start snooping around saying, 'Oh, Tom Zutaut's checking out this band because his assistant was there.'"

Why did he not want that?

Because if another label finds out that someone like a Tom Zutaut is checking out, and is interested in a band, *they* start to get interested, and then the price of the band skyrockets because it ends up in a bidding war.

I'd also fly around the country and see bands. One of the first tapes that I played for Tom out of those six hundred was this band from Seattle. I thought they were really good songwriters. Tom said, "This is a great tape. Why don't you go check them out." And I'm like, "Yes, great, I get to travel!" **When I got up to Seattle and got off the plane and got in my rental car, I thought, This is great—someone's paying me to go listen to music. This is life for me. This is what I want.**

You sign that band?

I went back up to Seattle with Tom to see them again, but live, they weren't what we wanted them to be. They weren't as great as we hoped they'd turn out to be. You gotta know when something is kind of putting your feelings over the top and really just putting a charge in you. And the whole thing just wasn't doing it. Their live show was saying no, it's not enough to make them a great band.

Great songs aren't enough?

There's just got to be an overall specialness about the band. You look for great music, great songs, a vibe personality. And also, people who are willing to work; people who I would think can go through the whole process of becoming a mega-musician.

A lot of bands don't realize that making a record for two months is a lot of work and can be damned tedious and damned frustrating. And also touring. Touring is fucking hard work, you know? In one city one night, another city the next night, and having to sleep on a bus or sometimes on someone's floor. You don't want some mamma's boys that don't want to tour.

A band may have some talent, but they might not be able to organize themselves enough to make it happen. Or they're a little too fucked up on drugs and it's gonna catch up with them a little too soon. You see stumbling blocks like that. Usually though, if a band is great, if they're a great live band and they write great songs and play great, you'll work with them through whatever other kind of bullshit they have.

So how did you go from tape listening to being an A&R guy?

I would just observe and pick up everything that I could—asking the assistants questions, you know, "What's going on?" I'd try to pick up information about studios and how the billing process was done and learn about contracts, so if the time was right I could become a full-fledged A&R person.

Last year I told Tom, "I'm getting a little frustrated. I'm ready to make a move. I'm ready to sign a band." He said, "You have to go out and find a truly great band. You have to find something that you are willing to die for." **He put pressure on me and said, "This is your one shot. If it doesn't happen, you're back to ground zero."**

Were you scared that you might blow your one shot on the wrong thing?

When you hear something great it just clicks. You don't even analyze it—it just clicks inside of you and you forget everything else. You're just taken by it. The first band I signed was this band Sloan. I heard their tape and went to go see them on the road in Vancouver. There was like twenty people there in a place that held about two thousand. They were having all kinds of equipment problems, but I just saw that they were having a great time. They were just enjoying themselves and not worrying about the other stuff. They were playing for the occasion and not taking themselves too seriously, which I liked.

What's your involvement after you sign a band?

You've got to figure out how the record needs to be made. You've got to make sure that you're making the right record for that band. They might have the great songs, but putting that into a record is one of the more difficult things of the job, really. If the band's just a straight-ahead rock band, then maybe you just need to get them a producer who can just capture them live while they're in the studio; just recreate that. So you find the right producer for that.

When they're in the studio making the record, you're overseeing that record. It's your responsibility. You're representing the company, so you've got to make sure that you're getting the best product possible. So sometimes it's fine-tuning things: "You're playing that too fast," or, "You're not singing that with enough energy," or, "That guitar solo's not happening." You know, anything like that.

You'll get that involved?

You try to let the producer and the band do their jobs. **You try to come in with an outside ear, with fresh ears.** Records take about two months to make, and sometimes when the producer and the band is locked in the studio for a month, they can lose objectivity on what they're doing. So sometimes you have to come in and say, "You've gotten off track."

Is there ever any conflict?

Oh yeah, it's not easy. Musicians are sensitive people. When they create something, they want to stick to that. I try to let musicians be themselves, really. But if I feel that a producer has guided them in the wrong direction and it's not really representing them, then it's my job to tell them, even though they might be convinced of what the producer's said.

What are some problems?

It could be a band not wanting to do a certain song that they've written, but *you* know that that song is their best fucking song for this record. You're gonna fight to have that song on the record. Ultimately I'll leave that up to the band, but I'm going to make sure that if they feel differently about it, that they feel stronger than I do. That's when I'll back down. **I don't think I've ever had anyone throwing fists or anything, but it can be really touchy.**

You could be mixing a record and the guitar player might be playing some guitar part that doesn't make sense. And you might say, "You're out of your mind. That doesn't go on that record. That doesn't fit on that record." And they're like, "But I play that. It's this new thing that I'm trying."

Do they ever go, "Fuck you, you're just a suit"?

Yeah. But that's a matter of when you sign a band, to make sure that you're seeing eye to eye musically. The bands come up with the music. I can't write songs. I have to realize that and be sensitive to that myself. But usually when you start working with a band, they'll start bouncing ideas off you.

You've also got to try to keep the record on budget, on your contractual budget. Sometimes that goes over.

Why would it go over?

Oh, god. A singer getting sick. In one case, a guitarist was recording an album out of his home town and he got homesick, and his guitar playing just went downhill. It was such a struggle to get the record finished because he was so homesick for his girlfriend. Ultimately she ended up flying out and the record got done.

That's pretty temperamental.

So often musicians are eccentric and out of their minds; that's what tends to make them so interesting. It tends to make for exciting music too. If a lot of people met their idols they could end up really disappointed.

Why, because they're nuts?

Yeah. Really. That's the way it is. I was at a real nice restaurant with this band Jackyl. This guy from BMI music had taken us out. And the band asked the guy, "Hey, you ever seen a Cornish game hen?" And this guy's like, "No, never have." And all of a sudden all five members of the band pull down their pants and lift up their balls and say, "This is a Cornish game hen." And then they bumped each other's balls—in the middle of this restaurant. And I'm like, "Wow." People were pretty stunned.

The singer from that same band interrupted a lunch that was going on between one of our promotion people and a radio programmer. **He interrupted their lunch in the restaurant by coming in with a chain saw, taking a chain saw to their table, and carving the name "Jackyl" into it.**

Why?

Just to make their point. Just so they would know the band. He knew this lunch was going on, he wanted to have an impact, and it worked for him. But he also got sued by some of the people in the restaurant, obviously just looking for money by saying they were scared out of their fucking mind—that there's this long-haired dude with a chain saw coming in and grinding up the table.

How do you deal?

You can't control people. These people are going to be who they are. Once you realize that, you're a little bit more at ease.

How about the drug thing—how do you deal with that?

It hasn't come to the point where I've been afraid that someone's gonna die, or I felt like it's completely affected their work in a *negative* way. I've seen band members waste their life on that shit. You see 'em get clean and then, you know....

Do you like for your bands to do wild things to get press?

I like it to be real. I wouldn't want to stage anything. I definitely think there's some truth to any kind of publicity is good. But I don't go around looking for a band, like, "Oh, this band's going to get in trouble—that will be great." The music has got to be first. But I definitely like it when a band is kind of edgy. **The best times of rock-and-roll music to me is when I see a band and I feel like I'm gonna die.** I feel like the whole place can fall apart at any minute. I think rock and roll should be threatening.

Is your job done when the record is done?

At some companies A&R is just signing the band and making the record, and then they hand off the record to the product manager who looks after everything after that point. At Geffen an A&R person not only signs the band and makes the record, but is the product manager too—looking after everything. I kind of act as a manager within the company for that particular act. I've got to look after the artwork. Make sure the band's image is presented in the right light. Make sure that the art director knows what the band is trying to get across. The videos, the promotions, choosing singles.

Choosing singles?

OK, you're done with the record. You know that this one song is absolutely amazing, but your promotion people say, "No, we like *this* song. It's going to be a lot easier for us to get on the radio." You have to let them know that it might not be the right song of this band for people to hear first. Like a ballad or something. A ballad may be easy to get on the radio, but you know that people who are really going to like this band are going to be the ones that like the song with the guitar and feedback on it, and not the ballad. So you've got to say, "Look, it's gonna be harder work to get this song on the radio...."

Does promotion ever to say to you, "Todd, I can't do anything with these guys."

Yeah, and that's when you're like a promotion person to them, because you're trying to sell them on your group. That's why it's so important to sign bands that you love, because you come up against these roadblocks. You try to make the company understand this band that you've signed. You want them to do the best for the band and for the record. And they might not always see it or hear it right off.

What else can be frustrating?

Telling people no. There's always people trying to get record contracts, and 99.9 percent of the time you're saying no. And that's an incredible drag. "Who are you to say no? You're just one person." That's what their thoughts are. **It's not fun telling people no. You'd rather say yes and make their day. That's probably the worst part of it—saying, "Don't quit your day job."**

How about stress?

The stress that goes along with spending half a million dollars every time you put out a record. There's so many A&R people that come and go. **You don't sign a band that sells records, you're outta there. It's just a matter of survival.** Record companies have to have people that are finding bands that sell records. If they're not, they need to find someone who is.

How about the lifestyle?

It's virtually a twenty-four-hour-a-day job. You're constantly around it. **You get calls at three AM from musicians who are freaking out about something, or want to know something, or want you to bail them out of jail.** It's twenty-four hours. I'm always around music. It's always in the back of my head. I'm always thinking about it. "How can we market this band to get them across to people? Who am I going to get to manage this band? Who am I going to get to produce this band? Why aren't people responding?"

It's hard to have a girlfriend or personal life when you're constantly out and constantly working. It gets to be a struggle. If I go in the office at ten-thirty in the morning and I work until eight PM, and then I go out and see a band, or I go out and have dinner with a manager, or I go to the studio, or I go out and have a meeting with the band or a publisher...It's pretty nonstop. But that's the nice thing about it also, is that you're not always at your desk just doing that paperwork.

I try not to let it overdominate my life. I have to remind myself to do other things and see how other people live.

Words From On High:
Advice From the Vice President of Staffing Development at Sony Music on Breaking In

GLORIA BURNETT

Vice President, Staffing Development, Sony Music, New York City

Background check—Sony owns Columbia (Bruce Springsteen, Billy Joel, Mariah Carey) and Epic Records (Michael Jackson, Pearl Jam), each of which has its own satellite labels, such as Chaos at Columbia. They also distribute a bunch of small labels such as Def Jam. Its offices are in New York and L.A.

Before I started the actual interview, I commented to Gloria how nice her staff was to me, unlike some other people at record companies—smaller ones even—who were real mean when I asked to speak with someone high up about doing an interview. Gloria responded, somewhat in their defense: "On one August day—between individuals calling from within the company and unsolicited calls—I averaged 110 calls. It's impossible. It can be very difficult, so you have individuals running interference. One thing we pride ourselves on, though, is the way and the manner we treat people over the phone.

"I just called a young woman back today who called two weeks ago asking about our college rep program and she thanked me so much. She was so thankful that I actually called her back. Don't put *that* in the book!" (Laughs.)

Absolutely not.

How do you go about hiring?

First of all, we have a list which is for internal people only that lists every opening. We try to promote and move our people as much as possible. Internal movement and development is very important to us.

For entry level, 90 percent of the time you're talking about clerical positions. So for administrative assistants, the first things we look for are the skills necessary. We have a very sophisticated clerical staff. It may not matter to the hiring executive if this individual has A&R experience, or has even worked in a music company. It may not matter. We look for certain computer and clerical skills. There's generally too much work that needs to be generated. It's a plus if they've had an internship, because then they understand the flow of a music company, but the first thing we look for are the skills.

How many resumes do you get?

I would say we average between seventy and eighty a day. Then there are periods, like now, when people are getting out of school when we get even more than that.

Do you look at them?

Resumes become a source for us, especially for recruiting nonexempt jobs. We look at and respond to every one of them.

When we're filling a position, we go to agencies, we look at our write-in mail and employee referrals. Temping is a good way. You're in the building, you know the people, you get to know Human Resources, you get to know the departments.

What impresses you in an interview?

Communication skills. They have to be able to express their interest, express their desire to get in to the company.

It's important to show that?

Yes. Definitely.

How do some people not do that?

They come in, they don't show enthusiasm, they're nonverbal. They're very nice, but they're shy. You have to be able to present yourself in a positive manner, and, unfortunately, I don't have much time to try to pull things out of you. I just don't have the time, although I will spend five minutes trying to make an individual feel very comfortable. So work through the nervousness. You're dealing with an executive that has a short period of time.

I'm also interested in someone who has done their research. How much do they really know about us? Do as much research as possible about the company. Call ahead of time and say, "Can you send me information about your company?" Read the annual report. Read the trades. Look at MTV. Find out what's going on.

I'll tell you what turns me off in an interview: the arrogance, the attitude that "I am entitled." It can show itself in different ways—the way they present themselves, their body language. You might ask them, "Why do you want to be in this industry?" And there's a look of, "Why are you asking me this? I'm here. Why are you asking me why I want to be in this industry?" And they'll give a short answer: "Because I like it." Or, "My uncle's in the industry."

So the type of person you look for?

We look at the overall personality. People do not operate in a vacuum. You have to look at how they're going to interact with everyone else. We are strictly a team effort here. So you constantly try to match up personalities. And you don't have to be bubbly and sweet all the time. Now, how do you get a sense of how they're going to fit in? It can be from the way the individual asks me questions, even. Questions are very important. It shows someone who wants to learn. We are interested in individuals who are eager to learn.

Are grades important?

We do not harp on grades. They're just a bench mark. It gives you a feel for the person. Will it be a deciding factor if the person gets the job or not? Not really. But that depends upon the hiring supervisor. Suppose two candidates are completely equal. Will the grades give leverage to the other? Maybe, depending upon the department.

Any creative accounts of someone trying to get a job here?

An individual, a young guy out of school trying desperately to get in, would constantly call. But he was very nice, not offensive, not arrogant, not obnoxious. He would call and call and call and call. He would send resumes. This was at our old building. Next to that building there used to be a brownstone there. He had his resume printed on a sheet and he hung it from the top of the brownstone. He got a job.

I had an individual constantly call me. A nice kid. He'd call me and call me and send me resumes. One day I get a brown paper bag with a string around it with my name on the bag. Something was in this bag. I look in the bag and I see a bottle of Windex. There was a note attached that said, "I will do anything to get into this company including windows." I said, I like that. I know he was seen by some-body. Did he get a job? I'm not sure.

Here's an interesting story. I was very impressed with this. An individual was referred to me by an employee. A very nice, intelli-gent guy, from a very good college. He was currently in an executive trainee program, a wonderful program at another company. He said, "I don't want this, I want to be in the music business." I said "You're not coming into this business. What are you going to do? You're going to start off as a secretary." I told him that he should stay in that program. I had no idea what might come up for him, but I told him he could stay in touch with me.

About three weeks later my receptionist was out ill, so they called for a temp. I walk in and this young man had quit his job and is now there as my receptionist. He had called the office to find out which temp agencies we used. I walked in and I'm saying, "I don't have an appointment with you." He said "No, I'm your temp for today." I said "What do you mean you're my temp for the day?" (Laughs.) I said, "Your parents paid for you to go to this school and you quit your job?" I said, "Give me your parents' number. I'm calling them now, because if my kids ever did this I'd kill them." (Laughs.) He was really a great kid. He temped for two or three days. I spoke to my manager and I said, "We've got to get him in here. We just have to." He temped for a month or so and we got him a job.

How about kids getting stuck entry level once they're in?

We try to make them think beyond that one area. It's very important for individuals to realize that sometimes you have to move laterally to move up two steps. And people don't get that through their heads because society says only move forward. Sometimes it's necessary to reposition yourself. Say you're in publicity and you want to get into A&R and there's an assistant position at the same level in A&R. Consider it; you want to get into the department. When you're starting out, you also should network and become known throughout the company.

Moving up the Ladder

10

From Being an Assistant to Having One

WAITING FOR SOMEONE TO KICK THE BUCKET

Somebody dies. Somebody quits. Somebody retires. Somebody gets sent to jail. When you're an assistant and you don't want to be an assistant anymore, you want to be a real person, these occurrences never seem to happen. You're just waiting for someone to keel over at their desk and be carted away down the service elevator.

What's worse, the people above you with the jobs you want are, in most cases, baby boomers. Those mid-thirty, nowhere-near-retirement, healthy, Chinese-chicken-salad–eating, Stairmaster-climbing, mountain biking, trying-to-make-up-for-all-the-drugs-they-did-in-the-seventies, type of people. In other words, they ain't going nowhere—by death or by choice. They've got a mortgage, a kid, a Saab, stock options; they're there for life. There to make upstarts like yourself crazy.

First Problem: This Ain't IBM or Apple

Generally, the companies within the eight industries covered in this book are cottage industries in a sense. Mom and pop shops. They do not recruit on colleges. They do not have training programs or career development offices like you may find at Apple Computer or Pfizer Chemical. They're ladderless industries with no promotion line to wait in.

So how do you go from being this low-life human coffeemaker to being a real person? It's actually quite simple. I'll tell you what it is. I'll fill some more pages with a bunch of advice and stuff. But ultimately it all comes goes back to the same thing, which is absolutely crucial. Alright, here it is: You've got to want it. That's it. Whoever wants it the most gets it.

Fortunately, or unfortunately, this may go against how you thought it worked, i.e., sleeping with the boss, nepotism, being a kiss-ass, being really smart and charming, blah blah blah. A little of all of these won't hurt you and might be necessary (now, I'm not saying to jump in bed with your boss), but without that *je ne sais quoi*, that burning desire, the want, the desire to prove yourself—you ain't got a chance.

So if you don't really want it, travel around the world, watch a lot of TV and get really bored until you do. Because in order to do the stuff that I'm gonna lay out, it's absolutely necessary.

Keeping You in Your Place

Alright, say you're lucky and someone decides to give you money, a job, because the schmuck before you who used to answer the phone, type things, get coffee, pick up the boss's dry cleaning, water the plants, etc., got sick of it, decided it wasn't worth it, gave up and went home.

Funny. When they hired you, you *thought* you heard them say, "We're looking for smart people who are ambitious, who will grow with the company, blah blah blah." Well, they're not going to attract you to the job by saying, "We want someone who's going to be content answering the phones and doing all the shit work with no chance of advancement."

What am I getting at? I think it's this: When you're hired as an assistant, you're there to provide assistance. (Clever, huh?) Think about it. They've dipped into their profits to hire someone to make their lives easier and to help them do their jobs better. **They haven't hired you thinking, "Oh, won't he eventually be able to do my job great one day?"**

So the sad truth is, nobody really cares if you move up or not. I know, it's a bummer. But it's worse. Not only does no one care, there are actually people like yourself—competitive, power hungry, ambitious overachievers—who don't want you to succeed, who would gladly step over your dead body to get ahead of you. To get that promotion.

Stop. Hold it. Back up. What I've just said is probably the biggest fallacy a young person believes about the working world—that you get "promoted." Listen up 'cause this is important. Nobody says, "Hey, you've been doing a great job. Here's your reward: You're promoted." Get over that idea now. I'm telling you, if you ever move up the ladder, get "promoted," you're not going to be grateful to anybody but yourself.

A Word About Smarts

There's something you've got to understand. When you're talking about moving up the ladder, being smart and competent is, like, maybe half of it. What it all comes down to is results. Are you the person who gets results or not. That's what matters. Nobody really cares if you went to Harvard or Central Connecticut State College once you're in the door. They're looking for workaholics. Especially in the consolidating-three-jobs-into-one nineties.

Having an Opinion

One thing that separates the people who move up the ladder from those who don't—something that doesn't show up on standardized test scores and is not emblazed on your diploma—is an opinion. Do you have one or not? You can be the best assistant in the world. Always on time, very organized, willing to stay late to complete a task, always cheerful and energetic. These are great and absolutely necessary qualities one must have to get ahead. But they mean nothing if you, as a person, don't have your own sense of taste, convictions, and ideas—all of which I will classify as having an opinion.

You could say that there might be a problem with having an opinion. Hell, yours could be wrong. You know what? It doesn't matter. Better to have an opinion and to voice it (as long as you can support it) than to not have one at all. Your bosses are bosses just for that reason: They have opinions and ideas which they then carry out. So if you hope to ever move up in your company, you must be willing to assert an opinion and stick to it—just as your boss would. Even if they don't agree with you, at least they know that you're thinking, that you have ideas, that you're someone who's not interested in being an assistant or receptionist all your life.

Consider Emily Gerson-Saines's situation when she was an assistant at ICM talent agency. She said, "I worked really long hours there and very hard. More often than not I worked until nine at night. But just working very hard doesn't mean anything."

Working until nine at night doesn't mean anything? If that won't get you ahead, what will? Emily goes on to explain,"I talked to the agents about ideas—who I thought were good actors—and I think they started to respect my taste over time. They would listen to my suggestions about actors for certain parts and such, and then they gave me some small movies to cast. Some of the people I suggested for parts wound up getting offers."

Even though Emily was just an assistant, she thought and acted like an agent—the job title she wanted. She eventually got it.

While some employers don't really care if you have an opinion or not—they just want their lives made easy—others expect it. Laurence Schwartz from New Line Cinema says in his interview, "What I look for is people who have ideas of what to make films about."

I love that quote. It's so simple. He's an executive at a film company who is responsible for making films. And if you're going to make a film, you have to have a subject, an idea. That means having an opinion of what would make a good film. The simplicity of that quote can be applied to every job. If you work for a newspaper and want to move up, you have to have ideas of what's newsworthy. Or say you work for a book publisher, you have to have ideas of what material is worth investing money in to publish it.

Don't Take My Word for It...

Jenna Hull from HarperCollins: "You have to have a really strong opinion, I think, in some ways even if you're wrong a lot. You're always going to be gung ho over a book that is just going to die without a trace. You go into these meetings saying, 'I want *this* much money. It will sell *this* many copies.' And people are going to argue with you. I was just very sure of my own taste."

Any job that I would classify as a hot job requires that you have an opinion—that you have ideas. If it doesn't require that, then the job is probably boring and unchallenging. So get used to the idea of being someone who has something to say.

Salesmanship: Selling Your Ideas

When you realize that you've got something to say, you then have to sell it. Therefore, a persuasive personality is a must. TV, film, publishing, advertising, the art world, in general, you're talking about industries that attract confident people. I don't think someone would even attempt landing one of these elusive glamourous careers if they weren't confident, if not arrogant. These are big ego industries whereby in order to be successful you must be persuasive.

You're selling. Whatever it is, you're selling. You're selling your idea of what to make a TV show about, what book is worth publishing, why a certain actor would be great for David Letterman to have on his show, why you should make a certain product over another one, why a potential client should use your company's services over another one's.

I'm not sure what good this does you as a reader. Either you're someone who is convincing and outspoken or you're not. I'm not sure if it's something you can practice on your dog. But go ahead and try. We'll do a little *What Color Is Your Parachute*–type exercise. Try to convince your dog that, in fact, he *would* be happier sleeping outside in his dog house that is presently being attacked by pellets of hail than inside on the nice cushy sofa. If you don't have a dog, pretend. How did you do? Is the dog outside? If not, you might consider being an accountant or something.

Don't Take My Word for It...

Listen to Jeremy Spiegel (producer, "A Current Affair"), "I'm like a salesman sometimes. I mean, to be a producer on a TV show like this, you have to be a salesman. You want to hear me be a salesman? (Picks up the phone) Hi, this is Jeremy Spiegel from 'A Current Affair.' We took an interest in your story. It's very compelling and I think it would be something to bring to national attention; we're a nationally syndicated show...."

Author's note: If you can convince someone to come on "A Current Affair," well, then, you're doing alright.

Book editing. Publishing. Seems pretty docile, right? A little ivory towerish, a little removed from the real world. Basically, a place for bookworms. Not! Listen to Jenna Hull from HarperCollins about what it's like for an editor to get their company to buy a book they want to edit: "When you want to acquire something, you get called into this frightening meeting where they all want to say no to you, and you pitch your brains out. There's a lot of pitching all the way along. I talk to people and they're like, 'Oh, I love books. I love to read. I should go into publishing.' And in some ways it's not suited for people who like to be quiet and read a lot, because there's a lot of other garbage that you do."

Writer's Disclaimer...Apology...Advice (Whatever)

Does all this just sound too ghastly and frightening? Am I driving all of you away from even joining the workforce, leading you towards a hunkered-down-in-your-parents'-basement lifestyle? Listen, I know this whole selling thing sounds pretty ugly, but if you believe in what you're selling, then it's easy. Don't worry about it. If you don't, if you're trying to sell Disney on some lame movie that you think has no redeeming qualities at all (hmm, hard to imagine), or sell Sony Music on some band that's all hair, period, then your job is not only going to be difficult, it's also going to suck. So what's my advice? As I said in the "Strategies for Landing the Hot Job" chapter, try to work for a company that produces things that you either like or believe in.

A Mix of Confidence and Arrogance

When we're talking about selling and/or having an opinion, it requires a degree of confidence and arrogance. Because when you're saying, "I think we should do this"—whatever it is—in effect, what you're saying is that you should do it instead of the way it's been done. Instead of doing it somebody else's way.

Consider Robin Danielson's thoughts on what makes a successful advertising copywriter: "It's generally a group of extremely egotistical young men, and the system makes them that way. Because **in order to get work sold in a bullpen environment, it's the person who says, 'I've got the biggest dick,' that's the guy who wins.** A lot of times the work is relatively equal. The stuff that gets through is very often just somebody who's willing to say, 'I am king of the fucking world.' So successful creatives are trained to be assholes."

"I think you have to have a certain amount of self-confidence," says Laurence Schwartz about being a film exec. "I don't think you have to be a killer. That's not appealing to me, people who have that shark mentality. Although I can't say that that's not a good thing to have, because a lot of the people that make it are all about that."

Good News for Wallflowers

I've got some good news for you docile types. I think the only thing you need to do as an assistant when it comes to demonstrating that you're not a wimp, that you can put up a fight, that you can swim with the sharks, blah, blah, blah, is just stick up for what you believe in. Which goes back to having an opinion and sticking by it, which means...

Don't Be a "Yes" Man

When you're starting out in the real world, you should want nothing more than to please your boss, and so, it can be easy to completely lose your identity. You find yourself agreeing with him about the stupidest things. From hating the movie that he saw last weekend (which you actually kind of liked), to hating mayonnaise on bologna sandwiches as well. With one boss, I actually took the time to say, "Yeah, I hate mayo on bologna too." Why would you do it? **It's like I was on a neverending date with my boss, always afraid of hating or liking the wrong things.** Your boss is going to respect you and think that you actually have a brain if you disagree with him once in a while.

But if you're lucky enough and your boss hands you a letter or report he wrote or something and says, "What do you think?" If you don't especially like it, well, you better say something like, "I like it, but maybe it'll be better if you add this, or take out that." When disagreeing, or making suggestions, use a little diplomacy. But you know that.

The Relationship You Want

Basically, the relationship that you want to establish with your boss, that you *must* establish, is that of a peer. **Yeah, you're still that chump who's picking up dry cleaning and watering cacti, but that doesn't mean that you have to *act* like an indentured servant.** Because if you don't get him to think of you as a peer, as someone capable of doing what he does, then he'll never give you that opportunity. How do you do that?

Walk the Walk; Talk the Talk

A lot of this whole business thing is a game. It's posturing. It's a matter of giving people a certain impression. Making them think that you're smart, that you're on the ball, that you're promotable. And a lot of that is demonstrated by an image. It's why you see obnoxious twenty-four-year-old movie execs running around in faux Armani suits, hopping into their leased BMWs.

It's a way to carry yourself. The way you talk, the way you look (we'll get to this one in a while). Having a presence. When you and Mr. Thirty-five-year-old executive are talking while waiting for the elevator, an outside observer shouldn't be able to tell that you don't have the same job as the aforementioned balding guy next to you.

Just don't act like a punk. Try to act at least a little professional. When I go visit my friends (who have real jobs) at work, I can spot the serious low-level intern or assistant who wants to be promoted from the punk who's bouncing off the walls.

The Image Factor

This is the best advice you'll ever get on appearance. By Robin Danielson:

"It's not necessarily about looking neat, it's about looking important," Robin points out. "It is really true to dress for the job you want, not for the job you have. The thing about advertising is, the first question is, 'Can you go to the client?' **If you want somebody to feel like they can trust you to do the job of the person that's above you, then every day you should** *look* **like they could trust you to do the job of the person that's above you.** Even if you think you know what you're doing that day and don't think you need to be dressed up to be doing any of it. The first time you might get the chance to do something is when it's spontaneous, not when it's planned. When somebody says, 'Oh shit, who can do that?'

"I had a girl who worked as the account assistant and she basically got herself stuck for a good six months longer than she needed to, purely on the basis of the way she dressed. I mean, people are not going to pull you aside and tell you, 'Cut it out.' People aren't going to be that nice to you."

Style + Confidence = Importance

I think the first thing Robin said is right on, the part about not necessarily looking neat, but looking important. It's totally true. In the entertainment biz, image is definitely a factor. It's not about a shirt and tie, it's about *the* shirt and tie. The fact is, and I really believe this, a sense of hip style with attitude goes a long way in the entertainment biz. I'm not talking about lip rings and leather, nothing too wild. Fashion that you see in *Details* or *Vogue* magazine. You know, not the Brooks Brothers, Laura Ashley, Banana Republic crap. If you can pull off something that's a little different, it shows confidence, a little arrogance, and an awareness of what's going on out there.

WORD INTO ACTION: THE WORK

Showing your boss that you have a brain. Proving to him that you have prowess beyond channel surfing. That just because you're an *x*'er, doesn't mean that you're a vidiot.

Don't Give Me No Lip

A lot of entry-level people are stupid. They're like, "I'm hot stuff, I'm a graduate." Wake up baby, you're at the bottom. Yeah, maybe they've tossed you some bone of a title with the word "associate" in it. Truth is, you ain't much more than Alice from "The Brady Bunch." You're there to do the crap that nobody else wants to do. Picking up your boss's dry cleaning or someone's mother at the airport. Getting coffee. Straightening your boss's desk.

Not fair? Not what you were hired for? Listen, if someone's given you a job, you're lucky. The only reason you're there is because someone with energy and endurance that you can't even fathom created something from nothing and is now able to offer people like you money. So in my book, employers are god. They should be able to ask you to do anything, even if you don't think it falls within the realm of your responsibility.

Really, give up the notion of being above anything right now. If your boss tells you to do the dishes and if you do it begrudgingly, you're being foolish. He's not doing it to punish you. In his mind, his money and manpower is being spent best by having you, rather than someone else, do it. **Complaining isn't going to urge him to have someone else do the dishes. Demonstrating that your time is too valuable to do that crap will.**

Who Are You?

If there is one quality that all of the successful young people interviewed share, one thing that stands out so clearly as being a major reason why they advanced in their careers, it would have to be enthusiasm to work. Just the willingness to do anything. So, as John Verrilli says, "You either establish yourself as a hard worker or you don't." And people are going to notice.

Becky Coleman has some good advice for someone starting out. "I'll do people favors and hire them if they really want to get in as a P.A. (production assistant—entry level). I'll open the door for them. But unless they really kick it in, I'll never ask them back. You know what I'm saying? You want people who really are hungry. And there just doesn't seem to be any of that anymore. I run into that so rarely nowadays. I want people who are like me; who just work like slaves to get where they want to go."

So, you've got two options. You're either going to be that person who just becomes so valuable that they can't live without you. Or you're not. You'll work relatively hard. Hard enough. And then you'll start bitching about the person who sailed by you and got the position you wanted to get. That person being the former of the two types. In every company there's always a pathetic whiner, "Whose ass did they kiss to get that promotion?" And the person who got the promotion.

"Trust Me"

Again, don't think of it as a promotion. What it actually is is their letting you do the work that they do. And the only way that's going to happen is if they trust you to do it. You have to ask for it and say, "Hey, can I do that?" They're not going to just hand it to you. (I'll get to this in a bit.) But before they'll let you do that, you have to prove yourself. You have to show them that if they do let you do something, you're going to do it great. **You have to show them that you are nothing short of a perfectionist.**

Listen to Becky Coleman about when she started entry level with a TV commercial production company. "They were so afraid to give away the slightest bit of responsibility to anyone because they might fuck it up. So if you can't sharpen pencils well, no one's going to give you the next step. So I literally would make sure that every single person there had sharp pencils and staples in their stapler."

And when you demonstrate to people that you're really conscientious and really thorough, it also makes them like you and grow to depend on you. As Becky goes on to explain: "If you subtly make someone's life really easy and then you go away for a minute, they realize you've been doing all these things. The easier you make other people's lives, the more they'll like you and need you around."

And that's an important thing. You need people to want and need you around. Because when you're an assistant, you're basically like the little brother or sister nobody wants around, unless it's for something like getting somebody's lunch. It can be cliquish. People who've been at a company for a while will probably want to exclude you from things that they do.

But if you're busting your ass for them, they're going to pick up on it. And then when they're hanging out talking about a strategy for marketing the film *Three Men and a Grown-Up Sex Vixen*, maybe they'll let you throw in your two cents. If you've busted your butt for them, they'll be cool and allow you that courtesy. They'll indulge you. You've earned the right to their ears. To be heard. If you've just done your job, however, without going out of your way to please these people and make their lives easier, then they have no reason at all to listen to you. In their minds, they don't owe you anything.

The Shit Work

Pretty much everyone I spoke with told me stories of how interns and assistants blew their chances by having an attitude about doing the shit work, about paying their dues. Greg Drebin from MTV says it best.

"A lot of people come in and are like, 'Well, I'm making copies but that's really beneath me.' But if you're making copies, be damn good at making copies. If you're just going through the motions and it's obvious that you're sick of it and you want to get out, no one is going to let you do anything. Because then it's like, 'Well, if I hire you, are you going to do the same thing to me?' Are you going to say, 'Well, yeah, he hired me to do this, but what I really want to do is this, so I'll just go through the motions here.' Uh-uh. I want someone who's going to be 110 percent."

So, as Ray Rogers from *Interview* magazine says, "Be psyched to do everything and they'll give you more."

And, as Spike Feresten from "Late Night With David Letterman" says, "You want me to get coffee, I'll get coffee."

A cynic or veteran might respond to the "be psyched to do everything..." quote by quipping, "Yeah, they'll give you more Rolodex cards to type out." They would have a good point. Hell, they'd be right. That quote should really read, "Be psyched to do everything and they'll *allow* you to do more." The stuff you want to do, i.e., the stuff your boss does, is something you're going to have to grab and lobby for. Read on.

Doing More Than What Your Job Description Says

Nobody has time to watch over you, to offer you things to do, to keep you challenged and entertained. They've got their own stuff to do. Yeah, they're going to watch after you and make sure you're doing your job, but that's probably going to be it. **Nobody is going to say, "You know, if you're interested in advancing here then you should do this and this."** It isn't going to happen. You've got to make things happen on your own.

Listen to how Jeremy Spiegel from "A Current Affair" made it happen for himself. "You can't come in here with the attitude that you're going to only do what they allow you to do. You've got to drive yourself to do more. I have no problem getting people coffee, but I really wanted to milk it (his internship) for all it was worth. I pushed myself and got myself into setting up stories, which is an actual position here. I said, 'Hey, can I start working on some stories?' And you know, at first they were a little hesitant...."

When I asked Ray Rogers from *Interview* magazine how he got to write his first record review, if they handed it to him and said, "Here, review it." His answer: "No. I was real persistent. If I hadn't pushed for that they wouldn't have given me anything. You know, they're not going to come to you with a little silver platter and say, 'We would be honored if you would do a review of this new record.' Or, 'We would be honored for you to write our next feature story on music.' You know, they're not going to come to you and do that. So you've got to fight."

On Your Own Time

So don't wait around for your boss to give you something challenging to do. Grab it. Tell your boss what you want to do and do it. It's going to mean doing things after work or coming in on weekends, because you're still going to have your old responsibilities to tend to.

Don't Take My Word for It...

A perfect example: After a year and a half of being a production assistant at Fox News, the next step for John Verrilli, as he saw it, was to become a writer. So what do you do, wait for somebody to say, "OK, you've been a great production assistant, now you're a writer?" No. You simply have to start doing the job you want. So John came in on weekends.

"At first they weren't paying me," John says. "And, so, I'd come in and wouldn't get paid. And then after a while when they started using my stuff they said, 'OK, we'll pay you.' And eventually they made me a writer on the weekends."

Same thing with Farrah Greenberg from *Elle* magazine. When an assistant stylist position became available, the reason Farrah got it is clear. She says, "During that year when I was assistant to the senior editor I would volunteer to assist one of the stylists when they needed help." So even though the job "was hard to get, because she was interviewing a lot of people," Farrah got the job because, as she says, "I knew how to do it."

Jeremy Spiegel: "A lot of what I'd do when I was an intern was stay after hours, because a lot of people work at night cutting segments. I'd work the phones until eight PM and then go back to the edit room and stay until three AM just to watch and ask questions and see how they put a show together. That's how I learned.

So, as Greg Drebin says, **"Nobody's job is so defined that they can't do something else."** Therefore, once you're in, it's really what you make of it.

You Don't Work in a Vacuum

I think someone you have to watch out for is the person you don't think you have to impress or watch out for. Not to make you paranoid or anything, but there are a lot of people out there who, in effect, act as spies, reporting back to your boss about the quality of work they perceive you're doing. Or more obviously, about something bad you might have done.

It was at one of my first real office jobs. It was a small office, about ten of us. The boss was out at some afternoon meeting or something, and his wife happened to be hanging out at the office that day. She was cool. I liked her. Nice woman. So, the boss gets back, and as I'm leaving the office at around six PM, he pulls me into his office. "Try to keep the personal calls to a minimum, OK?" he tells me. What was that about? I thought. Yeah, I had a late lunch at my desk while talking on the phone, but how would he know that? The wife. She was a snitch. Yeah, this is an obvious spy, but consider this story.

An Obnoxious Little Story

Here's a little story about something that happened to me last week. I'm writing my career book, it's four PM and I'm now thinking about plans for tonight. So I call my friend. This friend is vice president of a $55-million-a-year clothing company.

"Hi, is Joe there?" I ask the receptionist in the New York office. "No, he's not," she replies. Pause. "Is he out of town or just out for the day?" I ask. "I think he's out of town," she says. Pause. "So he won't be in today?" I ask. "I don't think so, but don't quote me on it." "Is he in the main office in Pennsylvania?" I ask. "I don't really know. Do you want me to find out?" she says. "Do you want me to wring your stupid little neck?" I want to say. Instead I think I said, "That would be great."

Fun huh? I think this is a wonderful little portrait of the type of person who will always be answering phones. Yeah, it's quite obvious that immediately she should have said, "Hold on one minute and I'll find out where he can be reached." Her bigger mistake though was demonstrating her utter incompetence to me, the caller, someone she doesn't know.

I, being friends with Joe, her boss, will most likely recount this little story to him. Maybe you're saying, "What's the big deal? God, this guy Charlie's a real prick." Well, maybe I am, I don't know. I just know that if I were my friend, I would be very upset that the receptionist I employ is useless and lazy.

Oh, my god. There's this receptionist at this record company that I called the other day. This person was so short and snappy with me,

I couldn't believe it. I think I must be a real jerk or something, because if I had known anybody high up at that company, I totally would have called and raised hell, and even exaggerated the extent of how rude this person was to me.

But the real issue at hand here is not how people like me might be unsympathetic egomaniacs. It goes beyond that. What it says to me, the caller, is that this person, this assistant, this phone answerer, this peon, can't hack the pressure. **When you are anything but cool and under control and charming, you're basically telling the world of callers out there that the simple duty of answering phone calls is too much for you;** that you crack under the slightest bit of pressure. So don't think it makes you sound important by sounding busy or by having an attitude when you answer the phone. It doesn't. It makes you look stupid, and it may get back to your boss.

But even if it doesn't get back to your boss (but I'm sure he will pick up on your little problem), you've got to realize that you're not making many fans out there. You're shooting yourself in the foot, when you should be kissing theirs. The people calling for your boss are the ones that, if you're good and very helpful to them, will probably wind up being your boss one day. It's how it all works.

That's how it worked for Michael Catcher. While in New York, Michael was helpful on the phone and impressed these casting directors in L.A. enough so for them to ask him to move out there and work for them. And, in a higher capacity. He says, "That's how I actually met my bosses now. They were casting different things from L.A. So when they got "The Wonder Years" for ABC, they called me in New York and asked if I would be interested in coming out there to cast "The Wonder Years" as a casting director. And I'm like, 'Sure.'"

So you made an impression on them when you were an associate with Deb and Don.

"They would talk to *me* and I would tell Deb and Don what the situation was. I was like a point man."

*Did you know that's how things worked, that that's how you
wind up getting jobs, from people that you talk to on the phone
in other situations?*

"No, at first you don't realize it. And it's funny because you *do*
burn bridges, because you don't know who certain people are, and
you *do* give them some attitude. Or you don't do the job as well as
they want you to and you have no idea who they are."

"Thanks for Being Patient. You're Next." Not!

By now it should be pretty clear that there is no promotion line.
You know, "OK, thanks for being patient. Here, you're promoted."
You can work and work and work and work, but sometimes you need
to put the heat on. You need to go to *them* and say, "I want more."
There are no rules for being promoted. Sometimes someone will
leave, and since you've taken it on yourself to learn his job, you
might get it. But only if you go to them and say, "Look, I've been
doing this and this and this. Give me a shot." Don't expect them to
come to you.

Oftentimes it's a matter of convincing them to expand the
department, in effect, creating your own position. Listen to how
Laurence Schwartz helped create a job for himself: "When my
internship was over, I didn't want to leave, and they didn't want me
to leave, so we sort of figured out together a way for me to stay. So
we came up with this idea for an apprenticeship, which had never
been done. This was an idea I had so that they could keep me but
wouldn't have to pay me a full salary while I did more of trying to
prove myself."

So you sort of created your own position?

"Yeah, we figured it out together. Nobody offered me anything—that's the important point. So at the end of the apprenticeship, they had to come to a decision on whether to hire me or not. I
was ready for it. I had done good work and had become really
involved in the projects and was valuable to the department, I think,
so they decided to hire me officially."

Listen to Emily Gerson-Saines on becoming an agent: "No one is saying to them (agent trainees) they're definitely going to become an agent. It's up to them whether they're going to be made an agent. You create your own destiny. To figure out how to become an agent is probably one of the sure signs of whether or not you could be a good agent. If you can figure out how to become an agent, then you get to be one. You have to figure out how to be indispensable to the company and show signs of promise. No one just goes down the hall and says, 'Oh, you're next in line, you're an agent.' No."

That's when it becomes crucial that you are well loved. Well loved by your boss and by just about everybody else that you work near. But especially by your boss. Because if you've been busting it for your boss, making their lives really easy, doing things before you're asked, blah blah blah, they might then rally behind you when you say, "Alright boys, it's been fun, but now I want *this*."

PERSONALITY DEFICIENCIES OF THE WORKINGMAN

The working world is a weird place. There's nothing else like it. It creates and breeds monsters. (It also explains why most grown people—your parents—seem so distant, sort of like a different species. Uptight and rigid. It's the working world rubbed off on them. You, as a child, take part of the blame, but work is the real culprit.) The dog-eat-dog-ness, the pressure of pulling your own weight, of performance, of office politics, of aging and not being where you thought you would be by now. It can all weigh large and heavy on an insecure person with a short fuse, creating a psychotic, abusive dickhead. (Watch out, it could happen to you.)

What's worse however, is the fact that abuse in the workplace is an accepted and generally tolerated affair. Since it's all about performance and the dollar, rules of conduct are tossed out the window. **So get over the idea that people are supposed to act a certain way. Hell, get over the notion that they even have to be human.**

In Conclusion, A Personal Story of Abuse From Your Author

I worked at a talent agency—won't name it—for this agent who was, in my opinion, Satan on earth dressed in a cheesy suit and sporting a bad, Napoleon short-man complex. A real fucking nightmare. But a really good fucking agent. He was a young guy who had a lot to prove. I hated him. I hated him a lot.

He'd come in in the morning, walk past me, and would never say hello. He'd go into his office and yell, "Get in here." I'd go in, take a seat, and he'd say, "Alright, what did you forget, what have you let slip through the cracks?" I'd say, "Nothing." He'd say, "Are you sure?" "Yes, I'm sure." Then an evil little smile would form on his face—he loved this—and he'd say, "Are you positive?" And then he'd ream me out over something usually really small that I missed or forgot. A real pleasant guy.

One minute he'd be throwing his pen at me because it had run out of ink—"Can I have a pen that works!"—and then, as if we were in a weird monster movie, he'd all of a sudden be really nice. He'd say, "Good morning" or something and pretend to be my best friend. Sometimes it would last for two days, long enough for me to think, "Hey, I might not have to sneak in to his apartment and kill him after all." Of course, the spell would break, he'd catch hold of himself, and let me have it.

He knew that I hated him. But that was OK because he hated me too. Why didn't he fire me? He couldn't. One of the partners of the agency liked me, and this agent was young and apparently had gone through a couple of assistants before me like water. No one lasted. I think the partner and the office manager knew my boss was difficult, and knew I was crazy to stay (anyone would be crazy to stay), and would therefore never fire me. It was kind of funny. Everybody in the company knew we hated each other, but it didn't matter. The work was getting done. It's all about the work.

The hatred and tension got so bad that the office manager finally pulled us into her office. We both screamed, blah blah blah. I said, "Fuck it, I can't work for you any longer. I hate you, OK, so fire me."

And they were both like, "Yeah, so, what's the problem? Why should we fire you?" "The problem is I hate you. Doesn't that bother you, that your assistant hates you? I'm fired right?" It didn't bother either of them in the least. I couldn't believe it. Then I said to the office manager, "Tell him he's got to be a little nicer to me." "Why?" the office manager asked me. "Because."

She went on to explain to me, to my amazement, that assistant abuse is a common thing in this industry, and that if you want to be an agent you've just got to deal with it. I said, "He can treat me however he wants?" She was like, "Yeah. There's a lot of people who want the opportunity that you have, so I guess that he can." He could be abusive and it didn't matter. There's lots of supply. I didn't have a leg to stand on.

But probably the funniest thing that happened in that little meeting was when I told them that I didn't actually want to be an agent. That I was using the opportunity to make contacts with producers. I thought this would piss them off, 'cause when I was hired I was like, "Oh, yeah, I definitely want to be an agent." It didn't piss them off. They looked at me incredulously. They were like, "You don't want to be an agent?" And I was like, "No." "How on earth," they asked me, had I managed to deal with the abuse? They were like, "You don't want to be an agent and you've been dealing with this amount of work and abuse. What are you crazy?" Some weird initiation-abuse mentality was going on big time.

After that, me and my boss had two weeks of bliss. He was really nice to me. He totally laid off of me. And then I got another job.

In retrospect, I realized that I was to blame for a lot of the abuse he gave me. Listen, the guy was under an enormous amount of pressure, and the work and life of an agent is an insane one. Just keeping up with the calls, and then the selling aspect—it's tough. He dealt with a lot of abuse and rejection all day long, so in his mind he thought, Why shouldn't I? It's a weeding out philosophy of, "If he can't deal with my abuse, he'll never be able to deal with the abuse that comes with the job of being an agent."

The thing is, if I had been into it more, if I really wanted to be an agent, I would have dealt with the abuse and worked my ass off harder so he would have no reason to yell at me about anything even remotely minor or insignificant. My friend who worked next to me, who worked for the partner who liked me, told me how he got reamed out, yelled at, called "stupid" and "lazy" every day for about eight months. And then finally, after eight months, it stopped happening because he became a really efficient, perfectionist working machine.

Sorry, it's sort of an obnoxious story, but I wanted to relate to you, somehow, the mentality behind abuse and of bosses in general.

One last word of encouragement from a very successful theatrical producer friend of mine, Peter Breger. Like everybody getting out of college, Peter and his friend were a little nervous about facing the real world. His friend's father pulled them aside and told them something which must have had an impact on Peter because he still remembers it. He said, "Boys, I don't want you to be too concerned about the world out there, because mere competence is everywhere mistaken for genius."

Good luck, friends. Charlie.